Lovers. Liars. Killers.

BLOOD AMBUSH

SHEILA JOHNSON

Author of *Blood Lust* and *Blood Highway*

DON'T MISS THE LATEST HITS FROM PINNACLE TRUE CRIME

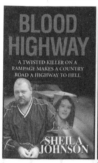

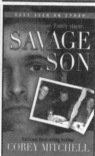

A NIGHTMARISH SCENE

When Jason Sammons and Ellis Williams saw a late-model SUV sitting partially hidden in some willow bushes in the pasture beside the road, they drove down to check it out. It just didn't look like the type of car someone would drive into a rough pasture like that, too nice and new to be driving around through the high grass and over the rough ground. . . .

Sammons glanced over toward the small pond a short distance away and noticed that something at the water's edge didn't look quite right.

"Man, what's that down there in the pond?" he asked Williams. "Do you see it?"

Sammons steered toward the pond to a place where he could get a better look at what he saw floating in the shallow water. He started driving slowly, but slammed on the brakes, his heart pounding, when he saw what looked like a body lying at the edge of the pond. . . .

When they stepped a few feet closer, they could see that it was the corpse of a woman, floating facedown in the brackish water. She appeared to have suffered horrific injuries to the head and back. There was absolutely no question that the woman was dead.

As the two men stood there, hardly believing they had stumbled onto such a nightmarish scene, Sammons noticed that some shotgun shells were lying nearby on the ground, two blue and one red, looking fresh and clean, as if they hadn't been lying there very long. He recalled hearing several gunshots while he and his friend were standing outside at his home, and he realized that what he and Williams had heard was more than likely the firing of the shots that had killed the woman in the pond.

BLOOD AMBUSH

SHEILA JOHNSON

PINNACLE BOOKS
Kensington Publishing Corp.
http://www.kensingtonbooks.com

PINNACLE BOOKS are published by

Kensington Publishing Corp.
119 West 40th Street
New York, NY 10018

All Kensington Titles, Imprints, and Distributed Lines are available at special quantity discounts for bulk purchases for sales promotions, premiums, fund-raising, and educational or institutional use. Special book excerpts or customized printings can also be created to fit specific needs. For details, write or phone the office of the Kensington special sales manager: Kensington Publishing Corp., 119 West 40th Street, New York, NY 10018, attn: Special Sales Department, Phone: 1-800-221-2647.

Pinnacle and the P logo Reg. U.S. Pat. & TM Off.

ISBN-13: 978-0-7860-2274-8
ISBN-10: 0-7860-2274-4

First Printing: August 2010

10 9 8 7 6 5 4 3 2 1

Printed in the United States of America

For Mary Coffey Wood,
a daughter of the Old South,
and the closest thing to royalty
I've ever known.

Acknowledgments

There are a great many people without whom this book would not have been possible. Their help has been appreciated, and, hopefully, none will be omitted. But if I should fail to mention anyone who lent me a hand with their information or expertise, please know I am very grateful.

District Attorney Mike O'Dell, Assistant District Attorney Bob Johnston, and their staff have, as always, been there for me with their help and support, and Cherokee County Circuit clerk Dwayne Amos and the courteous and competent ladies in his office have gone out of their way to assist me in locating information. I thank them for their patience and consideration.

Cherokee County sheriff Jeff Shaver and his officers, lead investigator Bo Jolly, Mark Hicks, Charles Clifton, Jimmy DeBerry, Tim Hays, and all the other sheriff's department personnel who worked on this case and offered their input, I thank you very much. I appreciate all your hard work, as well as that of the agencies that assisted you, the Alabama and Georgia Bureaus of Investigation, the Federal Bureau of Investigation, and the officers of the out-of-state departments who contributed to the investigation.

I would like to extend my thanks and appreciation to the circuit judges of the Ninth Judicial District, whose wise and thoughtful decisions I have reported on for many years. The people of DeKalb and Cherokee Counties in Alabama are fortunate to have two such dedicated public servants as Judges Randall Cole and David Rains to sit on the bench and devote their lives to the cause of justice.

Attorney Rodney Stallings has given me access to so much material that has helped me to understand this case and all the legalities and personalities involved; this book would not have been at all possible without his generous assistance, and I greatly appreciate his help and that of his staff.

Despite his impatience with me for "pushing the deadline," my husband, Tim Johnson, took the time to haul my copier up and down the courthouse steps, copy stacks of papers and keep them in perfect order, and lug huge file boxes in and out of offices for me. Without his help and support, there is little I could do in any area of life. I'm lucky to have him.

My heartfelt thanks go to Edie Comeaux, a sister of Barbara Roberts. Despite all the pain and worry, Edie loves her sister with all her heart and has made that very clear in all my contacts with her. Edie is a generous, loving, and devout person, and I greatly appreciate the touching contribution to this book that she wrote and allowed me to include, verbatim.

Finally I would like to thank Barbara Roberts herself. Her correspondence with me has helped give me a far greater understanding of bipolar disorder and related mental illnesses. Her story has shown me the consequences of insufficient or irregular treatment of mental illness, as well as the changes that can eventually result from regularly receiving the proper care. Thank you, Barbara, for your trust, and I will always wish you well.

1

Early evenings in April are a treat for the senses in almost any part of the country, but even more so in rural northeast Alabama. Pastures and fields are bright green with new growth, dogwood trees and fruit orchards stand covered in fragrant pastel blossoms, and the smell of freshly tilled soil carries for miles on the breeze. And sometimes, when the wind is right, the workers plowing the fields can catch the equally pleasant scent of the great lake that covers a large percentage of the area that makes up Cherokee County, Alabama.

Cherokee County adjoins the Georgia state line and is best known as the location of Weiss Lake, one of the finest fishing and recreational areas in the southeastern United States. Countless professional fishing tournaments are held year-round, drawing entrants from all over the country, and the hundreds of miles of shoreline have become lined in recent years with lakefront homes, docks, campgrounds, and boathouses.

The lake, which covers forty-five square miles, is a result of the Coosa River being dammed in the 1950s by the Tennessee Valley Authority (TVA) in order to provide hydroelectric power for a large portion of northeast Alabama. Construction of the dams caused the extensive flooding of hundreds of acres of farmlands on all sides of the river. The huge lake that resulted is surrounded on almost all sides by the fertile fields and pastures of the county.

Darlene Roberts left her job in Rome, Georgia, on the afternoon of Thursday, April 6, 2006, on her way home to Cherokee County, Alabama. It was a fairly short commute, and she and her husband, Vernon, enjoyed living out in the country. They had been married for four years, and had met where they both worked, at Temple-Inland Paperboard and Packaging, Inc., near Rome, where Darlene worked in personnel management and Vernon was a supervisor.

Vernon had gone for a doctor's appointment that morning, and had been told by his physician that he would have to start taking medication to lower his high blood sugar levels. He got back to work in time to meet Darlene and some friends for lunch, and told them about his diagnosis. Darlene immediately began planning ways that she could change their diet in order to help get Vernon's blood sugar levels down, and she assured him that they'd make it just fine with the changes that she had in mind.

Vernon left work a little early that afternoon

to do some painting and plumbing work around the house; he expected his brother to come for a visit over the weekend, and Vernon wanted to get things finished up before his guest arrived. He went home and started work, fixing a sink and painting the upstairs hallway, planning to have the jobs completed by the time his wife came home.

After she left work, Darlene gave her daughter, Heidi Langford, a ride to Heidi's home. Darlene often gave Heidi rides to and from work; it gave them a chance to spend time together, and sometimes they went shopping together. After she dropped Heidi off, Darlene stopped by Wal-Mart in Rome to shop for some of the foods that would work well with the dietary changes she had talked about with Vernon and their friends during lunch. Her shopping list included lots of fresh vegetables, flour tortillas, pinto beans, and other ingredients for a nice dinner of fajitas. She also picked up some chicken fingers, corn dogs, and a few of Vernon's other favorites that he could still enjoy while keeping his blood sugar level lowered. Before Darlene went into the store, she called Vernon on her cell phone. She told her husband where she was, and asked him if there was anything else that he needed her to pick up for him while she was shopping. They both ended the call as they almost always did, telling each other, "I love you."

Charles Edward Young Sr. and his wife and stepson, Ryan Kyle Tippens, enjoyed spending time on Weiss Lake, and they had a weekend house on the lake in the Wildwood Acres area in Alabama, where they kept their boat and often went fishing. Despite the pleasant weather on the afternoon of Thursday, April 6, 2006, clouds were beginning to gather rather quickly, and severe thunderstorms had been predicted for the coming evening. The Youngs and Tippens decided to move their boat from the lake house to a nearby campground with a boat launch they regularly used.

At around 5:30 P.M., Young and his wife were on their way to meet Tippens at the lake house, where he planned to take the boat out onto the lake and meet his stepfather at the dock at the campground to load the boat back onto its trailer. As the Youngs drove down Cherokee County Road 941 toward the lake, they saw an unfamiliar black Dodge pickup truck with a hard bed cover backed in at the double gates beside the entrance to a pasture and farm pond that adjoined the road. A few minutes later, Tippens drove past and also noticed the truck sitting beside the gate. He saw two people there—a large gray-haired man and a shorter woman. Tippens didn't think anything seemed particularly strange or out of the ordinary; people from the neighborhood often fished in the pond. He continued on his way to the lake house, got into the boat, and took it around the lake to the campground to meet the Youngs.

After the boat was pulled out of the water and secured onto its trailer, the Youngs started back down County Road 941. Around an hour had passed, and there was now a late-model white sports-utility vehicle (SUV) sitting a short distance down in the high grass and willow saplings of the pasture. The black truck was still in sight, but it had moved down to the end of the road at the intersection with County Road 182. Young Sr. noticed that the same two people who had been with the black truck earlier were still there, but now the hard cover of the truck bed had been raised.

A short time later, Tippens drove past, pulling the boat and its trailer. He, too, saw the same black Dodge pickup he had noticed earlier on his way to the campground. The truck was sitting beside the road, but it began to pull away as Tippens got closer. It looked to him like the truck was being driven by the same gray-haired man he had seen earlier.

Jose Luis Richiez was leaving for his home in nearby Summerville, Georgia, after a day on the job at Wildwood Acres Farms. Richiez had heard the local weather reports calling for possible severe weather moving into the area overnight, but he looked forward to the ride back to Summerville. On such a nice spring day, even with a few clouds beginning to gather in the west, it was going to be a pleasant trip.

Just before reaching the intersection of County Roads 941 and 182, Richiez saw a black Dodge Dakota pickup stopped on the side of the road with its hard bed cover raised. Thinking the truck might have broken down, Richiez was intending to stop and ask if he could help. As he got closer, he saw a man and woman fighting on the roadside beside the truck. The man was big, gray-haired, with a mustache, and the woman was smaller, wearing a light-colored shirt and jeans. Richiez was shocked when he saw the man hit the woman in the face and throw her back into the passenger side of the truck.

When the man hurriedly took off his shirt, tossed it into the back of the pickup, and jumped back into the cab, Richiez decided his safest move might be to mind his own business and continue on his way without stopping. As he passed the black truck, it pulled out onto the road behind him and closely followed him to a stop sign at the intersection. Richiez began to get uneasy; the gray-haired man had looked very big. When he pulled away from the intersection out of sight of the black truck, it didn't follow him any farther, much to his relief. Richiez didn't see the truck again, but he kept a close lookout in his rearview mirror all the way home, just in case.

While Richiez was being followed down the road by the black Dodge truck, another member of the Young family, Charles Edward Young Jr., was going toward his home on County Road 941 and noticed the white SUV sitting down in the pasture, near the pond. It looked to him like it might be stuck, so he stopped and called out to see if anyone was around that needed his help. No one answered, and no one was in sight at the vehicle or nearby in the pasture. Young Jr. started to walk down into the pasture and check on the condition of the vehicle, but he was wearing a pair of sandals and decided he'd better not try to push through the tall grass and into the field without having on a sturdier pair of shoes. He didn't notice anything else unusual in the pasture near the SUV, and thought that if anyone had needed help, the motorist had probably already left the pasture, so Young Jr. went on his way.

2

Jason Alan Sammons and his friend Ellis McNeill Williams were enjoying the spring afternoon. The two were at Sammons's house on County Road 182, having a beer out in the yard while they talked and put away some tools Sammons had been using on the job that day. Both young men worked hard, and they liked to relax after work and spend a little time together enjoying a "cold one."

When they heard a gunshot that seemed to come from the pastures down the road, they didn't pay much attention. In such a rural area, an occasional gunshot was nothing unusual. The vast majority of people who lived in the area were hunters, and still more people fished regularly, either at the lake or in the many ponds. And those who fished were likely to take a gun along on their fishing trips; snakes were very fond of the water, especially the farm ponds, where there were plenty of frogs and big tadpoles to attract them. When the two young men heard a couple more shots a short time later, they were still unconcerned.

About half an hour passed, and after the tools had all been cleaned and stored back in place, ready for the next day's work, the two friends decided to take Sammons's John Deere Gator all-terrain vehicle (ATV) and ride around the neighborhood for a while. Sammons grabbed Williams a beer out of the cooler and they started up the Gator and rode around over Sammons's farm; then they went across the highway and turned onto County Road 941.

When the two men saw a late-model white SUV sitting partially hidden in some willow bushes in the pasture beside the road, their first thought was that it might have been stolen or wrecked, so they rode down into the pasture to check it out. Car thieves often abandoned stolen vehicles off the road after they had been stripped. But this SUV seemed not to have been tampered with, so the men looked to see if its driver was in the pasture. When they found that no one seemed to be around, they pulled back out of the pasture and continued with their ride.

When Sammons and Williams turned around and started back down the road a short time later, they were still curious about the nice late-model abandoned vehicle sitting out in the pasture. They drove the Gator through the field down to the SUV again to have another look. This time they looked more closely and saw that there was, after all, some damage to the underside of the front of the vehicle, and it looked as though it might have been driven down and gotten stuck in the field. It just didn't look like the type of car someone would take down into a rough pasture like that, too nice and new to be driving around through the high grass and over the rough ground. Besides, it was sitting there with several bags of groceries in the back. They might need to call somebody, they decided, and report it, just in case there had been some kind of problem.

As they started to leave the pasture, Sammons glanced over toward the small pond a short distance away and noticed that something at the water's edge didn't look quite right.

"Man, what's that down there in the pond?" he asked Williams. "Do you see it?"

Sammons steered the Gator down toward the pond to a place where he could get a better look at what he saw floating in the shallow water. He started driving slowly, but slammed on the brakes, his heart pounding, when he saw what looked like a body lying at the edge of the pond. As he and Williams pulled up, got off the Gator, and carefully stepped a few feet closer, they could see that it was the corpse of a woman, floating facedown in the brackish water. From a short distance, it looked like she had suffered some horrific injuries to the head and back, and there could be absolutely no question that the woman was dead.

As the two men stood there, hardly believing they had stumbled onto such a nightmarish scene, Sammons noticed that some shotgun shells were lying nearby on the ground, two blue and one red, looking fresh and clean, as if they hadn't been lying there very long. He recalled hearing several gunshots while he and his friend were standing outside at his home, and he realized that what he and Williams had heard was more than likely the firing of the shots that had killed the woman in the pond.

3

At first, Sammons and Williams stood and stared, frozen in place, horrified by their discovery. Then they realized that they had to snap out of it, get moving quickly and call someone for help as soon as possible. Sammons couldn't get service on his cell phone in the low-lying area around the pond, and he knew that he was going to have to go back up to the road before he could make a call. The men backed away from the pond, jumped back onto the Gator, and carefully moved it away from the area so they wouldn't damage any evidence or disturb the scene. They were anxious to get some officers there as quickly as they could, but they took pains not to disturb a few patches of grass and weeds that looked as if they might have been recently walked through and flattened.

As they were hurrying out of the pasture, shaken by what they had found at the pond, a gold extended-cab Chevy pickup drove by the pasture on the dirt road at a higher-than-normal rate of speed, headed for the main highway. By the time Sammons and Williams got the Gator back onto the road, the speeding pickup had already disappeared out of sight down County Road 941.

Sammons pulled the Gator to a point on the road that was slightly higher uphill, to a place where he could get cell phone service, and he hurriedly called Cherokee County 911. After he told the dispatcher what he and his friend had found in the pond and gave the operator directions to the scene, the two men drove the Gator back to the pasture gate to wait beside the road for the authorities to arrive. It would be getting dark soon, and the coming storm was making the evening air unseasonably warm and muggy. It was not cold at all, but Sammons and Williams were shivering.

Todd Waits and his wife were going out that evening to the nearby town of Cedar Bluff, Alabama. They left home at 5:30 P.M., and as they returned home at around 7:00 P.M., they met a tan Chevrolet Stepside pickup truck going out toward the main road at a fairly high speed. Minutes later, after they turned onto County Road 941, they saw two men standing beside the road next to a John Deere Gator. The men, whom Waits recognized as Jason Sammons and Ellis Williams, began frantically waving for him to stop.

"Man, there's a woman down there, dead in the pond," Sammons shouted at Waits as he pulled up beside them. "I just called 911," he continued, "and they ought to get here pretty quick."

Waits could see that the two men were shaken, visibly upset by what they had discovered. He decided quickly what he should do.

"I'll take my wife on to the house, then I'll come right back down here," Waits told them.

When he had dropped his wife off safely at their home, Waits hurried back down the road to the pasture gate to wait with his frightened neighbors until the authorities began to arrive.

The three men didn't have a long wait; within a few minutes, the flashing blue lights of emergency vehicles lit up the darkening skies as law enforcement officers began coming up County Road 941 to the blue metal gate at the entrance of the pasture, and the cars of county deputies and investigators soon lined both sides of the road that stretched alongside the pasture.

4

When Cherokee County investigator Michael B. "Bo" Jolly was dispatched to the pond off County Road 941, he was one of a group of several officers who were the first to arrive at the scene. A 911 caller had reported finding a woman's body floating in a farm pond, apparently shot and killed. This was a very uncommon occurrence in rural Cherokee County, Alabama. When such calls went out on the scanner, they quickly drew responses from every officer and agency in the vicinity.

At that time, Jolly had been an investigator for the sheriff's office for three years, and had spent a total of seven years in law enforcement. He had served as the lead investigator on countless cases during that time, but this case would prove to be the main focus of his career for many months to come.

The 911 call had come in to the dispatcher just before seven o'clock, and by 7:10 P.M., Jolly and Deputies Kirk Blankenship and Kneely Pack had begun gathering at the scene, along with Drug Task Force officers Charles Clifton and Scott McGinnis. Clifton, commander of the task force, had arrived first, and had already started securing the scene. He had also identified the witnesses who had placed the initial 911 call, Sammons and Williams, and had gotten them and Waits started on writing their statements with details about how they had come to be at the pond that evening, and what they had found there.

When he arrived at the pasture, Jolly walked with Clifton down to the pond and looked at the body floating, facedown, not very far out in the murky water along the edge of the pond. It appeared to be the body of a Caucasian woman, probably in her mid-thirties, who had been shot several times at very close range, causing extensive damage to her head, back, and arms. The wounds appeared to Jolly to be consistent to those made with a shotgun. The victim was fully clothed in tan pants and a tan blouse, but a piece of light green plastic stretch wrap had been looped around her neck.

A short distance away from the pond, a late-model white Nissan Murano SUV had been driven into a clump of bushes in what looked to the officers like an attempt to conceal it from passersby on the road. The vehicle had not been wrecked, but there was damage to the lower front end, where it had been driven from the gate into the pasture, then through the mud and high weeds. When the Alabama license tag bearing the number *13BO341* was run, the SUV had not been reported stolen, and the name and address of its registered owner was determined. The address, the information revealed, was only a couple of miles farther down the road from the pasture. When they received that information, the officers knew that there was a strong likelihood that the driver of the SUV was, in all probability, the woman whose horribly mutilated body was now floating in the pond.

A short time later, Investigators Mark Hicks and Jimmy DeBerry and Cherokee County sheriff Larry Wilson arrived and joined Jolly and Clifton at the edge of the pond. Sheriff Wilson quickly decided that his department needed to call and request immediate assistance from the Alabama Bureau of Investigation (ABI), and the Alabama Department of Forensic Sciences (ADFS) was also notified that they would need to be en route. In the meantime, the daylight was rapidly beginning to fade, so the investigators began placing evidence markers and photographing the scene while they waited for the ABI agents and forensics personnel to arrive.

5

Vernon Roberts couldn't understand why his wife, Darlene, was not answering his repeated calls to her cell phone. She had called him earlier, around 4:45 P.M., to tell him she had just arrived at Wal-Mart in Rome, Georgia, to shop for groceries on her way home. She asked him if there was anything that he needed her to pick up for him, and said she'd be home soon. After they hung up, Vernon went back to the work he'd started as soon as he had gotten home, painting the upstairs hallway. When he finished, he worked on the faucet in the upstairs bathroom, then cleaned the bathroom in preparation for his brother's arrival for a visit. His work done, Vernon took a shower, expecting his wife to be home before he was finished, but she still wasn't there when he got out of the shower. He began to get concerned, and he called her to see if everything was okay.

There was no answer on her cell phone. Vernon called Darlene's daughter, Heidi, to see what time her mother had dropped her off at home after work. He told Heidi he couldn't get in contact with Darlene, and after trying unsuccessfully to call her mother's cell phone, Heidi called Vernon back and told him she hadn't been able to contact her mother, either.

Vernon told Heidi he was going to go out looking for Darlene, thinking that she might have had car trouble or a flat tire in an area where there wasn't a good cell phone signal. He got into his pickup truck and hurried down County Road 941, and as he drove, he tried again several times to call as he headed toward Rome. The calls continued to be unanswered; he still could only get Darlene's voice mail.

Vernon drove all the way to Wal-Mart and rode up and down all the rows in the parking lot looking for Darlene's vehicle. When he didn't find it, he turned around and started back toward home, expecting that they could easily have missed each other en route. He hoped that Darlene would be at the house waiting for him when he arrived.

Vernon was talking to Heidi again, telling her he was nearly home and would let her know if her mother was there, when he saw a large crowd of emergency vehicles at the pasture entrance and down at the pond, with their flashing lights, blue and red, lighting up the dusk. He told Heidi what he could see up ahead, only a couple of miles from their house, and he told her, "I think Darlene's been hurt."

He didn't have time to give Heidi any further information; when the officers saw Vernon's pickup coming up the road, they stopped him and checked his identification. They immediately knew that he was the husband of the victim in the pond, and they detained him, loaded him into a patrol car, and transported him to the Cherokee County Narcotics Office on the other side of the county, in Leesburg, Alabama, for questioning. They did not give him any information other than to tell that his wife had been hurt and they needed him to come with them so they could talk.

6

At around 10:00 P.M., ABI agents Jason W. Brown, Brent Thomas, and Wayne Green arrived at the crime scene where the Cherokee County officials waited for them. They all immediately began collecting evidence and taking additional photographs with the help of ADFS investigator Mark Hopwood. Cherokee County coroner Bobby Don Rogers pronounced Martha Darlene Roberts dead at the scene, and her body was transported to Cherokee Medical Center, to remain until it could be turned over to the Alabama Department of Forensic Sciences for autopsy.

Severe weather was on the way for the overnight hours, and the officers tried to work as quickly as possible before the coming storms moved into the area. There would be much additional work to do during daylight hours on the following day if weather permitted at all, but the scene would need to be carefully preserved during the night. It was decided that several officers would spend the night at the pasture to keep the crime scene secure, and the work of searching for evidence would resume as early as possible, on the next morning. In the meantime, Vernon Roberts was being held a distance away, in law enforcement offices in the Leesburg City Hall, being questioned by two deputies, who had not yet told him exactly what had happened to Darlene. Vernon was not at all pleased at being detained, and he was getting more and more disturbed at being held without an explanation and interrogated. However, the officers were determined to uncover any inconsistencies there might be in his account of his whereabouts during the time before his wife's body was discovered.

Lieutenant Jimmy DeBerry and Cherokee County Drug Task Force commander Charles Clifton knew, like all law enforcement personnel, that the spouse is almost always the first person who falls under suspicion when a husband or wife has been murdered. They left no doubt that they expected not only cooperation, but a complete and detailed account of Vernon's activities for the entire day.

The handwritten statement, given by Vernon Roberts at 8:45 P.M., said that he and Darlene had gotten up that morning at six o'clock as usual, and Darlene left around 7:00 A.M. to pick up Heidi and give her a ride to work. Vernon left home around 7:10 A.M. on the way to Temple-Inland Paperboard and Packaging, Inc., in Rome, Georgia, where he and Darlene both worked in the same building and were scheduled on the same shift.

Vernon said that he left his office around 10:00 A.M.

for a doctor's appointment and returned at noon in time to have lunch at the mill with Darlene and their friends Leesa Norton, Danny Alexander, and Lynn Willoughby. Vernon said that he returned to his office around twelve-thirty, and Darlene called him at four-thirty to let him know she was leaving work and planned to pick up Heidi, give her a ride back to her home, and then stop to get some groceries at Wal-Mart on the way.

Vernon said that he went home from work and started the chores he had planned to get completed on that afternoon before his brother arrived for the weekend, and he said that Darlene called him to see if he needed anything from Wal-Mart while she was there. After finishing his work and taking a shower, Vernon said, he was surprised that Darlene hadn't come home yet, and he grew concerned that Darlene didn't answer her cell phone. He called Heidi to see exactly what time her mother had dropped her off at home. He claimed that he told Heidi he was getting worried because he couldn't contact Darlene after repeatedly calling her, and he said that Heidi also had tried to call her mother and had no luck, either.

Vernon stated that he told Heidi he was going to look for Darlene; then he went to Wal-Mart, didn't find her there or anywhere else on the way back from Rome, and headed home, only to be stopped on the road, detained by the officers, and brought to the Leesburg office for questioning.

Vernon then signed a waiver of rights, and the interrogation began in earnest.

7

After confirming that his wife's name was Martha Darlene Roberts, Vernon answered the officers' questions with mostly the same information he had already given in his written statement. A few additional things came to light as he recalled details, such as a white convertible that came past his house while he was working on his chores, sometime between 6:00 and 7:00 P.M., turning around in the driveway of a house up the road, then driving back past the house, and a couple of shots he'd heard coming from the direction of the pond while he was outside the house, working on the pool. He believed, he said, that he'd possibly heard the shots after Darlene had called him for the last time, from Wal-Mart.

"I didn't give it a thought," he said of the gunshots. "That area is just covered up with deer and turkey, and she wasn't late yet, so I didn't think anything about it."

Vernon also remembered seeing Williams and Sammons on the Gator.

"I saw the two guys on the Gator, and I thought they were down there weedeating around the pond so people could fish better," he said, adding that Darlene's son, Benji, had talked about doing that same thing on one occasion, because the grass and weeds were very tall around parts of the pond.

"That's what I thought those guys were doing. I didn't care if they fished in that pond. It's not mine, so go ahead."

Vernon said that when he was stopped by the officers on his way home, "I knew there was something bad, wrong.

"Heidi called, and I said, 'Something's wrong, there [are] police cars all over, the ambulance . . .'

"Heidi is going to panic," Vernon said. "She was very nervous about her mother, when she wasn't able to get in touch with her. I went home thinking she'd probably be there already, but I got stopped. You said she'd been injured, but what happened? Did somebody shoot her?"

One of the officers said later that he had found it very odd that Vernon had not been more upset. He had not, at that point, been told whether or not his wife was dead, injured, or just exactly what it was that had happened to her, or why he was being interrogated.

"I just said to him that all I knew was that she was hurt bad," the officer said.

Heidi called Vernon's cell phone during the interview, and Vernon handed the phone to the deputy, who told her that she needed to come on over from Georgia, and the officers who would be there at her mother's home would explain to her what had happened when she arrived.

During the course of the questioning, Vernon had been becoming increasingly agitated, and as the questions grew more personal, tempers began to flare.

"What about another woman in your life?"

"Never!" Vernon answered emphatically. *"Never!"*

"Have you ever been in any trouble, or hit an ex-wife or anything?"

Vernon said the only trouble he'd ever been in was a charge of driving under the influence years earlier in Texas, and he'd never hit any of his wives. He had earlier reported his first wife as being Janice Dunaway, the mother of his two daughters, and his second wife was Barbara Ann Comeaux, who lived near Atlanta, he said. He and Darlene had been married for about four years.

"Who's mad at your wife?" Lieutenant DeBerry asked.

"Nobody," Vernon replied.

"Who's mad at your wife?" DeBerry shouted.

"Nobody!" Vernon shouted back.

"Somebody was mad at her and knocked her in the head! Did you knock her in the head?"

"No!" Vernon shouted. "I would never, ever hurt her, I cherished her with all my heart. We adored each other!"

Vernon claimed he would never be unfaithful to Darlene, no matter what.

"That's what makes me think that something's wrong," Clifton said. "Something might have happened today between you and her that might have caused you so much anguish. . . . There's no way, if you hurt this woman, that we're not going to find out."

"I told you on the way over here," Vernon said, "I worshiped that woman." He told the officers to have his hands tested for gunshot residue for having shot a gun that day. He and the officers then argued at length about whether he would get jealous if somebody hugged his wife, with DeBerry asking repeatedly if it would make him mad if a coworker or friend hugged his wife in front of him.

Vernon yelled, "My wife is injured and I'm sitting here listening to *this*? *This is crap!* I love my wife!"

Vernon was then asked if he'd found his wife with somebody else. He replied that Darlene had been taking antibiotics for a serious yeast infection.

"Do you think she'd try to be with anybody else like that?" he asked the officers, infuriated by their questions.

"There's no two people on God's earth that gets along all the time, never has a disagreement, never gets pissed with each other—it don't happen," DeBerry said. Vernon immediately disagreed, and said he and Darlene always got along.

"Now, if she's going to be okay and I ask her, will she say you never disagreed over anything? If there's something you need to tell us, tonight's the night. Extenuating circumstances could cause a man to do something he'd never do otherwise in a million years. We're offering you a chance to tell us now. Right now the district attorney will take everything into consideration—tomorrow'll be different. Right now, whoever hurt your wife is behind the event. They need to be out front of it."

Vernon talked again about his last call from Darlene when she called to see if he needed anything from Wal-Mart.

"The last thing I told her was that I loved her," he said.

"Is that what you said right before you shot her, looked her in the eye and told her you loved her? You told me you never let her out of your sight, that's what you said. Jealousy will eat you up. Now's the time to help yourself—"

"I told her that on the phone!" Vernon interrupted. "Look at the phone records! She called me on her cell phone from the Wal-Mart parking lot! I'm not worried about Darlene being unfaithful. I love my wife. I didn't have to worry about not trusting her because we genuinely loved each other, not because I was jealous of her! You did say she was injured, didn't you?"

"I'm going to say she was hurt bad," the officer said, repeating his earlier statement.

Vernon showed Clifton and DeBerry how to bring up the last numbers on his cell phone to verify the calls he'd sent and received that day. Then, as tensions eased a bit, he said that he and Darlene had a good life, living out in the country.

"My second wife hated it and couldn't handle it," he said, "and she moved back to Texas."

Vernon was asked if he'd noticed a hard-cover black Dodge pickup in the area that day, or if he knew anyone who owned one, and he said no. Then he was asked if he owned a shotgun. His wife's son, Benji, had left one at their house when he moved out after living with them for a time, he said. Benji had taken the shotgun, which had belonged to Darlene's father, and he'd had the barrel sawed off. Darlene took it away from him and hid it somewhere in the house, Vernon said, but he did not know where it was.

When he was asked if he and Darlene had ever had any trouble with Benji, he said Benji and his mother had argued over his continuing use of drugs, calling it a "knock-down, drag-out fight," after which Benji had moved out of their house and gone to live with his girlfriend in Rockmart, Georgia.

When asked if Darlene had any problems with her ex-husbands, Vernon said she did not. He made several disparaging comments about the character of one ex-husband, but he went on to say that she had never had "an ounce of trouble" from him. Her other ex-husband was the father of her two children, Benji and Heidi. There were no current problems with him, either, according to Vernon.

When the questioning concluded, Vernon agreed to his home being searched, and he was returned to the scene. A thorough search of the house, however, turned up nothing that could help with the investigation. So far, Vernon Roberts had an airtight alibi.

8

Investigators spent a late night at work at the pond off County Road 941, with Investigator Mark Hicks, Lieutenant Jimmy DeBerry, and Chief Deputy Tim Hays staying overnight in the rain to protect the scene. The following morning, Jolly and his team, along with a large number of other officers, reported to the pasture at first light to begin searching the area for evidence again, starting to comb through the tall weeds looking for anything they had not been able to see earlier. Quite a few items had been collected the previous night, before it grew too dark to do a detailed search, but the deep, stamped-down layer of grass surrounding the pond could be hiding many crucial pieces of evidence, which would be more easily uncovered in the light of day.

Among the first and most obvious items that had already been recovered at the scene the previous evening were three shotgun shell casings, two blue and one red, and their wadding, found lying in the mud at the edge of the pond. Each piece was carefully bagged and labeled, to be tested for evidence in the event that the murder weapon was recovered. Some long strips of white cotton gauze had also been found and collected, one lying near the side of the Murano and one farther away, out in the field.

Most of the green plastic stretch film had remained looped around Darlene's neck when her body was removed from the pond, but a couple of additional smaller pieces were found floating in the water; those had rough, jagged edges and looked as if they could have been ripped away from the main piece of green film by the shotgun blasts. They were all recovered and bagged.

The Nissan Murano was processed for evidence at its impound location, Larry's Tire & Towing, in Centre, Alabama, by Investigator Jolly on the morning of April 7, along with Vernon Roberts's brown GMC 1500 pickup truck, which had also been impounded until it could be thoroughly checked for evidence. There was nothing inside the pickup other than some personal items, which included an umbrella, a jacket, and some papers. A couple of red-brown stains on the headliner and passenger-side doorpost proved to be inconsequential.

The Nissan Murano, however, yielded much more pertinent evidence, including Darlene's bags of groceries in the rear cargo area containing a receipt from Wal-Mart in Rome, Georgia, dated 6:22 P.M. on April 6, 2006. There was also a recoil pad for the butt stock of a shotgun lying on the floorboard on the driver's side of the vehicle. A hair was adhered to the recoil pad, and it was carefully collected along with the pad.

There were several red-brown stains inside the Murano, and swabs were taken for analysis. They were located on the headliner, the door and steering wheel, and the passenger-side doorpost. Jolly also processed the Murano for latent prints, but none were recovered. Extensive photos were taken of both vehicles.

While Jolly photographed and collected evidence from the vehicles, the other officers continued to search the scene and found quite a few more items. Approximately ten feet from where Darlene's body was found, a chewed piece of gum lay on the bank of the pond. The back of a watch was also found lying nearby, and a broken bracelet—silver with pink stones—was found near the gate at the pasture entrance. Several other items, which would later prove to be unrelated to the case, were found at the pond, likely dropped there by some of the many people who had come there regularly to fish. There were also many footprints in the mud at the edge of the pond, but the water content of the soil was so high after the rain that the prints had very little definition, and photographs of the prints show them very blurred and containing standing water.

Two other items, which investigators believed would prove to be evidence in the case, had been found thrown out on the side of the road near the scene. Two traffic barriers marked *Floyd Co* with highway signs attached, one reading BE PREPARED TO STOP and the other MEN WORKING, were obviously the property of the road department in Floyd County, Georgia, and had very likely been picked up off the highway and transported over the state line into Alabama by someone other than Floyd County Road Department employees. They were tested for latent prints, but the Department of Forensic Sciences was unable to recover anything from them.

News of the murder of Darlene Roberts spread quickly, both in Cherokee County and in Rome, Georgia, with the news media reporting in detail about the discovery of her body in the farm pond. Her coworkers at Temple-Inland were shocked to learn that Darlene had been killed only a short time after they had last seen her leaving work for the evening. Ralph Stagner, the Temple-Inland plant manager, told *Rome News-Tribune* and *Cherokee County Herald* staff writer Kathy Roe that Darlene had been liked and respected by both management and employees at the plant.

"She was a true professional," he said. "We are all deeply saddened by this, and we will miss her. Our thoughts and prayers go out to the family."

Cherokee County sheriff Larry Wilson gave the press as many details about the slaying as he was able to disclose at that point in the investigation, saying that his officers knew the type of weapon used, but they had not recovered it.

"We'll see if we can come up with a motive and a suspect," he said. "We want to talk to anyone, neighbors, anyone who may have seen something." Wilson said autopsy results were not expected for several days, and he was concerned that the heavy rain and severe weather, which was expected, might destroy crucial evidence.

On April 7 and 8, officers fanned out around the community, going house to house to talk with any of the area's residents who might have information. Several had already come forward to report seeing a black pickup truck with a hard bed cover in the area at the time, and others reported having heard shots. Most of those who saw the black truck had been able to give a description of its occupants, a large gray-haired man and a smaller woman with brown hair. Some reported the two seemed to be fighting, and had seen the man hit the woman. Others reported that it looked as though the woman's face was red and she was crying.

Three of the officers conducted a roadblock on the morning of April 8 at the intersection of County Road 182 and County Road 941 in an effort to contact more possible witnesses. While there, one of the men, David Storey, noticed a garbage collection can sitting nearby with a bag protruding from it. Storey saw a paper sticking out of the bag with the name *Roberts* on it, and he and the other officers decided to check the bag in case it contained more evidence. A stained brown straw purse was inside, along with a pair of blue jeans and some paper towels that appeared to be bloodstained. They also found some blue masking tape with tan paint and what they believed to be bloodstains on it, with some hair stuck to it.

Those items, as it turned out, had no value to the investigation, since they had come from

Vernon Roberts's home improvement projects on the day of the murder, but another item inside the bag did prove to be useful. It was the hangtag from a brown Rosetti viscose tote, a new purse Darlene had recently bought and had been carrying on the day of her murder. The straw purse found in the garbage can had evidently been discarded in favor of the new one that Darlene had bought during a shopping trip with Heidi a few days previously. Since the new Rosetti purse had not been recovered at the scene, officers now had a good description of exactly what kind of purse they needed to be looking for.

Later on the morning of April 8, the investigators at the scene decided to try to search for the murder weapon in the murky pond. They thought it might have been thrown in there after the shooting. It would require some special equipment, which was requested and was soon en route. While the officers waited for it to arrive, a partial pair of eyeglasses was spotted, almost completely hidden in the weeds and grass. The left arm, lens, and nosepiece of the glasses were collected by Investigator Mark Hicks and were turned over to the ABI for testing. This would soon prove to be the most important piece of evidence that would be found at the scene, and it provided the investigators with the break they needed to move forward very quickly with the case from that point. But until the analysis of the glasses was completed, there were still very many interviews to conduct and statements to be given.

Sheriff Wilson told the press that there were "some possibilities" for suspects in the murder, but he did not disclose any further details. The owner of the broken eyeglasses would soon be identified he knew, and then much more information on the suspects would be made public, and arrests in the case would soon follow.

9

On April 12, ABI agents Brown and Thomas arranged to meet with Darlene's two children, Heidi Wynne Langford and Larry Benjamin "Benji" Langford, to take their statements and to get their help to develop as much background as possible on Darlene, her family and friends, and their relationships.

On the day of his mother's murder, Benji and his girlfriend had both slept late at their home in Taylorsville, Georgia, he said, then left that evening to go to a friend's home in Rockmart, Georgia. Later, they went on to another friend's house to shoot pool, and they didn't return home until around 6:00 A.M. It was the first time Benji had stayed out all night in quite some time, he told the officers.

As soon as they returned home early on the morning of April 7, Benji told the investigators, he saw all the calls on his answering machine and checked the caller ID. He immediately knew that something was wrong. He first called his former father-in-law, who hung up on him. He then called his aunt, and she told him that his mother had been murdered.

"Mom was my best friend," Benji told his interviewers. "The only thing I ever lied to her about was my drug problems. Mom didn't like it, and I got straight and moved in with Mom and Vernon and stayed for about three years, until a couple of months ago. Then I went off with a friend and stayed gone for a week. We argued about it when I got home, and I moved out."

Benji said he had called his mother on Sunday, April 2.

"I think I tried to talk about my ex-wife, about her not letting me see my son," he said. He and his mother had gotten into an argument, he claimed.

"She hung up on me because she thought I was being a smart-ass to her. I called her because she has always been able to fix any problem I had."

The investigators wanted to know some additional details about the shotgun that Vernon had told them was probably hidden somewhere in the house by Darlene. Benji had allegedly sawed off the barrel; then Darlene confiscated it and put it away in a secure hiding place.

"It was a bolt-action shotgun with a clip," Benji said. "I had cut the barrel off because it had a bulge in the barrel. I also had a belt that held shells. It was a twelve-gauge shotgun and I had several shells—buckshot and small game. The shells were red, blue, and yellow, three-inch shells, I think. Mom saw the gun after I sawed it off, and she thought I would get into trouble with it, and she took it and hid it. The gun should be at her house, maybe in the garage or in the room with the green carpet. She would have it hidden really well."

Benji told the investigators that his father, Larry Michael Langford, and Darlene got along when they needed to; they would never be together again, but they had a civil relationship.

"The only time they were around each other was my birthday," he said.

There had been incidents of abuse during their marriage, Benji claimed, saying that his father had treated his mother "like shit," slapping her and "slinging her around," and even pulling a gun on her at one point. However, he said that his father would never have shot her. Benji said he hadn't spoken to his father for several months prior to his mother's murder.

Benji then offered the investigators his own ideas about who might have been responsible for the murder.

"I think Vernon's ex-wife Barbara may have had something to do with Mom's death," he told them. "Barbara is crazy."

He said that Vernon had been talking to Barbara entirely too much on the phone "for the past couple of weeks, maybe about insurance or something. I don't think he should have been talking to Barbara on the phone."

The phone calls between Vernon and Barbara, he said, had made several of the family members mad, including his sister, Heidi.

Benji told the investigators about several incidents of alleged stalking and harassment that had taken place before and during his mother's marriage to Vernon.

"When Vernon and Mom married, Vernon had a Buick Riviera and a truck. I got Mom's car, and she drove the Buick. She didn't like it because it had been Barbara's, and she traded it for a new Thunderbird. Then Barbara went and bought the Buick and had a wreck in Atlanta, with a man."

Benji went on to say that Barbara had come to the home of Vernon and his mother about three years ago. She had been wearing a ski mask and overalls, and she had sneaked into the yard and attempted to spy on them while they were in the hot tub, nude, behind their house.

"Vernon saw someone in the yard, and he chased them and caught them. It was Barbara, disguised. He drug her by the hair to her car and made her leave."

Benji also said Barbara had vandalized Darlene's apartment, spray-painted her car, and put flares in the heat vents of her apartment, all before Darlene and Vernon were married.

Vernon took care of Darlene, Benji told the investigators, and he loved her. It was the happiest his mother had ever been, he said, being married to Vernon.

"I want to say Vernon didn't have anything to do with what happened," he said, "but something about this and Vernon bothers me. I know my mom wouldn't stop for anyone or pick up anyone, unless she knew them and trusted them. If she didn't know them, she wouldn't stop for them—no matter what the circumstances were—and she always locked her car doors when she got in to go anywhere."

10

When the investigators talked to Darlene's daughter, Heidi, later that morning, Heidi brought a few names into question that had not previously been mentioned. She claimed that two of the women who had worked with Darlene, and were allegedly two of her closest friends at Temple-Inland, were actually very jealous of her.

"She would act like she was her best friend," she said of one of the women, "but that was not true."

Heidi said the other woman's actions on the night of the murder were "strange," but she wasn't able to pinpoint exactly why she had gotten that impression.

Something had seemed to be wrong with her mother, earlier on the day of the murder, Heidi also told the investigators. She said that she did not know what the problem might have been, though.

Heidi and her mother had gone shopping together on the afternoon of Monday, April 3, to Goody's Family Clothing store, located in Rome, when Darlene had bought shoes, clothing, and the Rosetti viscose purse, which was, at that time, still missing. It was being sought as important evidence in the murder investigation.

Heidi mentioned Darlene's ex-husband, Ronnie Deems, and claimed that his marriage to her mother was abusive. During the years they were married, Heidi said, he had pulled Darlene's hair, beaten her, and attempted to run her over with his vehicle.

Heidi said Deems kept pictures of Darlene, Heidi, and Benji hanging on the walls of his home, but she said he had been told by the family not to come to Darlene's funeral.

The phone conversations between Vernon and Barbara were also brought up by Heidi during the interview, with her confirming Benji's statement that she did not like Vernon talking on the phone with Barbara. Heidi told the investigators about Barbara's alleged incidents of vandalism and harassment that had been directed toward Darlene and Vernon, and she told them that her mother had been seeing Vernon while he and Barbara were separated.

As far as she knew, no one had ever confronted Barbara about threatening letters she had allegedly written to Darlene, Heidi said, or about the vandalism that had been done to Darlene's vehicle.

The interviews with Darlene's son and daughter had brought up several points that caught the interest of the investigators, like the allegations of physical abuse they had made against both Darlene's former husbands. But they also had both mentioned Vernon's ex-wife, Barbara Roberts, in a way that immediately placed her prominently on the list of persons of interest. When Vernon Roberts came in for his scheduled interview that morning at 11:45 A.M., there were several new lines of questioning that the investigators planned to pursue.

As for the "best friend" of Darlene's who, Heidi had claimed, was very jealous of her mother, she and Darlene were, indeed, the best of friends, Vernon said. He said he had known the woman for many years, when he lived in Texas, where they had worked together at a Temple-Inland plant there.

Vernon said that Darlene had recently taken him to her father's grave and told him, "That is where I want to be buried." He also said that Darlene had told her sister about dreaming that she had been shot. He also told the officers that Benji Langford had broken into his sister Heidi's house at some point, but his statement did not indicate the reason for the break-in or what connection, if any, he thought it might have to the case.

When the investigators brought up the subject of Barbara Roberts, Vernon's first statement was that he did not see Barbara as being the one who killed Darlene. He then told the officers that Barbara and her boyfriend, Dr. Robert John Schiess III, had gone to Texas to attend her mother's funeral.

Since his first statements made on the night of the murder, Vernon's memory seemed to have improved somewhat concerning his activities after he left work on the day his wife was killed. A few minutes away from his home, he said, he had received a phone call from Barbara on his cell phone. He wasn't getting good reception and couldn't understand what she was saying, so he told her to call him back in around five minutes on the phone in his house. When he got home, the house phone was ringing, and it was Barbara, he said, who was calling him to give him some information on a place for one of his daughters to live. The girl was looking for a place in Georgia, but Vernon said he told Barbara it was too late in the evening, and not to worry about it. He'd take care of it himself the next day.

Barbara had told him on many occasions, Vernon said, that she was going to make arrangements for him to be her beneficiary when she died, and he told the investigators that she was not currently married. When they questioned him about the alleged vandalism and stalking incidents, he claimed that he and Darlene were not yet married when Barbara had come to the house dressed in a disguise to spy on them in the hot tub.

With both Benji and Heidi remarking on Vernon's recent regularly occurring phone contact with Barbara during their interviews, and with both of them saying that Darlene's family felt that it was "not a good idea," the investigators began to focus more closely on Barbara Ann Roberts and her boyfriend, Dr. Robert "Bob" John Schiess III.

11

Barbara Ann Comeaux was born on April 18, 1956, as the fourth child of a middle-class strict Catholic family in an all-American small town in southeast Texas. There would be three more children born into the family after her, which made her the middle child of a group of seven brothers and sisters.

Barbara's parents were said to be very well respected in the community, hardworking and very family-oriented, and they put a very high priority on providing their children with the best possible education that they could afford and building a strong foundation of faith in their lives. They raised their children according to their own values and standards. They expected that the children would maintain those values and standards when they reached adulthood, and, with the possible exception of Barbara, they were, for the most part, not disappointed.

In school Barbara was a high achiever who regularly made excellent grades and was very successful in many extracurricular activities. Learning came very easily to her, and she was talented in many areas, winning awards and contests frequently. Despite her accomplishments, however, she had very low self-esteem. In her elementary and middle-school pictures, there are few smiles to be seen on her solemn little face, despite her many achievements.

Barbara always loved animals and cherished all of her many childhood pets. And as she grew older, she was in demand as a much-requested babysitter, and she adored her little nieces and nephews, spoiling them at every opportunity. Barbara's teachers and other adults liked her quite a lot, but she didn't have much of a social life among her peers, having very few close friends apart from her sisters. She tended to have one-at-a-time "best friends" that she felt very possessive toward, which eventually became off-putting and caused the object of her attention to become uncomfortable and gradually begin to drift away.

Barbara didn't feel that she was very attractive or interesting to boys during her high-school years, and consequently she spent much of her time with activities like choir, where she won many state awards and contests. Her family members said she had a beautiful singing voice, and she was a self-taught guitarist, who spent countless hours sitting in her bedroom, practicing and improving her playing skills.

Acknowledged by her siblings to be the brightest one of the family, Barbara graduated at the top of her class from the Bridge City High School in

1974; then she attended college at Lamar University, Beaumont, Texas, where she completed a three-year course of training as a radiology technician, finishing the course with honors. She went on to work as a radiology technician at Doctors Hospital in Groves, Texas; Mid-Jefferson Hospital in Nederland, Texas; as a physician's assistant for Dr. Harvey Randolph in Groves, Texas, and as a technician at Bone Scanners Associates in Port Arthur, Texas.

After Barbara graduated from high school, she had worked and paid her own way through college. She had also paid for dance lessons, something she had always dreamed of and had wanted to take, but was an "extra" that the family budget just couldn't stretch far enough to afford. By all accounts, she was an excellent dancer, performing in public recitals and programs, and as her self-confidence grew to match her other abilities, her appearance began to change. Gone were the heavy glasses and prominent overbite—stylish clothes, makeup, beautifully styled hair, contact lenses, and braces transformed Barbara into the girl that all the men wanted to dance with when she went back to her high-school class reunion.

But the attention of those boys who now noticed and admired her seemed to make Barbara uncomfortable; she remembered all too well how they had ignored her throughout her earlier years. Despite all the outward changes and the seeming increase in her self-confidence, Barbara was still plagued by the same old deep-seated insecurities. Her photos from that period of her life show an absolutely glamorous young woman who is smiling, but the smile still does not show in her eyes, despite her obvious beauty.

There had been clues that Barbara was gradually developing psychological problems for years, but around this time, her family began realizing that Barbara needed help—more help than they could give her. They urged her to talk to professionals and get the appropriate medical care, but she chose not to follow her family's advice. They were disappointed with the choices she made for herself concerning her treatment. Barbara was beginning to slip closer and closer to the bipolar disorder that would come to rule her life for the next several decades.

Then Barbara met Vernon Roberts, and her world changed overnight.

12

Vernon Roberts was a handsome, charming man who had been divorced only a short time. Like many divorced men, he had lost almost all of his assets in the process. He had no money, no reliable means of transportation, and his child support was due. Barbara was immediately smitten with Vernon and she befriended him, helping him with his bills and child-support payments. In the process, she fell hard for him. He became the center of her universe, the love of her life, and she lived her whole life around him, doing whatever she thought would please him. Barbara gladly turned over control of virtually every aspect of her life to Vernon, and they were together for a few years until, on August 31, 1984, in Port Arthur, Texas, they were married.

The marriage lasted for seventeen years, but it grew increasingly turbulent as time passed and Barbara's psychological problems grew steadily worse. While she was still living in Texas, she began treatment for bipolar disorder. Later, though, she said that she'd had an extremely bad reaction to her medication and for that reason did not continue to take it. Several other drugs were prescribed by many other doctors for Barbara after that time, but none seemed to help without causing unpleasant side effects, which Barbara believed outweighed their benefits. She could not seem to find a long-term treatment that she was willing to continue.

Barbara had a history of various medical problems, along with her psychological difficulties, some quite serious. A series of surgeries, auto accidents, a hysterectomy, and many other problems plagued her for years and placed additional stress on her marriage. After Vernon and Barbara moved from Texas to Alabama, when Vernon was transferred to the Rome, Georgia, plant, Barbara's problems increased. She sought treatment at a Georgia mental facility in November 1999 because she and Vernon were having problems. Vernon was thinking about a separation, he told her. She claimed he said that he couldn't cope with her crying, depression, anxiety spells, and post-traumatic stress disorder (PTSD) symptoms. She also felt that he was embarrassed over her increasing mental problems.

After this course of treatment at the mental facility, her medication was adjusted and she was discharged, but she voluntarily readmitted herself again, a short time later, for another effort to find the right balance of prescriptions. During this time, her medications were changed numerous times while she received therapy, but on one occasion her problems with Vernon continued to plague her, even as she remained in the treatment facility. She stopped cooperating with her doctors and voiced some suicidal feelings. She expressed a great deal of hostility toward Vernon, who claimed that he feared for his safety. With her agreement, Barbara was transferred to another facility with a higher level of security. After discharge from that institution, she continued to receive periodic counseling, and she and Vernon remained married . . . at least, for the time being.

Because of her hysterectomy in the early 1990s, Barbara couldn't have children, and her pets had become her child substitutes, especially her favorite dog, Sheba, whom she loved dearly. A relative said that if Barbara and Vernon were out at a restaurant and Vernon ordered a T-bone steak, the exact same order had to be placed to take home to Sheba. After Vernon and Barbara moved to Alabama, Barbara was even more attached to her dogs, because she felt more alone and isolated than she had in Texas. They were her only friends and confidantes, and they gave her constant and unconditional love and devotion. When she listed her favorite activity on a medical information form, she wrote, *Playing with my dogs*.

In September 2000, Barbara once again sought admission to the first treatment facility she had gone to for help. She had been the patient of one of the doctors there since January of that year. She wanted to be admitted, she said, because her beloved twelve-year-old dog, Sheba, had become ill.

Sheba had lost control of her hindquarters,

having to drag herself around, with no control over her bladder or bowels. Both her veterinarian and Vernon were pressuring Barbara to put the elderly dog down, to put her out of her misery, since her illness was terminal and could not be treated. Barbara was heartbroken and couldn't stand the thought of giving up her adored best friend, her beloved pet. Finally, when Vernon was going out of town on a two-week business trip, he issued the ultimatum: Sheba would be euthanized before he returned, or else.

Accompanied by one of her therapists, Barbara took Sheba to the veterinarian on September 27, and Barbara stayed with the dog while Sheba was put to sleep. She then went straight to the treatment facility, tearful and afraid to go home by herself for fear of losing control of her impulses. She felt, she said, as if she had lost a child. After a year's time, Vernon was still talking divorce, leaving her living every day in a continual state of apprehension. She still loved him, she said, and wanted to continue the marriage, but she said she found it very demoralizing to sit at home, alone, with only the dogs for company. She and Vernon had been happily married, she said, until he was promoted and became a manager at Temple-Inland; then he became very controlling and demanding. She said he liked to "manage" her, as well as manage his employees. He was also ashamed of her, she said, for having problems with depression and for her admission to treatment facilities.

Barbara had become very dependent on Vernon,

despite his desire to end the marriage, and she had no social, spiritual, or family support. Her family was far away, she had few friends to confide in, and she had not gone to church regularly, as she had done earlier in life. She felt helpless, hopeless, and worthless, but she gradually became stabilized and was discharged from the facility on October 5, 2000, in a somewhat better state of mind. She had discussed the possibility of moving back to Texas to be nearer to her family, talked about resuming the church attendance, which she had missed, and said that she planned to continue with her therapy.

In February 2001, after endless months of constant threats of separation and ending their marriage, Vernon and Barbara Roberts were divorced.

13

Barbara met Dr. Robert John Schiess III in February 2004 on an Internet dating site called Kiss.com, where they both had pages posted. They began an online correspondence until they arranged to meet in person a few days later, and subsequently began dating.

Schiess was a successful neurosurgeon, one of a family that included several generations of medical doctors and surgeons, and aside from that, he was independently wealthy, a millionaire by all accounts. He attended Tulane University and the University of Florida, then attended graduate school at Wake Forest University's Bowman Gray School of Medicine in 1978, the same medical school his father had graduated from in 1954. Schiess completed his internship in general surgery at the University of Tennessee's Center for the Health Sciences, City of Memphis Hospital, in 1977 and 1978. His residency was spent at the Baptist Hospital in Memphis, where he was a junior resident in neurosurgery, and at Bowman Gray School of

Medicine, where he had a neurological clerkship in 1981. In 1982, he was chief resident of neurosurgery at Baptist Hospital; in 1983, he was chief resident of neurosurgery at Methodist Hospital; and in 1984, he was a senior neurovascular-neurosurgical resident at Le Bonheur Hospital.

During the course of his very distinguished career, Schiess had participated in many research projects, presentations, and professional publications, and had attended quite a large number of scientific meetings and conferences around the country. He had also had scholarly articles published in the *Neurosurgery Online* Internet magazine of the Congress of Neurological Surgeons. His private practices in Atlanta, North Carolina, and Georgia had been very successful, and he was acknowledged to be one of the most knowledgeable and highly respected physicians in his field.

All things considered, Barbara was tremendously impressed by the man and very flattered by his attention, and she quickly established a relationship with the wealthy, intelligent doctor.

During that time, Barbara was attending Coosa Valley Technical College to get her degree in mammography. She lived in Rome; Schiess lived in Conyers. They both occasionally stayed at one another's homes. "The whole time I was in college, I'd go back and forth," Barbara said.

After they were together, Barbara had the opportunity to meet Schiess's parents and stepmother, his three sisters, and his son and daughter.

Schiess also had accompanied Barbara on a few occasions when she visited with her family in Texas.

Schiess had been a practicing neurosurgeon up until a serious auto accident he and Barbara had on May 26, 2004, prevented him from being able to work; he had set up his neurosurgery practice and rented an office in Conyers, Georgia, and was still practicing in his office and making rounds at his affiliated hospitals at the time he and Barbara first met. Schiess was very generous with his new lady friend, and set up a checking account for Barbara to use, depositing funds in it as she needed. After their accident, he helped Barbara pay her medical expenses.

The accident—the worst traffic accident of the 2004 Memorial Day weekend—had taken place in Gwinnett County, Georgia, and Schiess was driving at the time of the crash. He and Barbara were returning from the hospital, where Schiess had completed making his rounds for the evening. Barbara had been driving up until around five minutes before the crash, since Schiess was dictating his medical reports from the hospital rounds. As it became darker, Barbara could not see as well as she was comfortable with; so they stopped and changed drivers. Then, within minutes, their trip home came to an abrupt and violent halt.

A woman, traveling in the opposite direction, talking on her cell phone, was intoxicated and impaired by drugs. It was believed she had passed out or had fallen asleep, going across two lanes of traffic. She then hit the median, went airborne, and landed on the driver's side of Schiess's vehicle. The woman survived the crash and subsequently went to jail.

Barbara and Schiess both suffered serious injuries and spent quite some time in the hospital. Barbara was taken to DeKalb Hospital in Atlanta, and Schiess was sent to Gwinnett Medical Center in Gwinnett, Georgia, where he was affiliated. Barbara's left arm and wrist were broken, along with her right foot and big toe. Most of her ribs on both sides were broken, there were other related problems with crushing injuries to her lungs, and she required surgery on her neck and arm. She was in the intensive-care unit (ICU) for almost two weeks, then spent another couple of weeks on a ward.

The accident took off the entire top of the car and pinned Schiess inside. He sustained a blowout fracture of his right eye socket and fractured his left femur. As a result, he had a rod inserted in his left femur from the hip to the knee. His right ankle had to be totally reconstructed, and he, too, had some lung injuries, along with other related problems. The injury that harmed him the most, however, was the permanent tremor in his hands, which marked the end of his neurosurgery practice. He could no longer operate, and it came as a crushing blow to him.

Both Schiess and Barbara experienced much long-term pain following their accident, and their recuperation was slow and difficult. Barbara said that she didn't remember much about the accident and didn't recall seeing the other car;

she only remembered hearing a huge explosion, the car stopped, and everything went dark.

"Ever since then, if I hear a loud noise, like [thunder], I go into a panic attack," Barbara said. "It's truly terrifying, like everything is happening all over again, and I can't breathe. It's horrible."

On their release from the hospital, Schiess hired a private-duty nurse to care for him at home around the clock, and since Barbara could not take care of herself, and could not be alone, he took her in and the nurse cared for her, too.

Barbara would require many more surgeries as time passed, and Schiess eventually closed his private practice in Conyers and began to suffer from a deep depression. He could no longer do what meant the most to him, and it had a tremendous effect on him.

"That accident drastically changed both our lives," Barbara later said.

14

On November 10, 2005, slightly less than five months prior to Darlene Roberts's death, Barbara and Schiess were involved in a bizarre incident with a Georgia State Patrol (GSP) trooper. As a result, they found themselves in handcuffs, taken to the Bartow County Jail.

The traffic stop eventually became so involved that the arresting officer's narrative of the incident took two pages of single-spaced, fine-print type.

That afternoon, as the officer was headed home from the GSP hangar in Kennesaw, Georgia, he was wearing his issued flight suit and had his weapon in a shoulder harness. He was driving his blue-and-gray marked patrol car, but since he was in his flight suit, he had no protective vest and was carrying no handcuffs or radio on his person. He had only his car radio and a pair of handcuffs in his patrol car.

As he traveled west on Georgia 20, he saw a black Mercedes-Benz parked on the opposite side of the median with its passengers—a man and a woman—standing outside the left rear of the vehicle. The officer was immediately alerted to a possible problem by the man's behavior; he had hold of the woman's waistline from the rear and was shaking her back and forth. He thought the woman might be in danger, so he turned around and went back to investigate. When he neared the Mercedes, he called the Georgia State Patrol headquarters in Cartersville, Georgia, and notified the radio operator of his location.

As the patrolman approached, he saw that the woman had gotten into the driver's seat of the Mercedes and the man was sitting in the passenger seat. He had noticed a lot of moving around while he had been talking on the radio, with both people reaching behind the front seats.

"I asked the male subject to step out of the car, and when he got out of the car, I immediately smelled a strong odor of an alcoholic beverage coming from him," the officer described.

"I wanted to separate the male and female subjects so I could ask the female in private if she was with the male by her own free will."

As soon as Robert John Schiess III got out of the car, he began cursing the officer and asking him for his name and badge number.

"He demanded to see my identification as I asked him for his. I asked him to step to the rear of the car, and I again asked him for his identification. He advised angrily that it was in the car, and once again demanded my badge number."

The patrolman went back to the Mercedes and asked the female driver, Barbara Ann Roberts, for her identification and for Schiess's. She reached over in the car and got a small black case, but Schiess began yelling to her not to show the officer any identification. She stopped and looked back at him, and the officer could see the ID in her hand. He asked once again to let him look at it. She very reluctantly produced her Georgia driver's license, then Schiess's, then stated, "But I was driving."

The patrolman told her that he simply wanted to know to whom he was speaking, but Barbara repeated, "But I was driving," with Schiess yelling the entire time for her not to show any IDs or give any information. He had noticed earlier, when he had stepped behind the Mercedes, that the car was registered in Rockdale County, Georgia.

At the time of this roadside fracas, Bartow County, Georgia, authorities were using all available personnel in an ongoing search of the nearby area for an escaped felon. Now that he finally had their IDs, the officer went back to his patrol car and called the Cartersville headquarters to let them know that Schiess was becoming increasingly agitated and Barbara was yelling something at him and pointing her finger at him. There was an extra pair of handcuffs in the driver's side of the patrol car, and the trooper decided it would be a good idea to get them. He saw Barbara was getting more and more upset as she was yelling back to Schiess and talking to someone on her cell phone.

"I was unaware who she might be talking to, but over the yelling of the male, I could hear her yelling for help on the phone."

The situation had reached a point where the officer felt that he needed to place Schiess into custody quickly so that he could de-escalate the situation, securing him so that he could safely speak to Barbara. As he got out of his patrol car with the handcuffs, he decided that, considering Schiess's intoxicated state and his refusal to cooperate or follow any of his instructions, the best thing to do would be to place the doctor under arrest for obstruction of a law enforcement officer.

"I went to the man and asked him to place his hands on the hood of my patrol car. He put his right hand on the hood of my car, and as he was about to place his left hand on the hood, he quickly brought it back. I grabbed his arm and asked him to place it on the hood of the car, and he jerked away and yelled at me to take my hands off of him."

The officer told Schiess two more times to place his hands on the hood of the car, but Schiess continued to yell and began calling the officer a fascist, a Nazi, and shouting several other inflammatory remarks. He started to repeatedly yell, "Name and badge number!"

The patrolman grabbed Schiess, and after a struggle, he cuffed both hands behind his back and attempted to lead him to the front of the patrol car, where he would be able to search him in front of the camera. Schiess was having none of that, and started to pull away. To prevent an escape attempt, the officer grabbed him and took him down to the ground, while Barbara continued to scream for help on the cell phone.

"Once on the ground, I felt he was somewhat secure. I felt he would not be able to get up on his own. I went to the radio to advise Cartersville to have any responding units to slow down because I now had the male subject in custody. While I was on the radio, an eighteen-wheeler pulled in behind me, and the driver asked me if I was all right or if I needed any help. I thanked him and told him I had the man under control now."

The officer then learned that Barbara was talking to the Cartersville station on her cell phone. The Cartersville operator radioed the other personnel that the trooper now had the male subject under control and told them that he was now talking to the female on the phone.

"I went to her and advised her to calm down and to have a seat in the car," the trooper said. "I asked her for the keys to the car, and when she gave them to me, I placed them on the roof of the car. When I asked her where she was coming from, she said, 'Rome.' I asked her if she had been drinking alcohol, and she said she had not. When I asked if she would provide a sample of her breath for a preliminary breath test, she said she would try."

While the officer was attempting to talk to Barbara, Schiess continued yelling insults and yelling at Barbara, telling her not to cooperate. After attempting to get a sample a couple of times with no results, the officer decided Barbara was not going to cooperate with the evaluation.

"I now went back to place the male into the backseat of the patrol car. I opened the back door and asked him to stand up, and he refused.

I then grabbed him to get him up and put him into the backseat. In doing this, I looked over my shoulder and saw the female reaching for something inside the trunk of the car. I could not see her hands, so I let go of the male and immediately went to the female and grabbed her and put her into the backseat of the patrol car. Then I went back to the male and tried again to get him to his feet. I had to pick him up to get him to the front of my patrol car to finish searching him."

The officer looked up to see Barbara halfway out the right-hand backseat window of his patrol car. The window lock was obviously unlocked, and she was not handcuffed.

"I hurried back to the back of the car and grabbed her. I got her out of the window and onto the ground. I opened the back door and told her to get into the car."

Barbara resisted, so the officer placed her into the backseat. At that time, a Bartow County sheriff's deputy pulled up behind the patrol car, and the patrolman asked the deputy to watch Barbara while he went to the driver's door and engaged the window lock and rolled up the window.

"I then spoke to the female and informed her why she was in the backseat. She verbally gave her consent to a search of the Mercedes, and the male continued his yelling and ranting as we looked through the trunk of the car. On reviewing the video of the incident, the male was yelling to the female, 'Call the police on your cell phone!' and she was yelling back, 'I don't have it!'"

Since both officers were in the assigned uniforms of their departments and were in marked patrol cars, the trooper stated later, he felt this was indicative of their condition at the time, since they obviously *were* the police.

After the officers searched the trunk of the Mercedes, the trooper noticed Schiess almost fall off the hood of the patrol car and into traffic.

"I went to him and pulled him to his feet and helped him to his knees in front of my car. In reviewing the video of this incident, the female makes a cell phone call to what I believe to be Bartow County 911. In talking, she gives her location as Georgia 20/US 411, right before the exit to get on I-75. That is seven-point-five miles from where this incident actually happened."

An investigator with the Floyd County District Attorney's Office stopped then and asked the trooper if he needed any help. When the officer explained the situation to him, the investigator made a recommendation as to the charge of reckless conduct for the female for going into the trunk while the officer struggled with her boyfriend.

"In reviewing the video, the female yells to the male, 'You shut up!' Then she asks him, 'What's the name of that road?' Then the investigator takes the male off to the side to see if he can obtain any information from him, and another trooper arrives at the scene."

The two troopers conducted a more thorough search of the vehicle; then the arresting officer returned to check on Barbara and asked her if she was okay. She claimed the officer had busted her lip, but when he asked her again if she was okay, she said, "Yeah." The officer explained to her again why she was put into the backseat of the patrol car. He told her that when he was trying to get Schiess into the backseat, her actions by going into the trunk of the car had presented an officer-safety issue.

The investigator who went to talk to Schiess said that Schiess stated, "She was cold, she was very cold. I only pulled over to put the top up." Then he retracted that statement and said that Barbara was the one who had been driving.

The Floyd County investigator went to talk to Barbara and explained to her that both she and Schiess were being charged with misdemeanor charges and told her that he had gathered all their medications from the Mercedes. Having completed an impound vehicle inventory, the trooper asked Schiess if he had any preferences for a wrecker service, since he was the registered owner of the vehicle. Schiess said that he did not care who towed the car, so the second trooper called the Cartersville headquarters and requested for the next wrecker service on the rotating list, Bulldog Towing.

During this time, Barbara was busy making more phone calls and said to someone that she would "need Mike's help." She then gave her location, then made another call, advising someone that she and Schiess had been en route from Rome to Atlanta, and the trooper had stopped because he thought Schiess was possibly assaulting her.

When the officers were ready to transport Barbara and Schiess to jail, Barbara complained that she was injured and needed medical attention, so the second trooper called and made arrangements to have an ambulance meet them at the jail. The arresting officer took Schiess to the Bartow County Jail for booking, and the other trooper took Barbara to jail. Once there, she was not allowed inside because of her complaint of injuries. The trooper then had to take her to the Cartersville Medical Center.

Schiess was evaluated by the jail's medical representative and was allowed to be booked; then the arresting trooper performed a state test of his breath. Standard field sobriety tests (SFSTs) were not performed because of the condition of Schiess and officer safety. Once the officer received the results, he released Schiess into the custody of the jail personnel. A short time later, Barbara was delivered to the jail, having been cleared by the medical center. She was then booked, as Schiess had been.

What had started as a simple trip home after work for one Georgia state trooper had turned into unexpected hours of hassle involving several officers from different law enforcement agencies.

15

In April 2005, Barbara sought treatment at a sports medicine and orthopedic surgery center in Atlanta for pain and weakness of her left forearm as a result of the Memorial Day, 2004, auto accident in which she fractured her left forearm and wrist. The fracture did not mend, and surgery followed on November 30, 2004. After removal of the surgical hardware, Barbara had spent the next five months in a cast.

In addition, Barbara had undergone two cervical fusions, and as a result of all her injuries, surgeries, and lingering problems, during her visit to the surgery center she reported pain that continually woke her up at night. There was constant nagging pain in her left arm and wrist, she said, with weakness and limitations to her wrist motion.

Her neurologic exam confirmed decreased muscle strength in her left forearm musculature, wrist, and decreased grip strength. There were significant limitations in her wrist motion, and there was atrophy noted in the muscles of her left forearm and left hand.

The examining physician reported to Barbara that there was evidence of left median nerve entrapment in the elbow, and exploratory surgery might be needed, and also reported his findings to her treating surgeon and to the doctor who had originally referred her to the clinic for examination.

Barbara's chronic pain and the medication it required was likely contributing to her increasingly impaired judgment.

16

Barbara Roberts and Bob Schiess were in Bridge City, Texas, to attend Barbara's mother's funeral while much of the investigation into Darlene's murder was beginning to come together. Barbara's mother had passed away on April 10, 2006, literally dying of a heart attack within minutes of learning that her daughter's ex-husband's current wife had been killed, and the Comeaux family had been devastated by such a shocking and unexpected loss. Barbara and Schiess arrived at the funeral home in Bridge City, Texas, and Barbara's nephew, Jeremy Jay Thomas, noticed that his aunt had shown up in old blue jeans and a T-shirt, which he thought was odd.

"Barbara didn't go anywhere unless she was dressed up nice," he said. She and Schiess had a rental car, which her nephew thought they had probably gotten at the Houston Intercontinental Airport when they had arrived in Texas.

"I noticed that Barbara had two black eyes that appeared to be a couple of days old," Thomas said. "I asked her what happened to her face and she told me she was learning to rollerblade and fell, face-first, into the end of a culvert."

Thomas didn't believe that statement for a couple of reasons, he told the authorities. First, the injuries didn't appear consistent to him with striking a concrete culvert or even a roadway. Second, Barbara had experienced some serious medical problems in the past, in addition to the 2004 car crash when she'd had to be Life-Flighted. Thomas, a deputy sheriff in Texas, based his opinion of the injuries because of his experience on the job as an accident investigator for the Harris County Sheriff's Office (HCSO). He thought that perhaps Barbara and Schiess had gotten into a fight, but said that he'd mentioned nothing to her about it because there appeared to be no problems at the time. His aunt didn't seem to be in any danger from Schiess, and they were, after all, gathered for the funeral of Irene Comeaux.

Barbara and Schiess were planning to stay in a nearby hotel, and since she and her nephew had always been close, she arranged for him and his wife to have a room there also—all of which was paid for by Schiess. Later, as Barbara and Thomas were walking around at the funeral home looking at the flowers that had been sent there for her mother's services, she found a card on one arrangement that said it had been sent by Vernon.

"Barbara looked at it, pointed it out, and said, 'Isn't this so sweet? He always loved Mama, and a couple of days after his wife is murdered, he still took time to send flowers to the funeral home for her.'"

Barbara had ordered and paid for the flowers at Wayside Florist herself, saying that Vernon had asked her to do so, but Vernon would later claim that he had never had a discussion with Barbara during which he asked Barbara to order flowers on his behalf or told her what to put on the card.

During that night, several of the family members were discussing Darlene's murder.

"Everyone knew that Barbara was still in love with Vernon, to the point of almost stalking him," Thomas said. "Other family members had told me that she would send Vernon e-mails saying that she had found God, and he would want her back, and that she wanted him to be happy."

On the following day, when the funeral services were held, Schiess did not attend; Barbara said he was supposedly too sick to go. After the funeral, Barbara asked if they could come and spend some time with her nephew and his family, and after staying in Beaumont a couple of days, they arrived at Thomas's home on April 17. That night, during a conversation about hunting, Thomas's wife was telling Barbara that she had gone deer hunting and shot her first deer. When describing how they had tracked the blood trail to find the deer, Barbara turned pale and said she'd rather not talk about it because it made her sick to her stomach.

Since several of Barbara's family were hunters and the whole family fished, it sounded strange to her nephew. Barbara had been around hospitals quite a bit, also, and it was odd that she would be squeamish about blood or about shooting a deer.

Barbara began talking that evening about what she had heard about Darlene's murder in the newspapers and on TV, and Barbara said that whoever had murdered Darlene had apparently robbed her because they stole all her grocery bags.

"That's when I told her that whoever did that was stupid to kill someone for groceries, and to take the groceries, because that bumped it up from a murder to a capital murder, and that was a death penalty–eligible case."

Barbara got really quiet when her nephew told her that, he said.

The following day, after a spa day for the ladies, the two couples went to a restaurant for dinner. The next morning, Barbara and Schiess left early for the airport. After they left, Thomas called his father and told him that he had a gut feeling that maybe his aunt Barbara had something to do with Darlene's death. His father told him that he had the same impression, and said that he had talked to some of the investigators on the case by phone. When Thomas called Investigator Bo Jolly, he learned that there had already been some major pieces of incriminating evidence pointing to Barbara and Schiess, an arrest was imminent, and there was a "pretty airtight" case against both of them.

17

In almost all police investigations, a veritable mountain of tedious detail paperwork is involved, far more than the public might expect. As soon as witnesses had reported a suspicious late-model black Dodge Dakota pickup seen in the area when Darlene Roberts was murdered, the search for the truck was on. Thousands of Department of Motor Vehicles (DMV) records from both Alabama and Georgia were searched for pickups matching the description of the one that had been seen by several of the witnesses. Investigators were looking for any trucks of a similar type that were registered to anyone who was in any way associated with Darlene Roberts. It took days for the search to begin narrowing down, but it finally paid off, with the investigators locating a 1999 black Dodge Dakota pickup registered in Conyers, Georgia, to Robert John Schiess III. Special Agent (SA) Brent Cameron Thomas, from the Alabama Bureau of Investigation (ABI), had been involved in the case from the start, interviewing and collecting evidence in Georgia.

He quickly confirmed that Schiess was currently residing at an apartment complex in Conyers.

Authorities had already learned from both Vernon Roberts and some of Barbara's family members, who suspected Barbara's possible involvement in Darlene's murder, that Schiess and Barbara were at that time in Texas. They had flown there to attend the April 13 funeral of Barbara's mother and would be flying back into the Atlanta airport soon. A photo lineup was quickly assembled and was shown to the three witnesses who had reported seeing a gray-haired man with the black truck, and they each independently identified Schiess as the man they had seen that day.

The witnesses had also described a white female in the truck with him. When a photo of Barbara Roberts was shown to the witnesses, they all said they believed she was the woman they had seen, and one man identified her as the woman he saw fighting with Schiess on the side of the road. Another of the witnesses had seen her in the truck, red-faced and crying.

An additional new witness had come forward with more information on the black truck. On April 13, two ABI investigators, Jason Brown and Brent Thomas, along with Cherokee County sheriff's investigator Mark Hicks, interviewed Leah Marie Stoker at her home on County Road 182. She told the officers that she had seen a black Dodge pickup truck, with the hard bed cover raised, on County Road 182, near its intersection with County Road 941, on April 6. Stoker told the officers that she had never seen that truck in the area previously.

The ABI had read the prescription on the broken pair of glasses found near the pond and SA Thomas began checking with optometrists in the Conyers area to see if they could locate the one that Barbara used. When Pearle Vision in Conyers confirmed that Barbara was a customer, Investigator Bo Jolly and SA Thomas obtained a subpoena for Barbara's records and traveled to Conyers on April 18 to get confirmation that the broken glasses belonged to her.

The trip to Pearle Vision yielded a bonus: When the officers got there, the staff at Pearle told them that Barbara had contacted them on April 7, the day following the murder, to order new contact lenses and glasses. She wanted to order a new eyeglass frame and lenses under warranty, and told them that she only had one side of the frame and one lens.

Andrea Knight, the Pearle employee who took Barbara's phone call, told her both lenses would be needed in order to cover her under the warranty. When she said she didn't have the nosepiece, the lost lens, and the missing half of the glasses, Knight asked her if she knew where they were, or had any piece that they could cover under warranty.

"She said that she did not," Knight reported, "then she started stuttering and getting very upset with me about it. She then went on about having to have them right away, and if we could start on them as soon as possible."

Knight told Barbara that Pearle would need payment over the phone, or she would need to come in to pay.

"She told me she'd been sick with a headache

and stomach problems, so I told her, no problem, we would get the lens started without her. We went over the lens options, then she needed to order contacts. She was starting to get upset with me because she said it was taking too much of her time."

Knight said that she and Barbara were on the phone for almost forty minutes.

"Once we got the glasses and contacts ordered, she gave me a MasterCard number," Knight said. "I went to enter the card through, and it declined. I called her right back within two minutes, and she sounded like she was sleeping."

Knight told Barbara about the card, and she gave her another MasterCard number, which processed through. The next day, Knight had to call Barbara back about what color she wanted her Transitions lenses to be.

"She told me that she wanted to refund the frame and use her boyfriend's black Silhouette frame, to go with gray lenses. I called her a few days later to let her know her lenses were here and she needed to pick out a new frame or bring us one to use. She said that her mom had died and that she and her boyfriend were in Texas, and said she would be back in a couple of days to get her lens order."

Barbara then arranged for Knight to ship the new contact lenses overnight to her in Texas.

After taking Knight's statement, Jolly and Thomas showed her the broken glasses that had been recovered at the crime scene. She and another employee, Danielle Lyn Anderson, positively identified them as being the same pair of eyeglasses that had earlier been made to order at the Conyers Pearle Vision for their customer Barbara Ann Roberts.

18

With a vital piece of evidence now positively placing Barbara Roberts at the scene of Darlene Roberts's murder, the investigators quickly began the process of obtaining search warrants for the apartment of Bob Schiess in Conyers, Georgia. They had learned that Schiess and Barbara had been in Texas for Barbara's mother's funeral and were due to fly home on the following day, so there was no time to lose. Since the officers felt that they had ample justification to request warrants, they immediately presented affidavits and applications for a search warrant in the Magistrate Court of Rockdale County, Georgia.

Special Agent Brian Johnston, of the GBI, prepared the paperwork after being assigned to assist SA Thomas, of the ABI, in the investigation of Darlene Roberts's murder. In presenting his credentials as part of the warrant application, SA Johnston stated he had spent over ten years in law enforcement and had been with the GBI for over five years. He also gave Thomas's credentials

as part of the warrant, stating that the ABI special
agent had been employed by the Alabama Department of Public Safety (ADPS) since 1997.
Thomas, Johnston said, was currently assigned to
the ABI Area II, which covered Cherokee County,
Alabama, and had been involved in the murder
investigation since its onset, and had provided
the pertinent facts and information to justify the
obtaining of the warrant.

Johnston began by outlining the circumstances
and details of the murder of Darlene Roberts, including a description of the green plastic film
found wrapped around her neck and the white
cotton gauze strips lying nearby at the scene. He
also told of the three witnesses who had observed
the black Dodge Dakota pickup, with a bed cover,
in the immediate area of the crime scene, near
the time of the murder, and the man and woman
they had seen with the truck and had subsequently identified from photo lineups as Robert
John Schiess III and Barbara Ann Roberts.

The murder weapon, Johnston said in his warrant application, was a 12-gauge shotgun, which
had not yet been recovered, and also missing was
Darlene Roberts's brown Rosetti viscose purse
and her cell phone.

The piece of broken eyeglass frame found at the
scene was described, as was the phone call Barbara
Roberts made on April 7 to reorder her eyeglasses
from Pearle Vision in Conyers, Georgia. She told
the clerk that she had broken her glasses and only
had the right lens and right arm remaining. The
warrant application described how SA Thomas presented the left lens, arm, and nosepiece recovered

at the crime scene to the Pearle lab tech, who identified them as being the same eyeglasses that had been sold to Barbara Roberts from that store.

The investigators, SA Johnston said, had determined that Schiess and Barbara were currently living on St. Clair Drive, Conyers, Georgia, in the Lake St. James Apartment Homes. Johnston said that based on the information outlined in the warrant application, he believed there was probable likelihood of finding additional evidence within the residence, specifically the missing shotgun, purse, and cell phone, along with additional amounts of green-tinted stretch wrap, cotton gauze, and the 1999 Dodge Dakota pickup truck.

The warrant was approved and granted, and the officers moved quickly to conduct a thorough search of the apartment before Schiess and Barbara were due to arrive at the airport on their return flight from Texas. Investigators headed at top speed to the Lake St. James Apartment Homes and began what would prove to be a very productive search, placing both Barbara Ann Roberts and Robert John Schiess III even more positively at the scene of the murder of Darlene Roberts.

Apartment number 714 was clearly marked with its numbers on the front door. It was located in building seven on the ground level, closest to building six. The officers entered the complex at the second gated entrance, located on St. Clair Drive, and went quickly to the correct residence.

On entering the apartment, the officers saw there were many indications that Schiess and Barbara had packed hurriedly when they left for Texas. Clothing, papers, and open suitcases were lying around on the bed and sofa, and one suit-case held some items that were wrapped together in green plastic stretch film, which appeared to be consistent with the green plastic film wrapped around Darlene Roberts's neck.

Officers also found the top of a box that had held a collapsible pistol grip butt stock, which in-cluded a free tactical butt pad. The picture shown on the box was, again, consistent with the butt stock pad that was recovered from the floor-board of Darlene Roberts's vehicle.

A digital camera found in the apartment held another key piece of evidence. The last picture on the memory card was a photo of Barbara, which she appeared to have taken of herself in the bathroom mirror of the apartment. It showed Barbara with two black eyes and a cut across the bridge of her nose. The investigators had already learned from Barbara's nephew, a deputy sheriff and an experienced accident in-vestigator in Texas, that Barbara had arrived in Texas for her mother's funeral with black eyes and a cut on her nose. He reported that due to his experience in dealing with traumatic injuries, he believed that his aunt's cut and bruises were consistent with someone who had been hit with a scope while firing a weapon. Barbara had told her family members that she had injured herself when she took a fall while rollerblading, but her nephew had found that hard to believe. Barbara had been in-volved in two serious traffic accidents in pre-vious years, he had told them, and, as a result, she was disabled.

The investigators found two new pairs of Rollerblades in the apartment, both still in their boxes and appearing to have been unused. They also found the package for a Weaver scope base for a Mossberg shotgun, and inside the package was an instruction booklet for a Tasco Red Dot optical sight.

Among the large amount of paperwork in the apartment were receipts for a Mossberg 500, serial number *R624708,* 12-gauge shotgun, purchased on November 7, 2005, from Piedmont Outfitters, located in Covington, Georgia. Piedmont Outfitters also carried in stock the R10 shotgun shells, the same type as those that had been recovered at the crime scene, and the collapsible stock and Tasco optical sight. The shotgun and its accessories, however, were nowhere to be found in the apartment. And neither was the missing purse and cell phone belonging to Darlene Roberts. The black Dodge Dakota pickup truck was not parked at the apartment, nor was it parked anywhere else at the apartment complex.

One of the most damning pieces of evidence recovered during the search was a group of records showing that Schiess had received shooting lessons from the South River Gun Club, based in Conyers. He had paid $395.70 for the lessons on February 27, 2006.

With so much incriminating evidence found in the suspects' apartment, Cherokee County, Alabama, authorities quickly obtained arrest warrants for Barbara Ann Roberts and Robert John Schiess III and faxed them to the GBI. The investigators had already received the date and time of the couple's scheduled flight from Texas back to Hartsfield-Jackson Atlanta International Airport. As soon as their plane landed, officers boarded before the passengers began to deplane. They hurried down the aisle, shoving some of the passengers out of their way in their haste to reach Barbara and Schiess and arrest them before they had time to react. The woman sitting next to the aisle beside Schiess was yanked unceremoniously to her feet and pulled out into the aisle. Schiess and Barbara were handcuffed, read their rights, and hustled out of the plane, through the airport, and to the Rockdale County Sheriff's Office (RCSO).

Once there, Schiess never once uttered a word, refusing to make any statement of any sort without an attorney present. On the other hand, Barbara didn't wait for her attorney, Steve Lanier, to show up. He had spoken with her by phone before the pair had left the Texas airport, and he had advised her not to give any statements, telling her he would be in touch with her the following morning. She and Schiess had called Lanier because they claimed they had heard some of the details of the murder from Barbara's family, and they expected that investigators would want to talk to them. Instead of waiting for Lanier, however, Barbara was frightened and disoriented, and she did not remember the importance of having counsel present when any statements were made. She began talking to the investigators without benefit of counsel, making the first of many long, rambling, and highly incriminating statements and admissions, which ultimately would seal her fate.

19

When Bob Schiess was taken into custody at the Atlanta airport, he had in his possession a black leather satchel. While he and Barbara Roberts were being booked into the Rockdale County Jail, the investigators searched the satchel for weapons and any other information that might possibly be related to the murder of Darlene Roberts. As they had earlier at the apartment, they once again hit pay dirt—the satchel was *literally* packed with evidence.

There was a receipt from Dick's Sporting Goods in Atlanta, showing the purchase of a pair of DBX Prowler in-line skates, a pair of DBX Aggressive in-line skates, DBX adult protective gear, a package of crew socks, and a bottle of Powerade fruit punch. The items were purchased on April 8, 2006, at 7:41 P.M. and paid for with an American Express card.

The satchel also contained thirteen downloaded and printed pages of an Internet document called "Frequently Asked Questions about

Fingerprints," and Schiess had printed pages one through fourteen of forty-eight pages. The information he had selected dealt with the fundamentals of the science of fingerprints. On the second page of the text, it asked the readers to describe themselves in order for the website to provide the best answers for their questions. According to the printout, Schiess had made inquiries both as a "law enforcement officer" and as a "criminal" about fingerprint information.

By far, the most crucial piece of evidence that was collected from the black leather satchel that day was a rental agreement. It was between Schiess and Aaron & Montana Self Storage, a Conyers facility located on Iris Drive, for leasing of space in Building A. The agreement was dated April 8, 2006. The spaces at the storage center were large enough to drive a vehicle into and park it.

The investigators had a strong hunch that they had just located the hiding place of the black Dodge Dakota pickup truck.

20

At 6:30 P.M., on April 19, Barbara Roberts was interviewed for the first time concerning her knowledge of the murder of Darlene Roberts and her possible role in that murder.

A large group of agents and investigators from both Georgia and Alabama had assembled in a room adjacent to the interview room so that they could listen to and view the questioning session. ABI agent Jason Brown, Cherokee County investigator Bo Jolly, and GBI agents Carter Brank, Jack Vickery, Wesley Horney, Boykin Jones, and Brian Johnston packed into the observation room, while ABI agent Brent Thomas and Cherokee County investigator Mark Hicks conducted the interview. For reasons not stated, this initial questioning session was neither filmed nor recorded, and the report was written from the officers' notes.

After being read her rights and signing a rights waiver, Barbara began to talk. And talk, and talk.

On April 6, 2006, the day of the murder of Darlene Roberts, Barbara said, she drove her Buick

Riviera to Rome, Georgia, in the afternoon, then went to the South Trust Bank. She claimed that she learned about Darlene's murder on the day of Darlene's funeral. When she was asked if she knew the whereabouts of the black pickup truck belonging to Schiess, she replied, "I have no idea."

The officers then showed her the pair of broken eyeglasses, and she claimed she did not know if they were hers or not. She had broken her pair, she claimed, by trying to in-line skate, and she said she had called Pearle Vision to have them replaced.

When she was asked if she had ever fired a shotgun, Barbara told the investigators that she could not hold or fire a shotgun because of injuries she had received in an automobile accident. As the questions became more and more direct, Barbara was asked if she had ever been in the field where Darlene was murdered. She denied that, but admitted that she had talked to Vernon Roberts on the phone that afternoon, and said they had talked about his daughter, Angela, and places that she might stay in Georgia.

When asked if her fingerprints would be on any of the shotgun shells that were found at the scene, she said they would not, because she was not strong enough to load the shells in the shotgun. That statement cast a bad light on her earlier claim never to have been at the scene, and Barbara said that she was not sure if she needed to talk to an attorney or not.

That put an end to the questions for the time being, while Barbara decided if she wanted an attorney, but after a few moments, she decided to continue talking. Since she had contradicted herself, and now seemed to be acknowledging that she had indeed been at the murder scene, the admissions began coming more frequently.

Barbara continued to claim that she really didn't know where the pickup truck was located, but she then said that she and Schiess did not go back to her house after the murder. She admitted that she was at the scene of the crime, but she said that she did not kill Darlene. She didn't want to be there at the murder location, she said, and claimed to be afraid for Schiess to find out that she had talked to law enforcement. Barbara asked the officers if she would still be charged with murder if she cooperated with their investigation.

There should not be anything at the murder scene with her fingerprints on it, Barbara told the officers, then contradicted her earlier statements once again by saying that she did not know the name of the storage buildings where Schiess had taken the Dodge Dakota pickup, but she would lead law enforcement to the location.

Barbara admitted that she was afraid of Schiess, who had anger management problems, she claimed.

"He starts drinking as soon as he gets up in the morning and doesn't stop," she told the officers. She also said she was afraid he would not be able to see his children anymore.

When the questioning turned toward the motive for the murder, Barbara said that in October 2005, Darlene had to go on a business trip to Texas. While she was out of town, Barbara said she went to visit Vernon Roberts at home and had sex with him while she was there. Later, she confessed to Schiess that she'd had sex with Vernon, and Schiess became furious. Barbara said that when she and Schiess went to Cherokee County on April 6, she thought Schiess was only going to talk to Darlene, but soon learned differently. His real plan, she said, was to have sex with Darlene to repay Vernon for committing adultery with Barbara.

The questioning had begun to more closely resemble a narrative at this point, with Barbara doing most of the talking. She had definitely warmed to her subject, and the details flowed freely as a picture of her version of the events of April 6 began to emerge.

Barbara admitted that she and Schiess had gone to Cherokee County, Alabama, on April 6, in his black Dodge Dakota pickup truck, stopping on County Road 941, only a short distance from Vernon and Darlene Roberts's residence. They pulled off on the left side of the road in front of a blue pasture gate. Schiess got out and raised the hood of the truck to make it look as though they were having trouble and had broken down beside the road, needing help.

When Darlene drove up to where they were stopped, Barbara said, Schiess waved for her to stop and Darlene pulled up to see if she could help him. According to Barbara, Schiess then pulled Darlene out of the car and made her lie facedown on the ground. He tried to use plastic cable ties to secure her hands, but he could not get them to work. Barbara said that Schiess then took some heavy cotton gauze to tie Darlene's hands and feet, then stuck some rolled-up gauze in her mouth. She said that he then used some of the green-tinted stretch wrap, wrapped around her head, to hold the gauze in place. When asked about where the shotgun was at this point, Barbara claimed that Schiess had it with him.

"I was freaking out at that point," Barbara said. "I thought that he was only going to talk to her."

Darlene then managed to work free of her bindings and jumped up and began to run into the pasture, and Schiess made Barbara get into Darlene's vehicle with him, she said. They drove into the pasture after Darlene, who ran down the fence line away from where her vehicle had been parked, until she got close to the back of the pasture and another fence.

Barbara said she and Schiess followed Darlene when she turned and started running toward the pond in the pasture. Darlene ran into the pond, then ran along the edge of the pond until she got to a place where some tall grass was growing along the edge. Barbara told the officers that Darlene lay down in the water to hide behind the grass, but Schiess followed her, pointed the shotgun at her, and shot her three times, point-blank, as she lay facedown in the pond.

"I was really freaking out," Barbara claimed, and said that Schiess hit her in the face with the stock of the shotgun, trying to quiet her and breaking her glasses in the process.

After the shooting, Barbara said, she couldn't remember where they had parked Darlene's vehicle. She remembered that she and Schiess got back into his truck and started driving back to Georgia. They threw Darlene's cell phone out the window of the truck somewhere on the side of the road along the way, and Barbara said that she threw Darlene's purse into a Dumpster behind a Texaco station in Rome, Georgia. The shotgun, she claimed, had been thrown into the Etowah River, on US 411 and Georgia Highway 20, as she and Schiess drove over the bridge. At first she said it had been wrapped in plastic and cement, then later said they didn't use any cement.

After they got back to Conyers, Barbara claimed, Schiess cleaned the inside of the pickup and later parked it in a new rental storage building in town. They threw away the clothes they wore during the murder in the Dumpster at the apartment complex.

Barbara admitted to the officers that she had worn a disguise during the crime, pulling her hair up and stuffing it under a black baseball cap, then wearing a big sweater with a hood pulled over the cap. She was also wearing a surgical mask over her face. Schiess, she said, didn't wear any sort of disguise.

She had wanted to tell Vernon what had happened, and that they hadn't meant to hurt Darlene, she claimed. Then she said that she had asked Schiess after the murder if he was worried that they would be caught by law enforcement, and he said that he wasn't.

"He said that he has a genius IQ, and that lawyers made Cs in college and police made Cs in high school."

It was a great deal of satisfaction to the "C-student" police officers present at the interview to know they had been given so much incriminating testimony against their two suspects, due to Barbara's making such a detailed and lengthy statement.

21

After the conclusion of her first interview, at around 7:50 P.M., Barbara Roberts told the officers she knew where the missing black Dodge Dakota had been hidden. She voluntarily agreed to escort the GBI agents to the location of Schiess's pickup truck. Thanks to the papers found in Schiess's satchel that had been confiscated at the airport at the time of their arrest, the investigators already were relatively certain they knew where the truck was parked, but corroboration from one of the suspects would add greatly to the importance of the evidence.

Barbara told the investigators that the truck was, indeed, located at Aaron & Montana Self Storage, and Barbara gave them the gate code and storage unit number. When the officers checked with the manager of the storage facilities, they were provided with records to the unit in question, A-66, which indicated that it had been leased to Robert John Schiess on April 8. The key to the lock on the unit, Barbara told them, was on a key ring that was inside the Schiess apartment, and she gave SA Jack Vickery her verbal consent to retrieve the key. Vickery went to the apartment and quickly found the key ring Barbara had described.

That night, at around eleven forty-five, SA Brian Johnston went to the home of Rockdale County Superior Court judge David Irwin to get his approval for a search warrant for the Aaron & Montana Self Storage Unit A-66, and the seizure of a black Dodge Dakota pickup truck, bearing VIN number *1B7GL22X7SS236977* and registered to Dr. Robert John Schiess III, which was believed to be parked inside the unit. After reviewing Johnston's affidavit giving information on the case and the investigators' reasons for believing the truck to be inside the storage unit in question, Judge Irwin signed the search warrant order and the warrant was executed at midnight.

After trying all the keys on the key ring that SA Vickery had brought from the apartment, police saw that none of them opened the storage unit. The Rockdale County Fire Department had to be contacted to come to the facility and cut the lock off the unit before it could be opened. When the door to the unit was finally rolled up that evening after midnight, and the waiting group of officers got their first look inside, the 1999 black Dodge Dakota pickup truck sat there—just as they had suspected, and as Barbara Roberts had told them it would be.

The investigators moved in and began photographing the truck from every angle and doing a preliminary check for evidence, and Milstead

Wrecker Service was called to move the truck from Aaron & Montana Self Storage to a secure storage area at the Rockdale County Sheriff's Office. There, it would undergo crime scene processing, and would yield even more evidence in the murder of Darlene Roberts.

22

The news of the two arrests in the Darlene Roberts murder case was the big story in all the area media, when it was confirmed that the exwife of Vernon Roberts and her boyfriend, a wealthy neurosurgeon, had been taken into custody. Investigator Mark Hicks confirmed to the *Post,* a Cherokee County newspaper, that the arrests had been made, and Sheriff Larry Wilson said the murder warrant had been executed on the couple by the Georgia Bureau of Investigation as they were deplaning at the Hartsfield-Jackson Atlanta International Airport. Wilson said that according to initial indications, Darlene Roberts had died of a single gunshot wound to the head, but he had no further details for the media.

Hicks would not comment on what kind of evidence had led to the arrests, and would not disclose any information as to the motive for the murder, but the hard work of all the agencies involved was continuing to pay off.

While some of the officers assigned to the case were interviewing Barbara Roberts and locating the pickup truck belonging to Robert John Schiess, other agents were actively pursuing other avenues of investigation. The GBI was working to assist the ABI and the Cherokee County Sheriff's Office (CCSO) in gathering information related to some of the paperwork found in the Schiess apartment and in the black leather satchel confiscated from Schiess at the airport. On April 20, ABI agents Jason Brown and Brent Thomas, along with Cherokee County investigators Mark Hicks and Bo Jolly, received information from the GBI on the South River Gun Club memberships of Bob Schiess and Barbara Roberts.

The South River Gun Club is a very popular, upscale organization, with facilities for all sorts of shooting sports. Large, well-maintained areas for trap and skeet shooting, target ranges, competitions, special events, and more are included in the benefits of club membership, and Schiess and Barbara had joined.

Several documents from the gun club had been found in Schiess's possession, along with applications and waivers of liability for both Schiess and Barbara, and a copy of the South River Gun Club shooting roster and the club's membership roster. There was also a copy of the Alcohol, Tobacco, Firearms and Explosives form that had been filled out by Schiess at the time he bought a Mossberg 500 12-gauge pump shotgun at JH Piedmont Outdoors in Covington, Georgia, and a receipt from the South River Gun Club for $395.70 for club membership fees for Schiess and Barbara, paid for with Schiess's Visa card.

The gun club was able to provide the investigators with the dates and times of all the occasions when Schiess signed in at the shooting ranges; on a couple of occasions, Barbara had also occasionally signed in for practice, but more often had merely accompanied Schiess to the club. Club staff reported that Barbara, due to her disabilities from her auto accidents, did not appear to have been able to lift and hold the shotgun comfortably.

23

Barbara Ann Roberts spent a sleepless night in the Rockdale County Jail on April 19, and by five o'clock the following morning, she began demanding to talk to an officer again. The investigators with whom she had spoken the previous night had been hard at work, long into the night, at the storage unit where the pickup truck had been located, and they had not yet reported in. Later that morning, after the jail staff was able to call in one of the investigating officers on the case, Barbara was taken to a room equipped with a video camera so that the interview could be taped this time.

The video gives a far better understanding of the mannerisms and body language of both Barbara and the interviewing officer. When it begins, it shows Barbara sitting alone at a table in the room, very still except for moments of fidgeting, twiddling her thumbs, and adjusting her glasses. The rest of the time, she waits motionless, staring straight ahead, wearing an orange jumpsuit, handcuffs, and leg shackles.

Investigator Mark Hicks, from the Cherokee County Sheriff's Office, was the officer who arrived to conduct the interview. Hicks was known for being respectful and low-key when conducting questioning sessions, and he wanted to put Barbara at ease. He entered the room and sat down at the table, saying, "Hey, Barbara."

Barbara sat up straight in her chair, leaned forward, and said hello to Hicks, who then asked her how she was doing.

"Good," she answered.

Hicks identified himself as one of the men who had questioned Barbara the previous evening, and she told him she remembered him, but couldn't recall his name. Barbara began to tell Hicks how she had "remembered some other stuff" during the night and had asked to talk to someone at five o'clock that morning.

"Okay, hold on just a second," Hicks told her. "I need to read you your rights again, every time we talk, and make sure you understand what your rights are. It's the same form that we read to you last night."

Barbara scooted her chair closer to the table to look at the form Hicks showed to her.

"It says you have the right to remain silent, anything you say can and will be used against you in court. You have the right to talk to an attorney and to have him with you, present with you, while you are being questioned. If you cannot afford to hire a lawyer, one will be appointed to you before any questioning, if you wish. You can decide at any time to exercise these rights and not answer any questions or make any statements. Do you still understand what your rights are?"

"Yes, sir," Barbara answered, "but I never had a chance to call my lawyer."

"Okay," Hicks said, "if you want to talk to your attorney, that's your choice."

Barbara hesitated for a moment, then began speaking in a slow, very precise manner.

"You know, um, there's just some questionable things, you know, after you lay back down and you start thinking, and you're not so tired, and things start coming to you, and stuff—"

Hicks interrupted, reminding Barbara again that she would need to sign the rights form before he could talk with her any further.

"If you want to talk to your attorney now, you know, you're telling me you want to do that, then we're gonna have to stop and I can't talk to you anymore, but if you want to continue, that's your choice."

"You mean I can't keep talking to you and still have him represent me?" Barbara asked.

"Ma'am, that's entirely up to you," Hicks answered. "Yes, if you have an attorney and you want to stop until he's here, that's fine. If you want to talk to me now, that choice is yours. I can't tell you to talk to me or not talk to me. If you want your attorney, that's your choice."

Barbara adjusted her glasses, then began to speak again in the same slow, deliberate manner.

"What I'm saying is, I don't mind talking to

you, but I'd still like the opportunity to talk to my attorney to let him know what's going on so that he can . . . you know what I'm trying to say . . . so that he can follow through with me."

Hicks continued trying, patiently and very politely, to be sure that Barbara understood that she had the right to have an attorney present during this questioning session and any others to follow, if she chose to do so.

"I think Brent explained all of it to you last night," he said. "I don't see a problem with you calling your attorney—if you want to do that before talking to me, that's fine. The choice is yours, Ms. Roberts, I can't tell you to talk to me. If you want your attorney, then we'll have to stop right now—and then when you notify your attorney, and your attorney can come, then we'll talk. It's entirely up to you whether you want to talk to me now or not."

Barbara adjusted her glasses again, then said, "Okay."

"If you want to talk to me," Hicks said again, "I need you to sign this form first. And if you want to wait until your attorney is present, then I'm gonna have to stop and leave."

That was not what Barbara wanted.

"No, I just want to try to be able for him to represent me. You remember when you said, if I can't afford one, then I would have to appoint one and—"

"Yes, ma'am," Hicks said, "speaking with me has no bearing on your attorney being able to represent you or anything like that. [Signing the rights form] is not saying that you don't want a lawyer to represent you sometime in the future. It's just saying that you are willing to talk to me today with your lawyer not being present."

Barbara was determined to continue with the interview.

"Right," she answered, taking a pen from Hicks and signing the form. "Now you were the one in the kind-of-colory shirt last night," she said to Hicks.

"This is the same color shirt I had on," he said.

"I must have been dreaming or something," Barbara said. "I could have sworn there was some guy that was not in a uniform that had just a colored shirt on."

Barbara wanted to be taken to the Cherokee County Jail in Centre as soon as possible, but Hicks explained to her that in order to transfer her, she would need to sign extradition in the presence of a judge or magistrate that afternoon; then Cherokee County could have a car there to pick her up early the next morning.

"What I would like to do is sign the thing," Barbara told him.

While she signed the extradition form, Barbara told Hicks, "I got hit in the head and lost my glasses, and I'm blind as a bat. They were some strong prescriptions, trifocals, and, you know, I can see you as a form, as a human being, but I can see color. I can tell you what you are wearing."

"Sure," Hicks said. Then the interview suddenly changed direction.

"Bob shot three shots," Barbara said abruptly, holding up three fingers, "okay, and he said, 'I bet that'll scare the shit out of her.' I did not see her move. I did not see no blood. I don't know how many shells were found, but only three shots were fired."

Barbara paused for a moment.

"I didn't actually see the bullet hit her, you know what I'm saying? I didn't see blood or nothing. Because when she was laying on the ground, like, um . . . the drawing with him yesterday . . ."

Hicks nodded and said, "Um-hm."

Barbara became more animated, gesturing as she went on with her story.

"She kept telling him, 'Let me go. I live about nine miles from here,' which I knew better than that, but I wouldn't say anything. 'I don't know who you are from Adam, you have plenty of time to get away.'"

"She was telling Bob this?" Hicks asked.

"I never said a word at any time or point of time or anything, because I knew she would have recognized my voice."

"Okay," Hicks said, "you don't think she recognized you when she saw you?"

"No, I don't think so," Barbara told him, "because she would not have been so cooperative as she was. She would have been . . . I know she would have been very more threatened because in other situations that come up that really had nothing to do [with this situation] she was, you know, 'I want you dead' type, okay?"

"Were you dressed like you normally dress?" Hicks asked. When Barbara said she was not, he asked, "How were you dressed that made you look different?"

Barbara told him she had on black pants, tan

tennis shoes, a blue hooded Hilfiger sweater, a baseball cap, with her hair tucked underneath, and the hood pulled up over the cap. She also said she was wearing wraparound sunglasses and a face mask. "You know, like people wear when they're doctors or like if they're mowing the grass or something like that, you know what I'm saying, that covers both their nose and mouth."

Barbara was beginning to talk faster and gesture more often with her hands, demonstrating what area of her face the mask had covered.

"You mean like a filter?" Hicks asked.

"Yeah, yeah, like that. So it wasn't . . . first off, she wouldn't have got out of the car. She would have ran my ass down." She leaned forward toward Hicks. "You know what I'm saying?"

"Yes, ma'am," he said.

"Because, I'm sure you've heard, just like he heard, you know, which has been said, 'If anything ever happens to me, go get Barbara.'"

Barbara was leaning back and forth in her chair by this time, gesturing with both hands and waving her arms as she spoke. She was becoming increasingly excited.

"But I never . . . I don't know how many gun shells, that is what's questioning [*sic*] me because, after we left, when we were leaving. And then—also something he told me last night—was how they recognized him was him taking off his shirt and he waved at a car. Now who has just shot somebody gonna wave at somebody? I don't know. I—I just think that he is saying and I'm thinking, 'I'm just going.' I didn't see blood. You know when I found out that she was dead? When my little sister called me, uh, the day before my momma died."

"Okay," Hicks said. "Did you think in the back of your mind that Bob had just maybe shot and scared Darlene?"

"That's what I really thought he had done," Barbara said. "And there were three shells, that's why I'm wondering how many shells were found, because we were hearing shots and we saw turkeys on the side of the road, and we thought that maybe somebody was turkey shooting."

"They could have been. I don't know," Hicks said.

"I don't know, either," Barbara told him. "I'm not gonna say they were or they weren't, I don't know what they was doing. I'm sitting there, laying, last night. I was thinking, you know, 'Yeah, he's got a bad temper and he's . . . he has temper problems, this and that and whatever,' and all this has to do with the fact that me and Vernon were having an affair, and me coming up honest with Bob about it."

"You had told Bob about the affair?" Hicks asked.

"That's correct," Barbara said.

"Okay, do you think that's why Bob went there that day?" Hicks asked.

"He went there to confront her," Barbara told him, "to tell her, and [the other officer] should have that on notes from yesterday."

"Bob was gonna tell Darlene about the affair?"

"Right, 'cause I had promised Vernon from the bottom of my heart that even if he died before she did, I would never tell her anything." Barbara began to cry and shook her head. "And I wasn't going to tell her anything."

"Okay, and you had told Bob about it, and Bob decided to go tell her?"

"Yes, and I think he was gonna do, like this"—Barbara motioned with her hands as if a mask was being removed from her face—"and she was gonna recognize who I was, and she would have been all upset and pissed off and run to Vernon, and shit would have been happening—things that were happening with us."

Barbara started to cry and got more excited, moving around in her chair and gesturing frequently as she spoke.

"It's all my fault. Vernon and me stayed in touch quite a bit. We talked back and forth two or three times a week and e-mailed each other. I never tried to call him at home—that was her house, you know what I mean, and I respected it."

Hicks, who had been listening without comment for a while, said, "I understand."

"And I never went over until he invited me over there. It was when he was on vacation, they were supposed to go to Florida but they weren't able to because she had some kind of meeting or something, and his brother was in town from Louisiana. And I actually came up the day before. And I rode along the side of the road and I saw them in the golf cart coming up, so I tried to hurry up and turn around, and the next thing I know, there they were, right there, and I put my hand up over my face. Me and Vernon made eye-to-eye contact. He knew who I was, and he mentioned later that his brother asked if it was me."

"Do you think that his brother might have recognized you, too?" Hicks asked.

"I think he might have," Barbara said. "And the following day, we got together and I thought we were just gonna talk, and he said he wanted to show me all the new stuff he had done around the house, this and that and all that kind of stuff. And I honest to God thought that was what we were gonna do. Well, before I get to the front door, we're already passionately kissing like this, you know, and next thing we're upstairs—this, that, and whatever, and this kind of stuff, you know, and all of a sudden the phone rings and it's his brother. He's calling, he's gonna come back. He's in Centre, he's coming back because he's forgot something. I don't remember what he forgot, he forgot something. So, and in order for . . . we didn't sleep in their bed, okay? We slept in the bed that we used to call the 'Angel Room.' He pulled the comforters and everything back, because he didn't want my makeup or my scent or anything like that on, that Darlene could recognize. I will be this explicit: he came so hard, he shit in the bed."

At this unexpectedly graphic disclosure, Hicks became red-faced and grew visibly embarrassed. After a slight pause, he said, "Okay. . . ."

Barbara continued to sniffle, fidget in her chair, and wave her hands in the air as she spoke.

"Now, Vernon would never touch Darlene in a million years. He would never slap her, he would never do anything. But I knew they were having a lot of hard times with her son, and a couple of times, he had given her an ultimatum, 'Either him or me.'

"She had even asked somebody that they worked with, at lunch, if they had an apartment to rent. She came to him and asked him how much they still owed, whatever, on that car that they still have. You know, there was some serious contemplation here going on.

"And during that time, we were talking a lot, okay? Now, I didn't come back that night, because her sister came over with her nephew and they cooked pizza, and the nephew spent the night—supposedly, they were going to be watching an Astros game or a Dallas game. I don't remember—it was a Texas game, it was football or baseball, I don't remember, because I don't watch any more of them. Come to find out the reason the little boy stayed there was because he had a girlfriend that lives locally there, that his mother does not approve of. He stayed on the phone and never watched the game. And I told Vernon, 'Now, look, don't let him disrespect you.' You know what I mean. 'You need to go in there and tell him, "I know what you are doing, this is enough. I'm not gonna do this behind your parents' back."'

"'Or if he comes and says, "Can I use your car?" tell him, "No, without a doubt, if you're gonna go anywhere, it's to your house."' You know, this kind of stuff."

Barbara had begun to cry and turned away from Hicks, sobbing, with her hands over her face.

"Barbara, did Vernon know that you and Bob

were coming up there that day to talk to Darlene?" Hicks asked.

"No, I didn't even know it," Barbara said, still crying.

"Okay, do you think Bob may have talked to Vernon and told him he was coming?"

"No, no, no, no." She was still crying and shaking her head.

"You don't think he would have done that?"

"No, because I think if Bob, if Vernon would have been there, too, he'd probably would have done the same exact thing. 'Cause of them both together, you know."

"You think he would have killed Vernon, too?" Hicks asked.

"I don't know if he killed Darlene! I don't remember. *I do not remember.* You would think, the way that thing read in the paper, you, this slaughter, this is how they put it, and stuff like that. Seems like you would have seen blood and stuff in the water. And you know, and in my mind . . . I pulled it up when my sister told me and I said, 'No way, because I was looking for homes in Rome.' That's why I was in Rome during that time, because I had went to see a banker and I was supposed to go see a lady with AACA, which helped people with disability get houses, and stuff like that, and I couldn't see her."

"Well, Barbara—" Hicks began.

"I even have all my money willed to Vernon and Darlene," Barbara said, leaning forward in her chair.

"Well, if you think about it, you know," Hicks said, "if Bob hadn't killed her, why did he throw the gun away? Why did y'all throw her purse away? Why did y'all throw your clothes away when y'all got home?"

"I know," Barbara began, waving her arms and moving around in her chair. "I know that part because my face was busted and we didn't know where the set of glasses was, and all that kind of stuff, you know. And he figured they might be able to find it, and I only had a little piece of glass, my face was gashed open, here I'm bleeding in her car, and you know what I'm saying."

"Who was driving Darlene's car? Was it you or was it Bob?"

"It was Bob," Barbara answered Hicks, then asked him if there were only three empty shotgun shells found at the scene. He told her he wasn't sure, since he wasn't the one who collected them.

"We started freaking when he realized that my, well, I knew right off the bat my face was slashed, but anyhow . . ."

Barbara said that in her earlier interview, she had been told that Bob waved at one of the witnesses and took off his shirt, and she raised up her head and looked, and that's when the witness recognized her, before she put her head back down.

"Why did Bob hit you?" Hicks asked.

"I think to get me out of the way, because, you know, I was kind of like, I—I, he hit me with the butt, the back end of the gun, kind of this way. (She demonstrated.) I don't know if it was just like a 'get out of the way' type thing. We never talked about it. We never talked about it."

"Were you saying anything when he hit you or anything?" Hicks asked.

Barbara seemed confused.

"I didn't know what was gonna happen, okay? I didn't know what was gonna happen."

"Did he hit you before or after—"

"Never, but he had a major fight with his father the month before . . . ," Barbara interrupted.

"Listen, listen," Hicks said. "Did he hit you before or after he shot the shotgun?"

"Before. That's what I'm saying. I didn't see. I knew there was a body there, but I didn't see red."

"Okay, that's why you couldn't see her, because he had already hit you with the gun and broken your glasses?"

"Correct," Barbara said. "I could see the figure of the person, but I couldn't see red. The way, you know, her being 'slaughtered,' seems like there would have been a lot of blood and gore. There was none."

"Well," Hicks said, "you know, I could understand if you didn't see, you know, a lot of things because, like you said, your glasses were broken and you could just see shapes and things like that. And if you had just been hit in the face with a shotgun butt, too, that would affect your vision some, too, you know."

"Well," Barbara said, "he didn't say something. He didn't say, like, 'Okay, now it's over. Now she's dead.' he just said, 'Maybe that will scare the shit out of her.'"

"Okay," Hicks said, "and after he quit shooting,

y'all just moved the car up there and y'all got in your vehicle and left?"

"Right, we didn't speed off. We didn't do nothing. You know, there's probably on the teleprompter [*sic*] of us going in, getting gas at the gas station, just calm like this, because I thought he was just gonna scare the shit out of her. I think that's what he did, too."

24

Hicks tried to learn more about the station where Barbara and Bob had stopped for gas after leaving the scene.

"You said earlier that y'all threw the purse in a Dumpster behind a gas station?" he asked.

"At the same gas station that we went in and got gas and I got something to drink. There should be something on their video." Barbara gave more specifics about the location of the gas station, and said the store's video should show her dropping a dollar while paying.

"I was kind of shaky. I really couldn't see, whatever, and stuff. I know the clerk noticed my face and, anyhow, she came back out there and she handed me my dollar back, and she said, 'Ma'am, I think you dropped this.'"

Having gotten sufficient information concerning the location of the gas station, Hicks then turned the conversation toward the whereabouts of the shotgun.

"One more thing I really wanted to ask you—

I think you told Brent what had happened to the shotgun. Can you tell me where you think it's at, since you've had time to rest and maybe [things have] come back to you a little better? You told him last night it was between Rome and Cartersville. Was it in the river? There's only one river between Rome and Cartersville, the Etowah River."

"That's what I told him," Barbara said. "I thought it was the Etowah."

"Were you driving the vehicle, or was it Bob?"

"He was driving at first. Bob can't see, there's certain distances Bob can't see. He had eye surgery."

"Were you driving when y'all were at the river, or was Bob driving?"

Barbara said that she was driving, and said that Bob threw the gun out of the truck window.

"You know why I think he threw it away?" she asked. "Because he put the shells in the gun with his fingers and he knew y'all were gonna get his fingerprints."

Hicks asked Barbara if the gun had been wrapped in the green plastic wrap that was found in the apartment and around Darlene Roberts's neck.

"It was wrapped in that plastic stuff way, way before that," she said.

"Okay, but when he threw it in the river, did it have the plastic stuff wrapped around it?"

"If I remember correctly, yes," Barbara told him. "But this is what's haunting me. He never said, 'Okay, she's dead.' He never said, 'Okay, that's the end of her.' He never said anything like that. He just said, 'I bet that scared the shit out of her.' And I don't remember seeing, you know,

I've cleaned many a fish and I know how much they bleed and stuff and they are slaughtered. I would have seen something. I would have seen red in the water."

"Possibly, or, you know, you might not have," Hicks said.

Barbara suddenly laughed loudly. "I don't know," she said, "I didn't see any." Then she paused and said, "That's not funny."

"No, ma'am, it's not funny," Hicks told her.

"No, it's not," Barbara said, "it's just kind of a hysterical laugh."

"It's not funny," Hicks said again, "but if your vision is as bad as you say it is, you may not have seen."

"I was standing right next to him," Barbara said. "His vision's off between a certain distance and a certain distance, and that's noted on the previous report, because that's why he couldn't see anything about what this guy had on, because he could not recognize nothing, you know. That's why I'm very, very curious about how many shells were found."

Hicks thought for a moment before answering.

"I'll tell you what, if they get you over and the judge signs your extradition papers, we'll come get you first thing in the morning and then I'll have Brent in our office, and you said, you know, you're more comfortable with Brent. You and Brent can sit down, and Brent can probably tell you a little bit more about the details than I can."

Hicks looked surprised when Barbara suddenly veered off on another subject.

"See, you know, there are other things that

come to mind. Like he'd always say his dad's name was Peter."

"You're talking about Bob?" Hicks asked.

"And his dad's name is Peter, and I've been around him many times, whenever he'd saved a person's life doing brain surgery and stuff and they would say . . . and they'd come up to him and say, 'You saved my mother's life, you saved my wife's life.' He'd say, 'I didn't. God did. He just gave me the instruments.' I told [Brent] that yesterday, too."

"Barbara," Hicks said, "I don't have all the answers. I can't tell you, I wasn't there. I can't see through your eyes and see what happened and why it happened, and—"

"It happened because I had an affair, that's why it happened," she said.

"You know, you and Bob were the only two that was there that could tell us what happened. I think you're trying to do the right thing, so let's see if we can get you to the people over here, where you can sign the papers and we'll come get you in the morning. I'll have Brent there as soon as you get to Centre. And then you and Brent, and if you want me to sit down in there with y'all, or just you and Brent, or whatever, and if you think of some more things between now and then, we'll be more than glad to sit down and talk to you."

Barbara and Hicks talked again about getting her attorney to be present if she chose to have him there for any further questioning, and Hicks assured her that if her attorney couldn't be there in Centre for any reason, a local attorney would be appointed for her. Then Barbara suddenly changed direction again and dropped what could prove to be a very important piece of information.

"You know, when my little sister called me and told me [Darlene] was dead, and I think that's when I called Vernon, his first words were 'What in the hell are you calling me for? What the hell are you calling me for?' and I'm going, 'I just found out.'"

Barbara began to sob.

"And if you had his phone bugged or whatever," she told Hicks, "you'll hear that. Because earlier, he's trying to act like he hadn't been around, 'cause he said, 'They say they saw a woman around one hundred forty pounds, light brown, light blond hair, that looked like you,' and this and that, and whatever, and all this kind of stuff. 'You could have done anything with your hair *since I haven't seen you in five years,*' and I said, 'No, man, we . . .' and he stopped me and said, 'My phone is being taped,' and stuff like that, so I was took away from it, you know?"

If Barbara's account of the phone conversation with Vernon Roberts was accurate, he clearly did not want to acknowledge that he might have spent some intimate times with her in the months prior to Darlene's death.

25

Barbara Ann Roberts and Robert John Schiess III were extradited to Cherokee County, Alabama, on April 21, 2006, as Barbara had wanted. She arrived early, and Schiess, who had not signed his extradition as quickly as Barbara had, was brought later. As soon as she arrived, Barbara immediately told jail officials that she wanted to talk with SA Brent Thomas again. Thomas arrived at the jail shortly before lunchtime, and he and Investigator Mark Hicks met with Barbara at 11:06 A.M.

Once again, they read Barbara her rights and told her that she would need to sign a rights waiver form before they could talk. Barbara then decided that she couldn't make up her mind whether or not she wanted to talk again without the benefit of having an attorney present. After about five minutes of deliberation, she told the officers that she wanted to have her attorney present before she made any statement or answered any questions.

She was returned to her cell without any further conversation, the interview ending with nothing having been accomplished except a trip to the interview room. Meanwhile, at the Cherokee County Courthouse, across the street from the county jail, District Judge Sheri W. Carver set bond for both Barbara and Schiess at $1 million each.

Over the next couple of days, while Barbara was still considering another session of talk with the investigators, Investigator Bo Jolly was preparing his evidence against Bob Schiess. He presented an affidavit for a search warrant to Judge Carver, asking for a blood sample from Schiess to compare his DNA to blood found at the crime scene. There was blood inside Darlene's vehicle and possible DNA samples that were recovered from other evidence that he believed would be a match to Schiess.

To justify his request for the blood sample, Jolly outlined the facts and evidence that tied Schiess to the crime, as well as Barbara's statements incriminating him. Judge Carver signed Jolly's request for the blood samples from Schiess on April 25, and the sample was collected at the Cherokee County Jail.

The next day, on April 26, Barbara once again asked to speak to the investigators. Since she had initiated the conversation, Mark Hicks and Brent Thomas were careful to advise her again of her rights, and she stated for the record that she did wish to talk to them without her attorney being present. She was told that she had the right to stop the interview at any time, which she said she understood.

During the following conversation, Barbara jumped from one subject to another many times, giving additional details on different aspects of the investigation. She first asked if the Cherokee County district attorney (DA) had been told that she had been cooperating with the investigation. She wanted to know if he might lower her bond because of the assistance she was giving the officers.

Barbara told the officers that Darlene wasn't chased with the car. At first, she said that she wasn't driving the car, that she was a passenger in the car. She then said that she didn't want to say who was driving the car, but a short time later, she said that Schiess was the driver.

Another claim Barbara made during this interview was that she and Schiess only had about three shells for the shotgun. A shot was fired at Darlene, she said, while she was standing about halfway across the pond.

Barbara said that the black Dodge pickup, in which she and Schiess had come to Alabama, had been backed in at the gate at the entrance to the pasture. Schiess had the hood up, Barbara said, and he stepped out and flagged Darlene down when she came driving up the road. Bob talked to her and she got out of the car, Barbara claimed; then Bob and Darlene struggled and he tried to tie her hands with some nylon ties, but they wouldn't work, so he used some gauze he had with him. She couldn't remember if the shotgun was lying on the ground at this time, and she didn't remember whether or not she gave Schiess the gun after he tied Darlene up.

"Somehow she got loose and started running to the pasture, and I chased her on foot," Barbara said. "Bob got into Darlene's car and drove it to the back side of the pasture and told me to get in the car, and I did."

Barbara said they drove around farther into the pasture, looking for Darlene.

"As we were driving around the pond, we saw ripples in the water, and then we saw her."

Barbara said that they stopped the vehicle and Schiess got out and shot at Darlene.

"I was hysterical then, and Bob hit me with the gun and broke my glasses, and he fired more shots," she said. "I never saw any blood and couldn't say whether the shots hit Darlene or not.

"I thought he just fired at her to scare her," Barbara continued. "We got back into Darlene's car and drove it back to the edge of the pasture, and left in the pickup truck."

Barbara then told the investigators what had happened to some of the missing items they had been searching for.

"The reason I took her purse was because I had touched it with my bare hands. The cell phone was thrown out onto the side of the road, and the purse was thrown into a Dumpster at a gas station in Rome. Then when we got home, we threw our clothes in the Dumpster at the apartment in Conyers."

On a surprising closing note, Barbara told the officers that the police still did not have the person who killed Darlene in custody. Vernon

Roberts, she said, was involved with the murder and had called her five times on her cell phone on the day Darlene was killed. She also told them that while at Vernon's house the previous October, when they were having their alleged liaison while Darlene was out of town, Vernon had told her that he couldn't afford another divorce.

Barbara had one more piece of information for the record; she claimed that while she was being held in the Cherokee County Jail, a deputy in uniform had come into her cell and beat her on the back of the legs, leaving bruises. The officers photographed the bruises, but Barbara apparently did not have a name for her alleged assailant. She was returned to her cell, and the investigators wondered how long it would be before she summoned them for their next conversation.

26

Despite her inability to wait until an attorney was present to speak with the investigators, Barbara had managed to secure the services of attorney Steve Lanier of Rome, Georgia. Lanier, in turn, was working with a local attorney in Centre, Rodney L. Stallings, who was also representing Barbara as her local legal advisor. Lanier was a veteran attorney with an established practice, and Stallings was a younger, up-and-coming lawyer whose office was a very short distance from both the Cherokee County Courthouse and the county jail, where Barbara was being held. Stallings, a former Auburn University football player, would be in a position to do the local legwork so essential to such cases, and had the ambition and energy to tackle the job. He was going to find, however, that defending Barbara was going to be tough going. He would eventually end up doing far more of the work on this particular case than he had expected to be doing when he first signed on.

One of the first actions Stallings took was to file a motion to reduce the $1 million bond that had been set for Barbara, as had also been set for Schiess. He claimed that the amount of bail set in the case was excessive under the facts and circumstances of the case, that Barbara could not make bail in that amount, and that the recommended range for a Class A felony under the bail schedule could be as low as $5,000.

District Judge Sheri W. Carver answered the motion with a court order denying the request for a reduced bond.

She also modified the original terms of Barbara's bond by adding that she would surrender her passport and not leave either Alabama or Georgia. In the event that Barbara was able to post bond, she would not be allowed to enter into Cherokee County, except to assist in the defense of her case.

Judge Carver specified that Barbara would have no contact with the victim's family or the victim's former place of employment, and no unwanted contact with the codefendant in the case. She would immediately inform the court of any intent to change residency or address.

With the last item of the order, however, Judge Carver made a modification that allowed Barbara more of a chance to post bond and be released from the jail.

In addition to the above modifications, the order read, *this Court makes notice of the general bonding practices in this area requiring Defendants to post approximately ten percent of any bond amount, consequently the Court further modifies the bond originally* *set in this matter so as to allow the Defendant to post a cash bond in the amount of twelve and one-half percent of the original bond amount or $125,000.00.*

Said funds shall be paid into the Circuit Clerk's office for Cherokee County, Alabama and upon payment and receipt of such funds by the Clerk's office the Defendant shall be entitled to be released from jail subject to the conditions previously stated herein and previously ordered by this Court.

That sum of money was no problem for Schiess, who was a multimillionaire with easy access to that amount of funds. It was not long at all until both defendants posted the stated percentage of bond and were released from jail and on their way back to Georgia together.

27

In accordance with Judge Carver's revised court order, attorney Steve Lanier obtained Barbara's passport on May 1, 2006, and sent it to Rodney Stallings to turn over to the clerk's office, as required. He also informed Stallings that both Schiess and Barbara wanted to attend the graduation on May 13 of Schiess's son from the University of North Carolina at Asheville. Barbara requested to get the court's permission to attend the graduation with Schiess, and Lanier asked Stallings if he had any advice or suggestions regarding the request. Stallings handled Barbara's request, which was then prepared and given to the court.

Judge Carver approved the travel request after it was submitted, and both Barbara and Schiess were granted the court's permission to attend the graduation ceremonies in North Carolina. Specific times were stated for their departure and their return, both of which were complied with.

On May 4, Barbara's defense submitted a request for a preliminary hearing, petitioning the court to set down a date on the grounds that Barbara had been charged with a felony, but had not been indicted. Her lawyer stated that Barbara had a right to a preliminary hearing under provisions of the Code of Alabama. The request asked that the court would set down a date, time, and place for a preliminary hearing in Barbara's case.

Also in May, the state filed a motion to continue. It asked that the reconvention of the preliminary hearing for Barbara be continued, until at least June 21. In support of the motion, the state said the following:

1. The defense had consented to the motion.
2. A continuance would aid the cause of justice by allowing Deputy District Attorney (DDA) Scott C. Lloyd to prepare for his extensive grand jury duties.
3. A continuance would not affect the interests of the defendant, as the state had agreed that the matter would not be presented to the May/June 2006 session of the grand jury, and the defendant was on bond with no serious restrictions on her liberty.

The continuance was granted, and the case was planned to be presented to the October 2006 grand jury session.

In the early summer, while Barbara and Schiess were out on bond prior to the grand jury session in October, Barbara decided she wanted to attend an out-of-state spiritual retreat. The retreat was, in fact, quite a long way out of state; it was held in Wolf Creek, Montana, and was a five-day residential retreat called "Through the Eye of the Horse: Explorations in Original Medicine." It was held at Blacktail Ranch. Its purpose, according to its promotional materials, was to explore what indigenous tribes considered *our own unique qualities and gifts that we bring to the world*. Many other New Age phrases, like *nature as a healing force* and *the source of your most authentic self*, were used, along with the statement that participants would *experience being witnessed by a herd of horses and a Circle of humans that are committed to seeing our strengths and bright potential*. Retreat attendees would *have the opportunity to witness in a new way the exterior and interior landscapes of all who come together at this time and in this place*.

Blacktail Ranch was described as *the home of a Sacred Cave that calls all who visit this land to come and spend ceremonial time visiting the cave, as others have done for thousands of years before us*. The eight-thousand-plus-acre ranch, located between Great Falls and Helena, Montana, also was home to one fork of the Dearborn River, which the retreat literature said would be *calling you back to your most instinctual self*.

It would have been practically unheard-of for any court to grant permission for such lengthy and distant out-of-state travel, especially for such a purpose, to a person who was out of jail on bond after being arrested as a murder suspect awaiting indictment, but two of Barbara's doctors wrote letters in support of her attendance. The persons who were conducting the retreat also wrote to Rodney Stallings to verify that Barbara planned to attend the retreat, they had accepted her as a potential participant, and that she had agreed to furnish them with copies of the permission letters from her psychiatrist and psychologist that she would be furnishing to the court.

At the time, the fee of $1,195 included workshop activities, materials, supplies, lodging, meals, horse time, and trail ride. Deposits of $400 would hold the prospective attendee's space, with the balance due by August 10. A preworkshop questionnaire for participants asked for some background information, including what the attendee hoped to get out of the experience, whether or not they had experience with horses or with shamanism, what their creative outlets or practices were, and if the person was meeting regularly with a counselor or spiritual advisor. The questionnaire also asked if the prospective attendee was currently in psychotherapy and/or taking medications for anxiety or depression, and, if so, to please specify.

Barbara's psychiatrist said that she felt it would greatly benefit Barbara's mental health to attend the spiritual retreat, and her psychologist wrote that he wholeheartedly supported her decision that she needed more long-term, in-patient treatment than she could receive locally. He felt, he said, that Barbara desperately needed to have more therapy than he could provide on an outpatient basis due to the intense and extreme stress she was experiencing due to the criminal charges and the withdrawal of support, care, or concern by her family. He expressed that he hoped her request to enter such a treatment program would be facilitated.

Rodney Stallings knew that there was little or no hope that Barbara's trip to Montana would be permitted, but he gave his best attempt to get approval, despite what proved to be the overwhelming odds of failure.

28

While Rodney Stallings was gathering evidence for Barbara's defense, he asked her to contact several people to provide statements or references concerning her physical abilities. One of these, her firearms instructor in a class she had taken on February 5, 2006, sent Stallings some detailed information on Barbara's activities in the class and her reaction to the areas covered by the training.

The class was conducted by Venture Outdoors, an outdoor educational, family-oriented company, which had an outstanding reputation. Venture Outdoors provided much more than firearms education and training; they also instructed in fishing, hunting, hiking, and many other areas of outdoor recreational training for all ages.

The instructor told Stallings that Barbara had taken a basic information class on the use of handguns and shotguns for home defense. During the class, the instructor said, they mentioned that if a person could not or was not willing to take a life to protect their own life, they recommended they not own a gun for personal defense.

"If you cannot shoot someone to protect yourself," the instructor said, "that person could take the gun away from you and use it on you."

Barbara had many questions, the instructor said, and seemed to have a problem with that concept.

"I recommended a couple of books for her to read and suggested she think about all that would be involved before she made her decision. Then, if she chose to pursue her training to the next level, to contact us for information on private (one-on-one) classes and our personal-defense class."

The instructor said that during the live-fire portion of the class, Barbara had a problem pulling the trigger of several handguns due to the lack of strength in her hands. As for the shotgun, the instructor said that with the lack of strength in her arms and the type of movement she would need to use in her home for personal defense, they suggested that Barbara not use the shotgun.

After that original meeting with Barbara, the instructor said, she had received no additional training classes, and they had never heard from her again until she asked them to send Stallings the letter.

29

On May 10, despite her wishes to travel to Montana, Barbara had violated the terms of Judge Carver's revised court order stating that she would not attempt to have any contact with Darlene's family.

That evening, Barbara called one of her brothers in Texas and asked him if he would contact Vernon for her. She wanted her brother to relay a message to Vernon and tell him that he was in danger. The investigators on the case, she claimed, thought that Vernon wanted Darlene out of the way so that he could get back together with Barbara again.

"She said that she was being told that if she goes down, Vernon is going with her," the brother told the investigators. He said that once Barbara saw that he was not buying her story—he told her he didn't believe Vernon was involved in Darlene's murder in any way—Barbara then changed her mind. She said that if he thought

Vernon wasn't in any danger, there was no need to call him.

"Later that day, I realized that May tenth was Vernon's birthday," the brother said, "and this was Barbara's way of getting in touch with him to let him know she was thinking of him."

He didn't call Vernon at that time, but he told him of the conversation a few days later when Vernon got in touch with him. Vernon was very displeased that Barbara was trying to contact him and attempting to use her brother to do so, but both men were surprised and dismayed when, the following month, she tried once again to persuade her brother to relay a message to her ex-husband.

On the late afternoon of June 7, 2006, Barbara called her brother to ask him once again to get in touch with Vernon for her. He stopped her in midsentence by telling her that if he did get in touch with Vernon, he would report it to the police. Barbara mulled this over for a minute, then decided that she wanted her brother to contact Vernon, anyway.

It was Darlene's birthday week, she said, and she was concerned about Vernon. She wanted her brother to tell him that the investigators had said that either she or Bob had told Darlene about Barbara's affair with Vernon, and she wanted him to know that hadn't happened.

Barbara's brother called Vernon and told him about the conversation, then sat down at his computer and e-mailed details of the conversation to Investigator Bo Jolly.

30

The following day, Vernon Roberts called the Cherokee County District Attorney's Office to tell them of Barbara's failed attempt to get in touch with him. He was incensed that his ex-wife had been allowed out on bail, and was made even more furious by her attempts to contact him, insisting she had information he needed to know.

Vernon said that Barbara had wanted to contact him on Darlene's birthday and let him know that neither she nor Bob had mentioned to Darlene about the alleged love affair, and that Darlene died never finding out about it.

"In her opinion, this was supposed to give me peace of mind," Vernon said. "She claimed it is her understanding that the police think she and Bob drove out to the murder site to give this information to Darlene."

Barbara's brother had told her that he had reported to the authorities her first attempt to contact Vernon, and that he would do so again, but she wanted him to call Vernon, anyway.

"This exchange of information through [Barbara's brother] is, in my opinion, just another way that Barbara's conception is that the law doesn't apply to her," Vernon told the district attorney's office, asking that the calls be used to persuade the judge that Barbara was ignoring the court order, and her bond should be revoked.

"She needs to be incarcerated, where she belongs, until a jury decides differently," Vernon said. "I need the peace of mind that I will not be her next victim."

That same day, a notice for a court appearance was issued, alerting Barbara and attorney Rodney Stallings that the preliminary hearing on her case would be held on July 12 at the Cherokee County Courthouse.

At the July 12 hearing, District Judge Sheri W. Carver ruled that probable cause existed to believe that the offense of which Barbara was accused had been committed, and that she was therefore bound over for action by the grand jury for Cherokee County, Alabama, as was Schiess for the separate charges against him.

Vernon Roberts went to the authorities at the end of July with another complaint about his ex-wife, this one considerably more weighty than the attempted phone messages. He said that on July 26, around 4:45 P.M., he was returning home from work and noticed Barbara following him. In order to be sure it was she, he pulled over and let her pass him. When he saw it was, indeed, Barbara, he said, he followed her car to get the license plate number.

When Barbara pulled over about two and a half miles from Vernon's house, he stopped and confronted her, wanting to know what she was doing that close to his home. According to Vernon's affidavit, Barbara told him she was going fishing and had missed the turnoff. She had decided to drive to Fosters Bend Road and circle back. She opened the trunk of the car and showed Vernon a rod and reel, a cooler, and some worms, all of which, he said, appeared to be recently purchased, to prove she was going fishing.

Barbara told Vernon she had moved to Rome, Georgia, and was bored sitting at home, so she decided to go fishing.

Vernon said he asked Barbara what reason she could possibly have had to murder his wife, and he said she told him she didn't do it, and that he would find out she was innocent at the trial.

"She then went back to her car and brought back a Bible and wanted to swear on it about her innocence," Vernon said. "I told her to stop with the sideshow and tell me the truth."

Barbara told him, he said, that he had someone who hated him and he would find out who that person was at the trial. He asked her who the person was, and Barbara asked him if he knew anyone who had a tattoo of an Indian Head on his shoulder, with long feathers that extended down below a short-sleeved shirt.

"I told her that Darlene's son had a tattoo like that, and she said she didn't want to know any names, and for me to keep that person in mind."

Vernon said that Barbara then asked him why he denied asking her to buy flowers for her mother's funeral. He told her, he said, that she was crazy if she thought they had a conversation about her mother's funeral, or about what he would have wanted to say on a card. She told him that he had been drugged out on medication when they had that discussion.

Barbara asked Vernon, he claimed, not to contact the police about her being in the area.

"I told her I was going to let the authorities know as soon as I got home. She said, 'Well, I guess I'll be picked up tonight.' I didn't respond, and she went and got back in her car and left."

On being notified by Vernon Roberts of this incident, the state immediately filed a motion to revoke bond, stating that Barbara had violated the conditions of release by changing her residence without first notifying the court of her intent to do so, engaging in other conduct constituting an attempt to violate the conditions that she have no contact with the victim's family, and that she not enter into Cherokee County, Alabama, except to assist in the defense of her case.

The motion went on to describe the incident Vernon had notified the authorities of, when he confronted Barbara within two and a half miles of his home in an area where she had no legitimate business, and she had displayed fishing tackle and claimed to be there to go fishing.

The motion stated that Barbara had told Vernon she had moved to Floyd County, Georgia, and said that the prosecution had not been advised of any change of address, as had been required by the court:

This conduct is made more disturbing by the fact that the defendant has engaged in other attempts to have contact with Mr. Roberts since her release by asking her family to "send word" to him about certain matters relating to the murder of Mr. Roberts' wife, even after having been told that Mr. Roberts did not desire any contact from her—even indirect contact— and considered such attempts to constitute violations of the conditions of release.

The state had not previously filed a motion to revoke bond based on those first two attempts at contact, the motion stated; however, Barbara was now escalating the forcefulness of her attempts to initiate contact, and the state claimed it feared for the personal safety of Vernon Roberts.

The motion then requested that the court issue a warrant for Barbara's arrest for violating the conditions of her release.

31

On July 31, District Judge Sheri W. Carver issued a court order requiring Barbara to appear in her courtroom on August 3, to show cause why her bond should not be revoked.

In Barbara's response to the state's motion to revoke bond, filed on August 1, Stallings listed several points for the court's consideration as to why the bond should not be revoked.

The state's allegations were untrue and required proof, said the response: the affidavit lacked authenticity, the information presented was an attempt to enter hearsay statements and was due to be stricken, and Barbara had not changed her address and had no intentions to do so.

Barbara was in the state of Georgia and not in Cherokee County, Alabama, when Vernon Roberts stopped her as she was going about her own business, and Vernon commenced harassing and cursing her, whereupon she ended the unwanted contact by leaving, Stallings claimed.

This is a futile effort by the State to incarcerate the Defendant in a malicious attempt to garner power over the Defendant for purposes of coercion and intimidation in order to obtain a confession, the response read, then asked that the motion to revoke bond either be dismissed or a date be set for a hearing on the motion with the state's witnesses, Vernon Roberts and Barbara's brother, present for cross-examination.

After the hearing was concluded, Judge Carver issued a court order denying the motion to revoke bond, but modifying the previous conditions of Barbara's bond. The order required both the Floyd County and Conyers residence addresses to be verified with the court within five days, that Barbara would have no contact—either direct or indirect—with Vernon Roberts or any other member of Darlene's family, even if the contact was initiated by someone other than Barbara, and that Barbara would not enter Cherokee County except to assist in the defense of her case. Also, in any event, she would not travel within five road miles of the home or workplace of Vernon Roberts, and the court should be notified in writing of her need to travel into Cherokee County in aid of her defense. The other conditions of her previous bond would remain the same.

32

As the members of the grand jury of Cherokee
County, Alabama, were being readied for their
October 2006 session, ABI agent Jason Brown and
Cherokee County Sheriff's Office investigator Bo
Jolly traveled to Parkwest Medical Center in
Knoxville, Tennessee, to interview James "Jim" An-
thony Captain, Parkwest's manager of neuro-
sciences. Captain had been friends with Robert
John Schiess III since May 2000. Captain had con-
tacted Jolly on October 18 to tell him that he'd had
several phone conversations with Schiess during
which Schiess had made several disturbing remarks
concerning his involvement with the murder of
Darlene Roberts. Jolly quickly contacted ABI agent
Brent Thomas, who called Captain and arranged
for a meeting with Brown and Jolly.

Captain told the officers that he had been
friends with Schiess since May 2000. He lived in
Schiess's apartment for ten months in 2002, with
Schiess moving back in for the last four months,
and the two men being roommates during that

period. They had kept in touch ever since Captain had moved out that November, and Captain had called him several times in May, June, and once in early August.

Captain had surgery in March 2006, and his wife had a note attached to Captain's chart when she learned that Barbara and Bob were going to visit him in the hospital during his recuperation. She said in the note that her husband had company coming in from Georgia, a retired neurosurgeon who "tries to throw his weight around" and demand that things be done and who to contact about Captain's treatment. Mrs. Captain said for the staff not to let Schiess make any decisions regarding her husband's care, and to call her if Schiess became a problem, or call security and have him sent off the premises. She also said he might request or try to see Captain's chart, and followed that statement with the words—capitalized and underlined—*NO, NO, NO!*

As it so happened, during their visit to the hospital, both Schiess and Barbara had to be escorted out of the building by security for causing problems.

Captain said that the first time he spoke on the phone with Schiess after his surgery was in early May. Schiess was quiet at first, and Captain asked him how things had been going.

"What," Schiess said, "you haven't heard?"

"No, what?" Captain asked.

"Barbara and I have been arrested and accused of murder."

Captain was astonished to hear this, and asked, "Whose murder?"

Schiess told him that it was Barbara's ex-husband's wife. They had been arrested at the airport, he said.

Captain then asked, point-blank, if Schiess had been there at the scene, and Schiess said, "Yes."

There were a few seconds of silence following this statement; then Schiess said that it had been done with a shotgun. He rambled for a few moments, then asked Captain what he would do if someone threatened his family. Captain told him he did not know.

Schiess then made another startling statement, saying to Captain that his sister had told him to stop killing people. Then he said that a shotgun was a perfect weapon because it did not leave a ballistic trail, such as rifling.

"I soon got off the phone with him," Captain said.

The next time Captain called, a few days later, to see how Schiess was doing, Barbara answered. When he asked to speak to Schiess, she told him that he had checked himself into an alcohol and drug treatment program and was not there.

"I asked her if he was still drinking and taking pills, and she said he was. 'Well,' I said, 'maybe a treatment program is where he needs to be.' We talked a little longer, then ended the call."

In Captain's third phone call to Schiess, a short time later, Schiess said that he had sent his mother a shotgun, which Captain said that he believed was a birthday present.

In the August phone call, Barbara answered and told Captain that Bob was out. Barbara told Captain that she had her preliminary hearing, then told him that the investigators were looking for Darlene's son, Benji, who had been missing, she claimed, for the past few weeks. She said that Benji and his mother had been arguing before the murder, and she thought that he had committed the murder.

"We shortly ended the phone call," Captain told the officers, "and I have not contacted Bob or Barbara since."

Captain told the officers of several other statements Schiess had made to him at various times. He said on one occasion that his father would not give his weapons back to him because he was afraid that he would hurt someone or himself. Schiess said that he told his father, "What makes you think I don't have a weapon now?"

Schiess also told Captain that Barbara was the weakest link in the case against them.

In early May, Captain said that Bob called him and wanted him to go to North Carolina and pick up some equipment and a riding lawn mower at a residence while the homeowner was at church. Schiess said he would have to force open the garage door and take the equipment, and that Barbara would stand watch at the end of the road while he did it.

"I did not meet or go with him," Captain said. "He called several times on that Sunday morning and left a message saying he was waiting for me to arrive."

Schiess told Captain that the reason for taking the equipment and lawn mower was that this person owed him money for a land deal that fell

through, and the individual would not return his
deposit that Schiess had put down.

One of the most telling comments Schiess made
to Captain came during a conversation about a
news event that included mention of the death
penalty.

"I said, 'I believe in the death penalty,'" Captain said.

"Bob got quiet, then said, 'Jim, I may face that
one day.'"

33

During the October 2006 term of the grand jury of Cherokee County, Alabama, many cases were sorted through and dealt with, either by indictments or by being no-billed, but none had received the publicity and public attention of the charges brought against Barbara Ann Roberts and Dr. Robert John Schiess. Newspapers, television, and radio news had followed the case of Darlene Roberts's murder, the arrest of Barbara and Schiess, the charges against them, and their extradition from Georgia to Alabama. Now it would be up to a group of seventeen Cherokee County citizens to determine whether the two would be tried on the charges recommended by District Attorney Mike O'Dell.

When Barbara received a plea bargain offer from the district attorney's office, prior to the grand jury session, offering life with eligibility for parole in exchange for a guilty plea, instead of the death penalty, attorneys Steve Lanier and Rodney Stallings were very much in favor of her giving it some serious consideration. But for some reason, Barbara expressed very little interest in the offer, which might have amounted to the difference between life and death for her.

Lanier, Stallings, and Barbara met to discuss the offer, and both attorneys were dismayed to learn their client was so disinterested in such an important opportunity to better her situation.

The two attorneys believed that Barbara would be expected to testify against Schiess in the event she decided to accept the plea bargain.

"What if she takes the plea, then totally exonerates Bob?" Lanier asked Stallings. "I think they're relying on the statements you've previously made," he added to Barbara, "but if you do a one-eighty on them, saying he wasn't involved in any shape, form, or fashion, then I'd think all bets are off.

"I think they're expecting full cooperation to testify against Bob. If you play a 'stand by your man' kind of thing, then they'll probably say—"

Stallings interrupted to tell Barbara, "That's what worries me about you having all this contact with Bob." Stallings had been concerned for some time that Barbara and Schiess were continuing to live together after they had been released from the Cherokee County Jail on bond pending the grand jury indictments that were very likely about to be issued.

"I think she's somewhat locked in by her prior statements," Lanier told Stallings. He then told Barbara, "They've got enough right now to indict on capital and get a conviction on capital on you and Bob, based primarily on evidence at the scene and witness statements. What they're wanting is if you'll testify against Bob, then they'll offer you a life with eligibility for parole. Just let me know tomorrow. Think about it, pray about it, and let me know tomorrow.

"There's been very little death penalty litigation in Cherokee County, Alabama, and there are not many lawyers locally that have even done a death penalty case. The death penalty is an all-or-nothing war. If they ask for the death penalty, you have to go all out because there's so much at stake, and the alternatives are not pleasant. You have an opportunity. You know what the options are."

Lanier and Stallings were concerned that Barbara did not understand that if indicted by the grand jury for capital murder, she and Schiess would be rearrested and most probably held without bond for quite some time until the lengthy trial process was completed.

"Vernon Roberts is extremely upset about the way this case is being handled," Lanier told Stallings, "specifically, them being out on bond. So you've got a victim's husband disgruntled, applying pressure. I've never known of a death penalty defendant being out on bond."

34

A grand jury motion had been filed by Barbara's attorneys prior to the session asking that the evidence introduced before the grand jury be recorded and transcribed, with the defendant agreeing to pay for the employment of a court reporter to record and transcribe the minutes and testimony.

The motion also asked that prior to considering the charges against Barbara, the grand jurors be asked several questions, starting with whether any of the grand jurors were related within the sixth degree to the prosecutor, the accused, or the deceased. The other questions dealt with whether any of the grand jurors had expressed or formed any opinion as to Barbara's guilt or innocence, and whether or not any of them had any prejudices or biases either for or against Barbara, or if they could be perfectly impartial.

The defense asked that any grand juror answering any of the foregoing questions in the affirmative be excused from the grand jury room during the consideration of Barbara's case. The attorneys also asked that before any state witness testified, the prosecutor would ask them if they had ever been convicted of any felony or crime involving moral turpitude. It was requested that all answers to the questions and all votes of the grand jury be recorded and a copy delivered to the defense.

The defense asked the court in a separate motion to question each of the grand jurors individually on pretrial publicity. The motion claimed that prior to, and after, Barbara's arrest, there had been extensive, intense, and prejudicial publicity by the local and national news media concerning the investigation of Darlene's alleged murder and the facts surrounding Barbara's alleged involvement in it.

Prior to the grand jury's vote, the motion said, the court should question them individually on whether they had a preconceived opinion against Barbara because of the publicity preceding the indictment proceedings. This action, the motion said, would protect the defendant's due process of law and her right to a fair and impartial, qualified grand jury. Those jurors who had formed an opinion against her due to the publicity, the motion said, should be disqualified, and if there were less than twelve remaining qualified grand jurors, the court should not permit them to consider or vote on an indictment in the case.

Another motion was titled "Motion for the Recordation of the Entire Grand Jury Proceedings and for a Copy of the Grand Jury Minutes." In support of the motion, the following was stated:

1. The district attorney of the Cherokee County Superior Court had informed the attorney for the defendant that the charges against the defendant were being presented to the grand jury.

2. The investigation of the defendant's alleged involvement in the murder of Darlene Roberts and other alleged offenses was conducted by local, state, and federal law enforcement officers. These police agencies conducted numerous scientific tests on particular evidence, which, based on information and belief, was being presented through expert witnesses to the grand jury.

3. The district attorney's presentation of the case against the defendant was based solely upon circumstantial evidence. Various witnesses would testify, based on information and belief, before the grand jury, as to numerous details that described these circumstances.

4. The defendant had a due process right to have the testimony of the witnesses recorded so that she might, through her attorney, subsequently examine that testimony to prepare her defense in the trial of her case.

5. The law of the state of Alabama did not preclude the recordation of the grand jury proceedings. The recordation of the entire proceedings would not inter-

fere with the proper functioning of the grand jury. (Recordation is the most effective restraint upon prosecutorial abuse of the grand jury process.) The stenographic transcription of the grand jury proceedings would improve the administration of criminal justice.

6. Recordation of the grand jury proceedings would not violate the secrecy of those proceedings. Upon a proper showing by the defendant, the grand jurors might be required to disclose everything that occurred in their service. The minutes of the grand jury proceedings might be sealed by the court until such time as the present grand jury's term had expired, prior to the defendant's trial.

7. The defendant had a right to examine the grand jury testimony of the state's experts who testified concerning the results of scientific tests that allegedly connected the defendant to the crime(s) charged. The defendant also had a right to examine the testimony of the state's witnesses who testified to details of the circumstances that allegedly connected the defendant to the crime(s) charged.

These points, the motion claimed, would need to be addressed in order for Barbara's defense to prepare for her trial.

* * *

In a separate motion filed the same day, it was requested that Barbara's bond funds should be released upon either indictment or no bill by the grand jury. The funds, the motion said, should be immediately remitted to the law offices of Coggin & Stallings, attorney Rodney Stallings's office.

As the grand jury was convening, Rodney Stallings received a letter from Barbara's psychologist, who had spoken to him on October 30, saying that Barbara was in dire fear of being indicted and jailed until her trial. She was afraid that she would not have her medications or get psychological support, the letter said.

The psychologist said that Barbara's condition was fragile due to multiple physical and mental problems, and said that Barbara had stated in the past that she would rather die than spend years in prison. The psychologist told Stallings that she did not believe that Barbara could survive in such an environment. In the psychologist's professional opinion, to place Barbara there would be an act of gross negligence and disregard of human life.

Barbara's psychiatrist also wrote that she was concerned that Barbara would not be able to get adequate medical and psychiatric treatment at her current level of need from the prison system in Alabama, which could be permanently detrimental to her health. Barbara took five medications on a daily basis, the doctor stated, and saw a psychiatrist or a psychotherapist every week. The doctor asked that the court consider Barbara's special needs when making their disposition toward her.

Another of Barbara's doctors saw her regularly for her back pain, which followed surgery due to the many injuries she had received through the years in multiple auto accidents. He wrote detailing her genuine need to sleep with a pillow, which evidently had not been provided by the jail.

These letters and recommendations were duly furnished to the court, attached to a notice to the court of medical issues, which Stallings immediately began preparing.

After much legal maneuvering and preliminary work, the grand jury got down to the serious business of reviewing the case against Barbara Ann Roberts.

There were three counts listed on the indictment. In the first count, murder committed during a robbery, Barbara was alleged to have intentionally caused Darlene's death by shooting her with a shotgun during the time that Barbara was in the course of committing a theft of property, namely Darlene's purse. Barbara was accused of having used force or threatening the use of force against Darlene in order to escape with the property, while armed with a deadly weapon or dangerous instrument.

The second count charged that Barbara caused Darlene's death by shooting her with a shotgun during abduction, or attempted abduction, with the intent to inflict injury on Darlene or to violate or abuse her sexually.

The third count found that Barbara caused Darlene's death by shooting her with a shotgun during her abduction with the intent to terrorize her or another person, to wit: Vernon Roberts.

On November 2, 2006, Barbara Ann Roberts was indicted by the state of Alabama on the three counts, one count of murder during robbery and two counts of murder during kidnapping. The grand jury foreman signed the true bill released by the grand jury, and Circuit Judge Randall L. Cole ordered Barbara and Schiess, who was also indicted, picked up by law enforcement and returned to jail, to be held with no bail until the time of their trials.

To keep both defendants in this sensational case from being housed in the same facility, Barbara was transferred to the DeKalb County Jail in Fort Payne, Alabama, the adjoining county in the Ninth Judicial District of Alabama, and Schiess remained housed in the Cherokee County Jail.

35

As soon as her indictment came down from the grand jury, and Barbara was ordered to be held with no bail, attorney Rodney Stallings was ready with a motion to set bond for Barbara. Attorneys for Schiess, who was being charged and tried separately, also filed a similar motion on his behalf, both of which would be considered by Judge Cole.

In Barbara Ann Roberts's motion, Stallings told the court that Barbara, having been indicted by the grand jury, had previously been out on a cash bond since April 27. She had surrendered her passport to the Cherokee County Clerk's Office, as ordered by the court, on May 2. She had been available to be contacted at all times since then, Stallings said, either by his office or the court.

"The defendant has at all times abided by the conditions of her bond and orders of the District Court of Cherokee County, Alabama," Stallings claimed, a statement that might not have rung true if more mention had been made of Barbara's attempts to get messages to Vernon.

Stallings also claimed that Barbara was not a flight risk and had proven this by her actions since being bonded out in April. He also pointed out that Alabama law stated that in order for a defendant to be held without bond, the judge must be of the opinion that the proof of Barbara's guilt should be evident, or the presumption great, that she was guilty of murder in the degree punishable capitally, with clear and strong evidence of such guilt.

"The evidence presented does not meet the requirements of 'being clear and strong,' or the presumption great that the defendant is guilty of the offense in the degree punishable capitally," Stallings stated.

"The burden of proof rests on the state to prove the crime, to prove that it was of the highest degree, and to convince the judge that upon final trial, the judge would sustain a verdict pronouncing the defendant guilty and imposing the death penalty."

Stallings then pointed out that the recommended range for the crime of which Barbara had been indicted under the applicable bail schedule could be as low as $10,000, and the recommended range for a charge of murder was as low as $5,000.

On receiving Barbara's motion and a similar one from Schiess's attorneys, Judge Cole set a hearing date for November 16, and both motions, by mutual agreement, were consolidated for the hearing.

When Judge Cole issued his order following the bail hearing, he said that the defendants had been charged with the noncapital offense of murder initially. Bail was set by the district court, and both defendants paid the bail and were released. Then, when the grand jury returned three-count indictments against both Barbara and Schiess charging the capital offenses of murder during kidnapping and murder during robbery, the court ordered that they be arrested and held without bail. In order to be entitled to bail, Cole said, a person accused by indictment of a capital crime must overcome a presumption of guilt.

At the bail hearing, Cole said, the state relied upon the indictments and a portion of the preliminary hearing transcript to justify the "no bail" order. The defendants offered evidence of their educational backgrounds and professional achievements, and the fact that they had appeared for their preliminary hearings and, otherwise, complied with the conditions of their bail. Schiess also offered the testimony of family members, who testified to his good character attributes and his reliability.

"While the evidence shows that the defendants have had distinguished professional careers, and that they have complied with previous bail conditions, the court, upon consideration of the indictment, the evidence, and the law, finds that bail is due to be denied," Judge Cole ruled.

At the same time Stallings attempted to get his client released on bail, he also filed his notice to the court of medical issues to inform the court of Barbara's medical and mental situation, and the medications and therapy she would require while in custody.

In his notice Stallings said that Barbara had been prescribed medication that would be extremely detrimental to her physical and mental health if not taken as prescribed. He provided letters from her psychiatrist and psychologist, along with a list of her current prescriptions, which showed she was taking a total of nine medications prescribed by three different physicians.

Also noted was the fact that Barbara had appointments with her psychiatrist every other week and with her psychotherapist on alternating weeks, and that level of care needed to continue while Barbara was in custody.

Since Barbara's medical doctor provided a letter in her support, it was attached to the notice. It verified that she had undergone spinal surgery and required a certain-thickness pillow to prevent extreme pain and headaches. The letter from her psychiatrist was also attached in support of the notice's claim of her need for care while incarcerated.

Stallings then pointed out that the United States Supreme Court had stated that deliberate indifference to a prisoner's serious medical needs constituted cruel and unusual punishment under the Eighth Amendment and could give rise to civil rights cause of action, regardless of whether the indifference was manifested by prison doctors in their response to prisoner's needs, or by prison guards in intentionally denying or delaying access to medical care or intentionally interfering with treatment once prescribed.

Stallings concluded his notice by asking the

court to ensure Barbara's prescriptions be properly maintained and dispensed, that her current level of psychiatric care be maintained, and an adequate pillow be provided.

After receiving the notice, Circuit Judge Randall L. Cole considered it and filed the following order:

The Court having considered the Notice to the Court of Medical Issues filed by the Defendant, finds that the same should be granted. It is therefore ORDERED, ADJUDGED and DECREED that during the defendant's incarceration,

1. *The listed medications will be dispensed to the defendant as prescribed.*
2. *A pillow of appropriate thickness will be supplied to the defendant.*
3. *The defendant shall have sessions with a psychiatrist every other week and psychotherapist on alternating weeks.*

Barbara was, at that time, being held in the DeKalb County Jail, and soon began to claim that her medication was not being administered correctly despite the judge's order. In mid-December, her psychiatrist sent a letter to Stallings and to the jail's medical director stating that due to Barbara's diagnosis of post-traumatic stress disorder and recurrent major depression, it was imperative that she get her medication or she might decompensate and become suicidal. (A list of those medications followed.)

Stallings immediately filed a motion to require correct administration of prescription medication, claiming that the DeKalb County Correctional Facility had not administered Barbara's medications as prescribed. As a result, his client had become delusional, incoherent, scratched constantly at her skin, and appeared to be in a state of physical and mental breakdown.

As a result, Stallings said, it had become impossible for Barbara to assist him in her defense.

Barbara had reported, he claimed, that the DeKalb County Correctional Facility personnel had indicated that they planned to "wean her off her meds and would not fund additional doctor visits or prescriptions." This, he said, could have extreme adverse effects, according to Barbara's psychiatrist.

Stallings asked the court to remedy the situation immediately, and on December 18, Circuit Judge Randall L. Cole issued an order requiring the medical director of the DeKalb County Jail to provide the court a written report of the medicine regimen being administered to the defendant.

The DeKalb County Correctional Facility's medical director responded to the court order immediately with a detailed accounting of the medical treatment at that time being administered to Barbara.

In response to Ms. Roberts' claims that she is not receiving the medications as prescribed by her physicians, the jail's medical supervisor wrote, *copies of current medical records have been obtained from her*

physicians, and her medications, as prescribed by those
physicians, are [as follows]:

> *Protonix, 40 mg, once daily*
> *Neurontin, 600 mg, twice daily*
> *Celexa, 80 mg, once daily*
> *Seroquel, 100 mg, one or two tablets at bedtime*
> *Ativan, 1 mg, four times daily*

A physician affiliated with the hospital in Fort
Payne, Alabama, had reviewed Barbara's medication list, and had suggested one change in the
prescriptions, which the medical supervisor said
should allow Barbara to remain more lucid with
fewer peaks and troughs.

Barbara had been evaluated that day, he said,
and she was alert and oriented, ambulatory without assistance and with steady gait. She denied
any scratches or lesions, and there were no visible abrasions or contusions. The supervisor said
that Barbara did complain of nerve damage to
the left arm with some noticeable tremors. This,
he said, had been explained by Barbara's regular
physician with a diagnosis of paresthesia left
hand. Her vital signs were normal. There had
been no other changes in the medication during
Barbara's stay at the DeKalb County Jail, the
medical supervisor reported, but they would continue to reevaluate for changes in her health
status and adjust her medication as prescribed by
the physician.

Upon reading the response from the DeKalb

County Jail, Judge Cole issued the following order on December 19, 2006:

Based upon the medical records and nurse's notes provided to the court by the DeKalb County jail in a report dated December 18, 2006, it is adjudged that the defendant's "Motion to Require Correct Administration of Prescription Medication" is DENIED.

It appears that jail personnel are knowledgeable of defendant's medical needs and are responding to those needs appropriately.

During the same time period, Schiess had apparently been involved in a similar situation regarding his own necessary medications, for his doctor had written a letter detailing his diagnosis and his prescriptions. Schiess, he said, was a patient he had been seeing since October 1997, and who was suffering from a severe major depression with anxiety and panic, as well as posttraumatic stress disorder. He said that Schiess had been taking his current medications for a number of years, and it was critical that he stay on them. If the Cherokee County Jail could not supply those medications, it was imperative that Schiess be transferred to a facility where they could be administered, the doctor said.

If he is not maintained on these medications, he may have a seizure, the doctor wrote. *It would be dangerous for him to stop them.*

36

Investigators had remained hard at work on the Darlene Roberts murder case, even though they had made what they felt were rock-solid arrests, and they continued to compile every scrap of evidence they could uncover and check out every tip they received, no matter how insignificant it might seem. In early November, they had gotten word from a Temple-Inland employee that another former worker might bear a closer look, and Investigator Mark Hicks interviewed the man.

He had worked with Temple-Inland Rome, he said, and he was terminated on March 24, 2006. The day he was terminated, Darlene Roberts sat in on the meeting and took notes, since she worked in human resources.

"She did not fire me," the man said, "in fact, she and I had talked and she was looking at my case and was considering hiring me back. I never had any problem with Darlene. I had nothing to do with her death, and I didn't know anything or plan anything about her death."

The man said he had never met and did not know the people who were arrested for killing Darlene.

"The week Darlene was killed, I was working for a maintenance contractor, working at a Georgia Power facility in Cartersville, Georgia. I went in at five A.M. and worked until four."

That information was quickly verified, and the man was no longer considered a person of interest in the case.

Another potential piece of evidence was checked out, but proved not to be connected to the murder. A shotgun had been confiscated in Lee's Summit, Missouri, where Schiess's mother lived, and had been sent to the Independence, Missouri, Police Department for test-firing "in regard to a homicide in Alabama." Apparently, a shotgun similar to the one believed to have been the murder weapon had been in the possession of a relative of Schiess's or Barbara, and was in nearly new condition and in its box. Since James Captain had given a statement that Schiess had told him he had given his mother a shotgun as a gift for her birthday, if that was indeed the case, the weapon was of interest to the Cherokee County authorities. It was photographed, test-fired, and the shell casings were sent to Alabama authorities. There was no connection to the Darlene Roberts murder case determined, and the murder weapon very likely still remained where Barbara had claimed it was, wrapped in green plastic and lying at the bottom of the Etowah River.

37

A motion to dismiss indictment was filed on December 8 by William M. Hawkins Jr. on behalf of his client Robert John Schiess III, asking the court to dismiss his indictment and alleging that the grand jury issuing the indictment was not qualified to do so.

The grand jury, the motion claimed, was made up of individuals whose names had been drawn from the "master jury box" of Cherokee County. The master jury box, in turn, contained cards identifying the names of every person entered on the "master jury list" of Cherokee County. That list itself had been prepared and derived solely and exclusively from the register of licensed drivers in Cherokee County.

The list of licensed drivers of Cherokee County was not a fair cross section of the community, the motion claimed, and cited several references from previous court decisions around the country.

The grand jury that returned the indictment against the defendant was selected from a grand jury list that did not contain a fairly representative cross section of the intelligent citizens of the county, including all significant identifiable groups, the motion stated, and therefore the grand jury was disqualified to return the indictment:

The Defendant had no knowledge, either actual or constructive, of the illegal composition of the grand jury or the grand jury list prior to the time the indictment was returned against him. The Defendant had no opportunity to challenge the grand jury before the indictment was returned against him.

The Defendant insists that he is entitled to have a duly qualified grand jury consider the charges against him and determine whether or not to return an indictment against him. For this reason, the Defendant moves to dismiss the pending indictment in this cause.

As the indictment against Schiess was not dismissed, the motion failed to impress the court with its arguments.

Rodney Stallings also filed a motion to dismiss indictment on Barbara's behalf, on the grounds of inadequate notice. He asked that her indictment be dismissed on the grounds that it denied her of adequate notice of the charges against her and of the opportunity to prepare an effective defense. In support of the motion, the defense stated that Barbara was at that time before the court on an indictment dated November 2, 2006. She was charged with capital murder based upon her alleged involvement in the death of Darlene Roberts on or about April 6, 2006. The indictment, the motion claimed, charged Barbara with intentionally killing Darlene during theft/abduction. It did not specify what item(s) the defendant allegedly stole or attempted to steal, nor did it specify what weapon was purportedly used to commit the killing. Therefore, the motion stated, Count One of the indictment was impermissibly vague and deprived the defendant of proper notice of the charges against her, and called the indictment *devoid of any legal or factual specificity*.

Another motion to dismiss the indictment was based "On Account of Discrimination in the Selection of the Grand Jury Foreperson, and Motion For Discovery of Grand Jury Foreperson Data."

The court was being asked to dismiss the indictment returned against Barbara because of the systematic underrepresentation of blacks, women, and young adults (aged eighteen to thirty) in the selection of grand jury forepersons, citing sections of the Alabama Constitution, Code of Alabama, and the United States Constitution.

The motion stated that, upon information and belief, African-Americans, women, young adults, and other cognizable groups were systematically and discriminatorily excluded from serving as grand jury forepersons in Cherokee County, Alabama. The practice formed a pattern, the motion stated, and was part of a history in Cherokee County of the systematic exclusion of blacks, women, and young adults from the position of grand jury forepersons. This practice existed at the time the grand jury that indicted Barbara was selected, the motion claimed.

African-Americans and women constituted a

cognizable, distinctive class of persons in the community under both state and federal law, the motion said, and their intentional exclusion from the position of grand jury foreperson violated an accused's federal constitutional rights.

An additional motion charged that upon information and belief, the jury venire systematically underrepresented African-Americans, Mexican-Americans, Native Americans, women, and other groups, in proportion to those groups' representation in Cherokee County. That underrepresentation, the motion stated, was statistically significant and unreasonable in relation to the number of such persons in the community. In addition, the motion said, that underrepresentation constituted part of a history and pattern of discriminatory and systematic exclusion of members of those groups from the grand jury pools in Cherokee County. The motion sought dismissal of the charges against Barbara for that alleged discrimination among the selected members of the grand jury that indicted her.

Rodney Stallings had played the race, gender, and age cards, all in one fell swoop, but the effort failed to get the indictment against his client dismissed. However, he was not yet finished objecting to the makeup of the grand jury, and filed additional motions to determine the composition of the Cherokee County jury lists.

Stallings filed a "Motion for Order of Access to, Inspection of, and Copying of All Jury System Records," asking the judge to direct the Cherokee County officials who had direction and control over the jury system to provide access to, inspection of, and copying of any and all source lists, master lists, computer programming and data, and any other records in their possession, to a designated representative of counsel for the defendant, pursuant to Rule 16 of the Alabama Rules of Criminal Procedure, the Sixth, Eighth and Fourteenth Amendments of the United States Constitution, and the corresponding provisions of the Alabama Constitution.

Stallings noted that Barbara had filed motions challenging the composition of the grand jury that indicted her and of the jury panel from which her petit jury would be selected. Her motions alleged that the Cherokee County jury lists excluded large numbers of citizens who would otherwise qualify for jury service on account of, inter alia, their race, sex, age, or employment status. Those motions, Stallings said, were incorporated into the current motion by reference.

The defense also filed a "Motion for Order Permitting Discovery of Transcripts, Exhibits, Other Memorialization of the Grand Jury Proceedings, and List of Grand Jury Members."

The motion asked for discovery of the grand jury proceedings and for an order directing the clerk of the Cherokee County Circuit Court or the Jury Commission of Cherokee County to produce records pertaining to the grand jury proceedings culminating in Barbara's indictment.

In accompanying motions, dismissal of the indictment had been requested on a number of grounds challenging the propriety of the grand jury proceedings. To prepare evidence on those motions and to litigate those claims adequately, the motion said, Barbara's defense must have access to and copies of the testimony, transcript, and exhibits from the grand jury proceedings for the October Term 2006, as well as a list of the members of the grand jury that returned her indictment.

In answer to Barbara's motions, Judge David Rains issued a court order addressing the several issues that had been brought into question, and this time, the requests in the motions were granted.

Judge Rains stated that he had considered defendant Barbara Ann Roberts's "Motion to Dismiss the Indictment Due to Systematic Underrepresentation of Cognizable Groups in the Composition of the Grand Jury" and "Motion for Order of Access to, Inspection of, and Copying of All Jury System Records." His order read that Barbara's legal defense would be allowed to conduct discovery concerning her claim of underrepresentation in the grand jury pool. He further ordered that the clerk of the Cherokee County Circuit Court would provide access to the defense of all the information and materials they would need to make an adequate determination as to whether the challenge to the composition of the grand jury was valid.

The judge ordered that a list of the Cherokee County grand jury pool members from, and including, 2000 through 2007 would be furnished to the defense, with data revealing each member's age, race, and sex.

Also to be made available was a list of the Cherokee County jury commissioners from, and including, 2000 through 2007, with complete information on each commissioner's age, race, and sex.

Barbara's defense would be given all the information, materials, memoranda, and reports concerning the selection process for Cherokee County grand juries, including jury questionnaires, source lists, and venire lists.

Judge Rains ordered that a date would be set, at a time agreed to by the jury commission staff and the defense, when a representative of the defense would be provided with access to all computer data concerning the jury selection system in Cherokee County. At that time, Rains ordered, the director of computer services would explain to the defense representative all phases of the computer system relating to jury selection or other related tasks, and that the representative of the defense would be allowed to copy any and all records, programming, and data used in the preparation and maintenance of the master lists, the periodic issuing of summons to jury duty, and any other aspects of the selection process.

Judge Rains also ordered that a hearing on the defense's motion challenging the composition of the grand jury pool would be scheduled when the ordered discovery was completed. At that time, he said, the defendant would be allowed to present evidence in support of the motion.

38

While Robert John Schiess III and his defense team had been filing for dismissal of his indictment on December 8, attorney Rodney Stallings had also been busy on Barbara's behalf, filing a motion to compel that indicated there might be some storm clouds beginning to form in the relationship between Barbara and Schiess. Having earlier filed a motion for the return of her $125,000 bail funds, Barbara filed once again; this time, because earlier that same day, Schiess had filed a motion to intervene regarding return of bond money. Evidently, Schiess was contending that he had furnished Barbara's bail and wanted it to be returned to him, instead of being released to her.

His motion to intervene asked the court to enter an order requiring the clerk of circuit court to return the funds currently being held as a result of the previous bond entered by the district court in the amount of $125,000. Schiess stated he was the party responsible for the payment of those funds to the clerk's office, and they were withdrawn from his assets and should be returned to him. The motion requested the court to issue an order directing the clerk of the circuit court to make those funds payable to Schiess's attorney, William Hawkins Jr.

In the motion filed for Barbara, Stallings said that the funds had been placed in the Office of the Circuit Clerk of Cherokee County and receipted to Barbara. She had duly filed her demand to release bond funds, and Schiess had filed a motion to intervene regarding return of bond money.

Stallings said that the defendant Barbara Ann Roberts argued that the money should be returned to her, pursuant to Alabama code and law, which he claimed stated that when money had been deposited instead of bail, if at any time before the bail was forfeited, the defendant surrendered themselves back into custody, the court must order a return of the deposit to the defendant upon producing proof of the surrender.

Stallings said that Barbara therefore filed her motion to compel the court to enter an order directing the clerk to immediately return the deposit of $125,000 to her, as she was incarcerated due to the court's denial of her bond upon indictment, on November 30, 2006.

With that considered, Stallings claimed, the defense petitioned the court, after due consideration, to enter an order granting her motion to compel and release of the funds in question, to release none of the money to Schiess without first holding an evidentiary hearing, and to grant any such other further and different relief to which she might be entitled.

The battle over the bond money continued on January 16, when a letter was presented to Dwayne Amos, the circuit clerk of Cherokee County, regarding the funds.

The letter sent from attorney William M. Hawkins Jr., on behalf of Schiess, asked Amos to please allow the letter to serve as a formal demand by and on behalf of Robert John Schiess III that the money currently being held in his office be returned to and made payable to said Robert John Schiess III.

As authority for the release of said funds, please find enclosed a copy of a promissory note executed on or about April 27, 2006, by Defendant Barbara Ann Roberts and witnessed by her attorney, Rodney Stallings, the letter said.

The promissory note stated that in the event that the money is not paid in full within six months of the signing of the note, Schiess would be entitled to any money due to Barbara from the circuit court in the present case and any subsequent court case.

Stallings immediately prepared a motion for the codefendant to be present, asking for a court order requiring Schiess to be present at the hearing on the bond funds dispute set for January 22, 2007, at 11:00 A.M.

The motion said that Schiess was presently incarcerated in the Cherokee County Detention Center, and that Barbara had a hearing scheduled on that day and time for determination of the return of bond money.

Schiess's attorney, the motion said, had written a letter to the court clerk demanding return of the bond money and referring to the promissory note from the defendant to the codefendant. The motion requested that a court order would be issued requiring the sheriff's office to transport Schiess to the courthouse for the hearing.

On January 31, the sum of $125,000 was returned to Schiess by order of the court.

39

On January 4, 2007, ABI agent Brent Thomas received a report from the North Carolina State Bureau of Investigation (SBI) in reference to a visit on December 12, 2006, that had been paid to the home of Robert John Schiess Jr., the father of Robert John Schiess III. Two special agents had spoken with the elder Schiess at his home and questioned him as to whether he had received a shotgun from his son.

Schiess Jr. told the agents that his son had never shipped any guns to his residence. His other son, he said, kept his gun safe there, but he did not have the combination to the gun safe, and it had not been accessed for around three years. His sons were not close, Schiess Jr. said, and they did not have contact with each other.

The last time he spoke with Schiess, his father said, was around eighteen months earlier, at which time they had a disagreement of a personal nature. He had learned about his son's legal problems from his daughter, who lived in Florida.

Barbara had claimed that someone had taken Schiess's guns from his medical office when it was closed, but according to his father, the guns in the safe in North Carolina were not the same ones.

Barbara's arraignment was set for January 25, 2007, and she would spend a very bleak holiday season in the jail. Her therapist had attempted to visit her and was refused the visit by the DeKalb County Jail officials, so attorneys Lanier and Stallings prepared a motion to the court and delivered it on January 12, asking for a continuance and for psychological testing prior to the arraignment.

Lanier and Stallings were just beginning to delve into some of the details of Barbara's long history of checking herself into psychiatric-treatment facilities, and they wanted to be sure she was evaluated prior to her arraignment. In petitioning the court for a continuance, they listed several points to consider, including the fact that her therapist had been denied a visit.

Lanier and Stallings also claimed that Barbara had attempted suicide while in the DeKalb County Jail and was at that time on suicide watch. The two attorneys said they had been informed by the state that they had knowledge of Barbara's having been admitted for psychological/psychiatric treatment on two occasions, and because there were several more such occasions than that, the attorneys would, by requesting a continuance, be better able to compile a thorough file on Barbara's previous treatment.

A thorough mental evaluation was requested in order that Barbara could properly plead for her arraignment, and the attorneys said that she might lack sufficient present ability to assist them with a reasonable degree of rational understanding of the facts and the legal proceedings against her. Her arraignment, they stated, needed to be continued so that adequate evaluations could be made in order to provide an adequate and proper defense.

Lanier and Stallings moved that the arraignment be continued until evaluations were performed, an order be entered allowing the visitation of Barbara's therapist and any subsequent visits he deemed necessary, and the medical and mental condition of their client to be determined by the appropriate evaluations.

On January 23, Circuit Judge Randall L. Cole issued a court order continuing Barbara's arraignment and permitting her therapist to visit with her in order to conduct a psychological evaluation. Barbara's Christmas season in the DeKalb County Jail had been depressing and lonely, but now she at least had hope that the new year would finally bring her a visit from one of the doctors she trusted and depended on . . . sooner or later.

40

During the early months of 2007, in addition to being visited finally by her therapist in the DeKalb County Jail, Barbara was in a continual state of frustration by the lack of time she felt that Rodney Stallings spent coming to see her. She wrote him on practically a daily basis, demanding that he come to the jail, but she did not appreciate the enormity of the amount of paperwork that was flying back and forth between Stallings, the district attorney's office, Schiess's attorneys, the Cherokee County Courthouse, the United States District Court in Georgia, and Vernon Roberts's attorneys. Motions, orders, summons, and more were being filed, issued, and answered on a continual basis by all the parties involved.

The latest entry into the field was a civil suit filed by Vernon's attorneys against both Barbara and Schiess, a complaint for wrongful death in the matter of Darlene's murder. Barbara was served a summons in that case on February 12, which required her to file an answer to the complaint within twenty days following service. News of the civil suit came as another blow to Barbara, but by this time she had no personal assets of any kind and was completely indigent. Schiess, on the other hand, was quite wealthy, so the suit was obviously not aimed primarily at Barbara.

There had been a surprising development a few days earlier, on February 6, that might have indicated that Schiess and his attorneys had somehow learned of the civil suit that was being prepared against him. Cherokee County investigator Mark Hicks had been contacted by the FBI and informed that Schiess was in the process of transferring funds to a Swiss bank. The total amount of the funds being transferred was close to $1.8 million.

Wachovia Bank had contacted the FBI, as is the standard operating procedure in a money transfer as large as this, and the FBI, being aware of the charges against Schiess, had informed Hicks. Hicks, in turn, passed the information along to Investigator Bo Jolly, the case agent in the capital murder case against Schiess.

Vernon Roberts, in his complaint for wrongful death, under Alabama law, stated that he was the surviving spouse of Darlene Roberts at the time of her death and that, as the personal representative of the deceased, was the proper party entitled to bring the action. He and Darlene, the complaint said, were both residents of Cherokee County, Alabama, at the time of her death. Barbara was listed in the complaint as a resident of Floyd County, Georgia, whose temporary address

was the DeKalb County Detention Center.
Schiess—said to be a resident of Rockdale County,
Georgia—had a temporary address of the Cherokee County Jail. Both were subject, the complaint said, to the jurisdiction and venue of the
Northern District Court of Georgia, Rome Division. The complaint stated the court had original
jurisdiction in the case because *there exists complete diversity of citizenship between the Plaintiff and
Defendants Roberts and Schiess, and the amount in
controversy exceeds $75,000.00.*

The complaint charged that on April 6, 2006,
the defendants, while acting in concert, intentionally, or as a result of their wanton and reckless
conduct, abducted, assaulted, battered, and shot
the deceased with a firearm. The deceased died
as a direct and proximate result of the afore-
mentioned gunshot wound. The defendants
then dumped the deceased's body in a pond off
Cherokee County Road 941 in Centre, Cherokee
County, Alabama.

The conduct of the defendants as set forth resulted in the death of the deceased, so they are
liable for the wrongful death of the deceased,
and the plaintiff is entitled to recover against the
defendants damages for said defendants' unlaw-
ful conduct.

The complaint went on to state that Vernon
Roberts, as Darlene's personal representative, demanded that the defendants be served with sum-
monses and processed as required by law, that
Vernon would have a trial by jury, and that he
would have judgment against the defendants for
damages in an amount sufficient to punish the

defendants for their wrongful conduct, and to deter similar actions, in excess of the court's jurisdictional amount to be determined by the enlightened conscience of the jury, plus an award of costs and expenses as allowed by law, and for such other and further relief as the court might deem equitable, just, and proper.

On March 1, Barbara filed her answer and motion for change of venue in the case, stating that she denied each and every allegation contained in the complaint for wrongful death and demanded strict legal proof.

Barbara also stated that she was currently incarcerated in DeKalb County Jail in Fort Payne, Alabama, and that the alleged activity occurred in Cherokee County, Alabama. Vernon, she said, was also a resident of Cherokee County. Therefore, she stated, the venue should be changed to the United States District Court, Northern District of Alabama, or the Circuit Court of Cherokee County, Alabama.

Despite Barbara's motion for change of venue, the case remained with the United States District Court for the Northern District of Georgia, Rome Division.

A videotape of Barbara's deposition was arranged to be conducted at the Cherokee County Jail on August 15, 2007, when she would be questioned by attorneys for Vernon and Schiess. Until that time, as she was penniless and had no assets of any kind that were subject to be lost, there would be far more pressing legal matters that would demand her time and attention.

Barbara Ann Roberts, convicted of the capital murder of Darlene Roberts. *(Photo courtesy of the Cherokee County Sheriff's Office)*

Dr. Robert John "Bob" Schiess III entered a guilty plea to the lesser charge of kidnapping. *(Photo courtesy of the Cherokee County Sheriff's Office)*

The body of Darlene Roberts floats in the shallow water of the pond where she tried to hide from Barbara Roberts and Bob Schiess. *(Photo courtesy of the Cherokee County Sheriff's Office)*

This spent shotgun shell was found in the shallow water of the pond where Darlene Roberts was shot. *(Photo courtesy of the Cherokee County Sheriff's Office)*

Cherokee County Investigator Michael B. "Bo" Jolley, lead investigator in the Darlene Roberts murder case. *(Photo by Tim Johnson)*

Lieutenant Jimmy DeBerry, left, and Cherokee County Drug Task Force Commander Charles Clifton questioned Vernon Roberts on the night of his wife's murder. *(Photo by Tim Johnson)*

Cherokee County Investigator Mark Hicks worked the crime scene and interviewed Barbara Roberts on several occasions. *(Photo by Tim Johnson)*

The broken eyeglasses belonging to Barbara Roberts were barely visible in the thick grass beside the pond. *(Photo courtesy of the Cherokee County Sheriff's Office)*

Investigator Mark Hicks points out the broken eyeglasses, a key piece of evidence in the case. *(Photo courtesy of the Cherokee County Sheriff's Office)*

Hicks and another officer show the location of the glasses in relation to where Darlene Roberts's body was found. *(Photo courtesy of the Cherokee County Sheriff's Office)*

These signs, property of the Floyd County, Georgia Road Department, were found beside the road near the crime scene.
(Photo courtesy of the Cherokee County Sheriff's Office)

Investigators believed the road signs were taken to be used to stop Darlene Roberts on her way home from work.
(Photo courtesy of the Cherokee County Sheriff's Office)

Several pieces of this green plastic film, the same material found around Darlene Roberts's neck, floated in the pond near the body. *(Photo courtesy of the Cherokee County Sheriff's Office)*

The bank of the pond was covered with footprints near the crime scene, but heavy rains and the muddy ground prevented positive identification. *(Photo courtesy of the Cherokee County Sheriff's Office)*

This broken bracelet was found near the place where Bob Schiess allegedly struggled with Darlene Roberts after stopping her car.
(Photo courtesy of the Cherokee County Sheriff's Office)

The damaged undercarriage of the Nissan Murano was packed with mud and grass from being driven through the pasture.
(Photo courtesy of the Cherokee County Sheriff's Office)

One of the entrances into the pasture where Darlene Roberts was murdered on April 6, 2006. *(Photo courtesy of the Cherokee County Sheriff's Office)*

The farm pond where the body of Darlene Roberts was found by two men out for a ride on their four-wheeler. *(Photo courtesy of the Cherokee County Sheriff's Office)*

This pair of women's in-line skates, still in their box, was found, along with the receipt for their purchase, during the search of the Schiess apartment. *(Photo courtesy of the Cherokee County Sheriff's Office)*

Also found during the search of the apartment was this carton for a tactical shotgun stock with a butt pad. *(Photo courtesy of the Cherokee County Sheriff's Office)*

Several items were found in the Schiess apartment, wrapped in the same green plastic stretch film that was found around Darlene Roberts's neck. *(Photo courtesy of the Cherokee County Sheriff's Office)*

Officers found the missing black Dodge Dakota pickup inside a storage building rented by Schiess. *(Photo courtesy of the Cherokee County Sheriff's Office)*

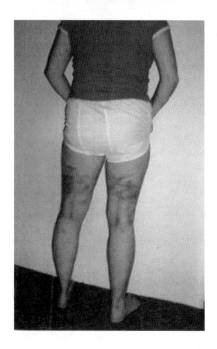

Barbara Roberts claimed these bruises on her legs were caused by a beating while in the Cherokee County Jail. *(Photo courtesy of the Cherokee County Sheriff's Office)*

This note was presented as evidence that Barbara Roberts was stalking and harassing her ex-husband, Vernon Roberts, and his wife, Darlene. *(Photo courtesy of the Cherokee County Sheriff's Office)*

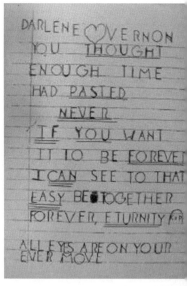

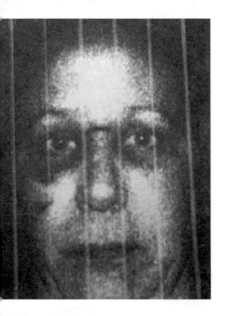

Despite the poor quality of this image, taken in the bathroom mirror of the Schiess apartment, the blackened eyes and injuries to Barbara Roberts's face are apparent. *(Photo courtesy of the Cherokee County Sheriff's Office)*

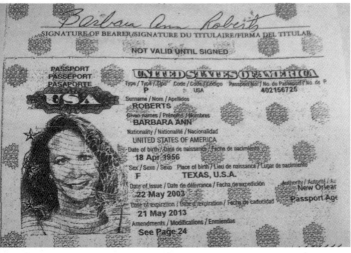

In this passport photo, taken in 2003, Barbara Roberts appears quite attractive. *(Photo courtesy of the Cherokee County Sheriff's Office)*

Attorney Rodney Stallings, seated, Barbara Roberts's defense attorney during her capital murder trial, and his legal assistant, Timothy Doyle. *(Photo by Tim Johnson)*

When he took office, Cherokee County Sheriff Jeff Shaver assumed supervision of one of Cherokee County's most important capital murder investigations. *(Photo by Tim Johnson)*

District Attorney Mike O'Dell of the Ninth Judicial District of Alabama, who headed up Barbara Roberts's prosecution for capital murder. *(Photo by Tim Johnson)*

Bob Johnston, Assistant District Attorney of the Alabama Ninth Judicial District, aided in the prosecution of Barbara Roberts. *(Photo by Tim Johnson)*

Dr. Robert John Schiess III and his attorneys stand before District Judge Randall Cole at a court appearance.
(Photo by Sheila Johnson)

Cherokee County Chief Deputy Tim Hays escorts Barbara Roberts back to the Cherokee County Jail to await return to Tutwiler Prison for Women following a court appearance.
(Photo by Sheila Johnson)

41

On February 20, 2007, Barbara revoked the durable power of attorney she had given to attorney Stephen F. Lanier on April 21, 2006, in Floyd County, Georgia. The revocation was signed and notarized in DeKalb County.

Then, on March 12, Barbara filed a copy of a letter to Lanier, a request for retainer amount and a notice of termination, with the circuit clerk of Cherokee County.

Barbara wrote in the letter that she had employed the Stephen F. Lanier law firm to represent her in the case number DC-2006-438F in Cherokee County, Alabama. The contract was for a $50,000 retainer:

I wish to terminate your employment and ask you to return the retainer as I understand you are demanding an additional $125,000.00 to represent me in the now CC-2006-461 Capital Murder case. I do not have the money to pay you and need the $50,000.00 retainer and the additional $15,000.00 you withdrew from my accounts to afford a defense.

Please send the refund to Barbara Roberts c/o DeKalb County Jail and send all legal documentation to Attorney Rodney Stallings in Centre, Alabama. You may deduct any mailing costs from the refund.

On the same day, Lanier filed a motion to withdraw as Barbara's attorney of record in the case.

Lanier maintained that Barbara was arrested on April 21, 2006, for a murder that occurred in Cherokee County, Alabama. He was retained and a legal representation contract signed by Barbara on that day for *representation of a noncapital* offense of murder. He was a licensed attorney and member of the State Bar of Georgia, and was admitted by the State Bar of Alabama to represent Barbara in the noncapital murder case prior to indictment.

On or about October 31, 2006, Lanier stated he was notified by the state of its intention to present to the grand jury of Cherokee County a capital felony indictment against Barbara. She was given an opportunity by the state to enter a plea of guilty to a noncapital murder offense with the possibility of parole. Barbara declined the offer.

Barbara was indicted subsequently by the Cherokee grand jury for a capital murder offense on November 3, 2006. The state of Alabama was seeking the death penalty in the case. Barbara was rearrested and her bond revoked due to this capital felony indictment, and she had remained in custody since her rearrest. Her cash bond of $125,000 had been returned to Schiess by order of the court on January 31. As a result of that court order, Barbara was therefore indigent and unable to retain Lanier's services in a capital felony case.

Lanier stated that his representation of Barbara was therefore concluded as a result of her indigence and by the terms of the contract, and Lanier respectfully requested the court to enter an order allowing him to withdraw as Barbara's attorney.

On March 29, Circuit Judge Randall L. Cole granted Lanier's motion to withdraw.

Judge Cole noted in his order that Lanier had stated he was retained and a legal representation contract was signed for representation of a *non-capital* offense of murder, that Barbara was later indicted for capital murder, that her cash bond of $125,000 was returned to her codefendant, Schiess, and that Barbara was therefore unable to retain Lanier for his services in a capital case.

Barbara had filed a notice with the court stating that she wished to terminate Lanier's services and requesting the return of a retainer paid to him.

The order stated that Barbara continue to be represented by attorney Rodney Stallings, whom she had also retained.

Judge Cole then advised Barbara that she was entitled to have counsel appointed by the court if, at any time during the course of the proceedings, she was indigent and unable to employ counsel.

42

On March 4, 2007, Barbara's psychotherapist had finally been able to meet with her at the DeKalb County Jail pursuant to Circuit Judge Randall L. Cole's order, which had permitted the visit along with the requested continuance of her arraignment pending further mental evaluation. The psychotherapist had evaluated Barbara following a one-and-a-half-hour interview, and his report was not encouraging.

Barbara was clearly in a state of agitation, he said, and was concerned that her medication was still not being administered correctly and that she couldn't get enough sleep in the disruptive, noisy jail environment. Since Barbara was on heavy medication, the psychotherapist spoke with the jail's medical director, who said he was following Barbara's medication regimen but would be willing to adjust the timing to accommodate her upon the prescribing doctor's approval.

Barbara talked to her therapist about a number of things she was upset about, and he reported that she gave no indication of paranoid or delusional thinking, but was frequently scattered, repetitious, disorganized, and often tearful. She was easily distracted, he said, and often lost her train of thought, but she told him that she could not survive in her environment—in pain, confined, heavily medicated, with limited social contact, and the fear of being put to death. She also reported constant pain in her hand, arm, and neck, and an inability to keep a steady focus.

Barbara's psychiatric problems were serious, but were undoubtedly exacerbated by her equally serious physical condition. A year prior to Darlene's murder, in April 2005, Barbara had been referred to, and had sought treatment at, a sports medicine and orthopedic surgery center in Atlanta for pain and weakness of her left forearm as a result of the 2004 auto accident in which she had fractured her left forearm and wrist. The fracture did not mend, and surgery to knit the broken bones had followed on November 30, 2004. After removal of the surgical hardware, Barbara spent five additional months in a cast.

As a result of all those injuries, surgeries, and lingering problems, Barbara reported pain that continually woke her up at night. There was nagging constant pain in her left arm and wrist, she said, with weakness and limitations to her wrist motion.

Her neurologic exam had confirmed that she was experiencing decreased muscle strength in her left forearm musculature, wrist, and decreased grip strength. There were significant limitations in her wrist motion, the examining physicians stated, and there was atrophy noted in the muscles of her left forearm and left hand. These problems alone were enough to seriously interfere with Barbara's ability to get a restorative night's sleep, but the addition of the continual noise, shouting, and the 24-7 blaring of the television made resting at night all but impossible.

The physician had reported to Barbara that there was evidence of left median nerve entrapment in the elbow, and exploratory surgery might be needed, and also reported his findings to her treating surgeon and to the doctor who had originally referred her to the clinic for examination. But there had been no opportunity for the surgery before Barbara was arrested, so the muscle, joint, and nerve problems remained.

There was no question that these problems, coupled with the mental and emotional distress Barbara was exhibiting and the continuing adjustments to her medication, were a source of her deteriorating psychological state. Clearly, Barbara had been in genuine need of the continuance of her arraignment in order to have time for a meeting with her psychotherapist.

43

As Barbara's jail time dragged on and she remained, uncomfortable and disgruntled, in the DeKalb County, Alabama, Jail, she continued to write to attorney Rodney Stallings on practically a daily basis begging, pleading, then demanding that he travel to Fort Payne on a frequent, regular basis and visit her. He was her only contact with the outside world, her only visitor other than doctors, and she desperately wanted to see someone other than her fellow inmates and the DeKalb County jailers. And all the while, even though Barbara felt forgotten, ignored, and neglected, the legal maneuvering in her case continued.

Barbara was even more unhappy and dissatisfied than ever, and in frustration she frequently clashed with the jail staff. As a result of one dustup with the jailers, she received two disciplinary charges in the same day. On one occasion she was written up for using profanity and making derogatory remarks to a staff member; later that same day, she was again written up, this time for disobeying the jail staff and once again making profane remarks. Things were not going at all well for Barbara in the DeKalb County Jail.

On May 29, 2007, Stallings filed a petition for a writ of habeas corpus addressing Judge Randall Cole, District Attorney Mike O'Dell, Cherokee County sheriff Jeff Shaver, and DeKalb County sheriff Jimmy Harris.

Stallings stated in his petition that Barbara was currently being restrained under an arrest warrant issued as a result of her indictment by the Cherokee County grand jury for murder during robbery and two counts of murder during kidnapping.

She was being held in solitary confinement, he said, at the DeKalb County Jail in Fort Payne, Alabama.

Stallings said that Barbara was receiving one hour per day to bathe and to make telephone calls, but she was allowed no contact with other persons similarly situated in the facility.

As a result of Barbara's indictment for capital murder, Stallings said, she retained his services to represent her in the charge, and Stallings's office was located in Cherokee County, Centre, Alabama.

Barbara, he said, believed he could better represent her if her detention location was correctly applied in the county where she was charged, Cherokee County, Alabama, by allowing more time to prepare for her defense.

Stallings told the court that Barbara suffered from

both physical and mental disease and required constant medications, which she claimed were not being administered correctly in the DeKalb County Jail. She was, he said, in need of medical treatment and could not receive the proper treatment while being incarcerated.

Stallings also told the court that Barbara was in need of mental/emotional and psychological treatment and, likewise, could not receive the proper treatment for those conditions while she was incarcerated. She was, he said, being held in an undue, cruel, and unusual punishment, with respect to her conditions and arrangements.

Stallings pointed out that Barbara was on bond after her arrest and reported to court—as ordered, reported her intentions to travel to her attorney's office—as ordered, and while at liberty, she traveled outside the state and freely and voluntarily returned. She lacked the financial resources to flee the country and had surrendered her passport to the court.

The petition then requested that the court grant Barbara's petition for habeas corpus or to alternatively transport her to the Cherokee County facility while awaiting trial.

The following day, on May 30, the state's response to the petition was filed by Assistant District Attorney (ADA) Robert "Bob" F. Johnston Jr., and made the following points: Defendants are required to file any petition for a writ of habeas corpus to the county in which they are detained. Defendants are required to file any petition for a writ of habeas corpus as a separate civil action and pay the appropriate fee (or a request to proceed in forma pauperis).

Johnston said that Barbara had met none of those requirements, since her petition had been filed in Cherokee County in a criminal action, not in DeKalb County in a civil action, and had not otherwise followed the procedure required by Alabama law. The state objected, he said.

That being considered, Johnston said, the state requested that the defendant's petition be summarily denied.

In June of 2007, Barbara had written a long, rambling letter to Judges Randall Cole and David Rains asking for their help in dealing with her attorney Steve Lanier. She was in the process of revoking his power of attorney and asking for the return of her retainer. In her letter she also took the opportunity to make several other allegations concerning the conditions of the DeKalb County Jail and the performance of its staff. From the composition of her letter, her mental and emotional condition seemed to have improved somewhat since the time of her initial arrest. She still was slightly repetitious, however, and jumped from one subject to another frequently.

Barbara claimed that Lanier should have returned funds of hers that she alleged should not have been used, and she said he would not return any calls. Then she said that she was being held in a twenty-inmate pod in which she was the only woman, and could not go downstairs to shower without having to listen to the vulgar comments of the men in the pod.

Barbara also complained about the return of her bond money to Robert John Schiess, then said that Steve Lanier was not legally an Alabamian lawyer, and said he was supposed to have been at the Atlanta airport to meet her and Schiess when they arrived and were arrested.

I strongly feel if he would have been there at the airport in Atlanta as he promised, everything would be totally different, but he did not, she wrote.

Barbara asked the judges to help her in any way they could, as soon as possible, to deal with Lanier. Then she claimed she and attorney Rodney Stallings did not get sufficient time to work on discovery because his time at the jail kept being cut short due to the jail staff claiming they were shorthanded. She said the prosecution did not want her back at Centre, at the Cherokee County Jail, and asked, *How do I help my case? It seems so slow, and time keeps running.*

Barbara wanted to know how she could see a psychiatrist every two weeks as she did before, at $1,000 an hour, whereas if she was out on bail, her insurance would pay for it. And how could she get orthopedic workups with no X-ray equipment? She was, she wrote, living in a pod of *just messy vulgar men* with *loud TV 24-7, never silence.* She still had not gotten a pillow for her neck, she claimed.

A list of other problems followed: not getting meds for neck, upper back, and arms, infected toe, both legs swollen, medical staff was a joke, the whole place was a joke. Regarding jail staff, *the best have quit. Over half the officers are new. It's a joke.*

Barbara closed her letter by saying, *I am being as honest as possible. I will not make it if I spend most of my time staring into space.*

With his customary polite formality, Judge Randall Cole acknowledged receipt of her letter, and told her he was providing copies to Stallings and to District Attorney Mike O'Dell. The judge told Barbara she had the option of filing a complaint with the Alabama State Bar and the Georgia State Bar. He provided her the appropriate names and addresses for both organizations in order for her to contact them directly.

He ended his reply by saying, *I am unable at this time to address other issues set forth in your letter.*

Barbara's stay at the DeKalb County Jail was clearly wearing on the nerves of everyone involved, and she fervently hoped, as did the jail staff, that she would soon be transferred back to Cherokee County. On June 20, 2007, both she and the DeKalb County Jail staff received some welcome news: Judge Randall Cole had granted at least part of the relief sought by her petition, and she would soon be returning to the Cherokee County Jail.

Judge Cole's order stated that Barbara had filed a petition that was designated as a petition for writ of habeas corpus, which was set for hearing on June 18, 2007, with Barbara, Rodney Stallings, and the deputy district attorney present.

The state had filed a response to the petition

and argued at the hearing that the petition was filed in the wrong county and that it should have been filed as a civil action with payment of a filing fee. The state also objected to the relief sought in the petition.

Judge Rains said that the relief sought by the petition appeared to be that the defendant should be allowed to make bond, and if not, her detention should be moved from the DeKalb County Jail to the Cherokee County Jail.

Habeas corpus, the judge said, was generally used to test the legality of a person's incarceration, and he said that Barbara had failed to provide sufficient proof that she was being illegally held. The contention of habeas corpus, he said, would not be allowed, and he instead considered the merits of her request as if it were part of a general motion or petition.

Concerning her request for bail, Judge Rains denied the request for reasons he had stated in a previous order of the court. As to her request that her detention be moved from the DeKalb County Jail to the Cherokee County Jail, Barbara claimed that incarceration in the DeKalb County Jail complicated her attorney's ability to work with her in preparing her defense, given the fact that his office was in Centre, Alabama. The district attorney's response to this request was that the court previously had permitted the sheriff of Cherokee County to make the decision as to where Barbara was incarcerated.

Barbara had been charged with a capital offense, the judge said. Therefore, it was essential that her counsel be permitted to consult with her, as was necessary, to prepare her defense. Without sufficient good cause showing why Barbara should be detained outside Cherokee County, Judge Rains ordered that her detention would be moved from the DeKalb County Jail to the Cherokee County Jail.

Other relief that had been requested, he said, was denied.

Barbara could hardly wait to climb into the back of a patrol car to make the short thirty-minute ride between the two jails. Now, she hoped, she would be seeing more of her attorney and could also be visited again by some of the ladies who worked for the jail ministries of churches in Cherokee County. She had been comforted by their visits during her previous stay in the Cherokee County Jail and looked forward to seeing them again. Now she would, at least, have the occasional company of someone other than "messy, vulgar men."

44

On August 15, 2007, at 9:00 A.M., the parties in the civil suit and their attorneys, along with a court reporter and videographer, gathered at the Cherokee County Jail to take Barbara's deposition.

Barbara was first questioned by Vernon's attorney, Andy Davis. He began by confirming Barbara's correct name, date of birth, Social Security number, current address at the Cherokee County Jail, previous addresses in Conyers and Rome, Georgia, her educational background, and her employment history.

He then moved on to ask Barbara where she had been born, what her maiden name was, and whether she had any relatives in the northwest Georgia area. He asked if she had any children, and if she had ever been involved in any lawsuits other than a divorce. Barbara gave information on how long she and Vernon had been married, who their divorce attorneys were, and whether or not she had ever been arrested for anything previously.

The only prior arrest Barbara had to report was for the obstruction of officer charge, which stemmed from the bizarre confrontation she and Schiess had with the GSP officer on November 10, 2005, in Cartersville, Georgia. She could not remember whether the year had been 2006 or 2005; attorney Rodney Stallings told her, "Just answer the best you can. If you don't know—"

"I don't remember, sir," Barbara told Davis.

"And was anyone else arrested with you at that time?"

Barbara told Davis that Schiess had been arrested along with her, and she said that the charges, as far as she knew, were for a DUI and an open bottle of liquor, and were still pending.

Davis asked Barbara if she had married Vernon on August 31, 1984, in Port Arthur, Texas, and if they had been married for seventeen years without having any children. That was correct, she confirmed. Then Davis asked if she had lived with Schiess, which she also confirmed.

Then Davis moved on to the subject of Darlene Roberts, asking if she had known Darlene while Darlene was working at Temple-Inland, prior to Darlene's marriage to Vernon. Barbara told him that she had known Darlene since 2001, meeting her following the divorce when "somehow, one way or another, we both ended up at Vernon's house at the same time. I don't remember exactly what the deal was."

When Davis asked Barbara if she had ever written Darlene any letters or e-mails, Stallings interrupted, asking if he could have a moment off the record with his client.

When the questioning resumed, Davis asked again about the letters or e-mails, and Barbara responded, "Take the Fifth."

"You're asserting your privilege, Fifth Amendment privilege, is that correct?" Davis asked.

"Just to clarify the record," said Stallings, "she's asserting her privilege under the Fifth Amendment, believing that those are part of the investigation that's currently ongoing."

Barbara was willing to answer Davis when he asked if she had ever received any letters or e-mails from Darlene, which she said she had not. Then Davis moved on.

"You didn't like Darlene Roberts, did you?"

Stallings immediately broke in.

"She's going to assert her Fifth Amendment. Would you rather her to say that or is it okay if I say that?"

"I'd rather her say it," Davis responded. "I think that's appropriate."

"I plead my Fifth, sir," Barbara said.

"Assert," Stallings corrected her.

"Assert my Fifth Amendment," Barbara restated.

"You had conflicts with Darlene Roberts, didn't you?"

"Same," Stallings prompted.

"Assert my Fifth Amendment right," said Barbara.

"You threatened Darlene Roberts prior to her death, didn't you?"

"No, sir."

"You threatened Vernon Roberts prior to the death of Darlene Roberts, didn't you?" Davis asked.

"Assert the Fifth Amendment right," Barbara answered.

Davis moved on to a series of questions Barbara had no problems answering, concerning when and how she had met Schiess, when they began dating and living together, how Barbara had gotten her volunteer job at Rockdale County Hospital, which of Schiess's relatives she had met and where they lived, who Barbara's relatives were and where they lived, when she had last visited Texas prior to her mother's funeral, and whether Schiess had accompanied her.

Davis asked Barbara if she was on any medications that day, and she said yes. When he asked what the medications were, she said, "I'll be honest with you. I really don't even know. They took me off the medications I was on and put me on what they wanted me on, so I have no idea what they are."

"You're talking about the medical staff here? And you're not sure what you're taking?"

"No, sir. I'm not on anything I originally came in on."

Davis wanted to know if Barbara was able to hear him and understand his questions, or if Barbara was having any memory lapses.

Barbara said that probably it would be the lack of her original medications, not the taking of her current ones, that would cause problems, but at that time they were not affecting her ability to respond to his questions.

Davis asked if Barbara had ever met Schiess's

ex-wife, and she said no. He asked if Schiess had ever told her about any other homes he had other than the apartment in Conyers, any office buildings he had an interest in, and if they had opened any joint bank accounts. She answered that he had set up a checking account that he deposited money in for her as she needed it. Then Davis asked if they had any brokerage accounts or investments together, and if Barbara was aware of any brokerage representatives that Schiess used during the time the two were dating.

Gregory "Greg" Price, Schiess's attorney, interrupted the questioning then.

"I'm going to interpose an objection on behalf of Dr. Schiess," Price said. "It appears that you're going into his economic circumstances, and I understand that this is a punitive damagement action." Price named some previous court decisions pertinent to the case, and continued, "It's improper during an action to go into the economic status of the parties until after, and if, a judgment is rendered."

"I understand your objection," Davis said, "but I think my questions right now are relative to the circumstances of which these two individuals committed the acts on Martha Darlene Roberts and relate to the motive. I think I have the right to cross-examine and ask her what her knowledge is, but your objection is noted, and I'll continue on."

Stallings asked for a moment off the record with his client; then Davis began again, asking Barbara if she knew of any brokerage representatives or any brokers that Schiess dealt with while the two of them were dating.

"We never really discussed his finances or nothing," Barbara said. "After the wreck we were in, he would help me out to, like, pay doctor bills, stuff like that and stuff, but it's not something we've discussed."

Davis asked again about the details of the wreck, which had gone on record as the worst in the state of Georgia over the Memorial Day weekend of 2004. He was primarily interested in whether or not Barbara or Schiess had made an insurance claim against the other driver, what insurance company had been involved, and whether anything had been paid to either of them as a result of the accident. Barbara told him that there had been no money to be had by a lawsuit, and that the driver of the car that had hit them had gone to jail.

45

Having exhausted the subjects of auto accidents and insurance money, Davis then switched over to the topic of membership in the South River Gun Club, asking if the couple had gone to the club, taken lessons, or practiced to improve their ability to shoot a shotgun or other firearms.

Barbara answered by asserting her Fifth Amendment right.

"Growing up in Texas, did you hunt and fish?" he asked.

Barbara told him she had fished, but she asserted her Fifth Amendment right again when Davis asked if she had done any hunting. She said that some of her siblings had hunted, but she was not able to give any details. Davis then asked if, when she went to her mother's funeral, she had discussed with her nephew, a deputy sheriff, how law enforcement conducted fingerprint detection and analysis.

"You were concerned about fingerprints showing up on items that were found at the scene of the murder of Darlene Roberts, weren't you?" he asked, and Barbara invoked the Fifth Amendment. This was the start of an endless stream of questions about the events of April 6, 2006, all of which would be answered by the assertion of Barbara's Fifth Amendment rights.

"And those fingerprints you were concerned about were not only yours, but also Robert John Schiess's, correct? On April 5, 2006, were you with Robert John Schiess at the Weathington Road residence in Rome? You and Robert John Schiess staked out the roadway to Vernon Roberts's house in order to ambush Darlene Roberts, didn't you? You were present with Robert John Schiess in Cherokee County, Alabama, correct? You came in contact with Darlene Roberts, didn't you? Robert John Schiess came in contact with Darlene Roberts, didn't he? You were in the possession of, either owning or had use of, a firearm, correct? You had a romantic relationship with Robert John Schiess, correct? Robert John Schiess had possession of or had access to a firearm, correct? You were present in a vehicle with Robert John Schiess, weren't you? That vehicle was not owned by you, was it? It was owned by Robert John Schiess, correct?"

In each and every case, Barbara had asserted her Fifth Amendment right not to answer due to the fact that the answer related directly to the ongoing criminal case. Rodney Stallings was ready to ask for a few minutes to confer again with his client. He requested a break, and the proceedings went off the record for a few minutes while he advised Barbara on what she was and was not required to answer.

46

Greg Price, the attorney for Schiess, had objected frequently to Barbara's being asked for information about his client that she had no personal knowledge of, such as exactly what Schiess's financial holdings and property ownership might be, and he stated his position once again when the deposition resumed after a short recess. But when Davis began his questioning again, it amounted to another long string of inquiries, almost all of which were answered by Barbara's statement, "Assert my Fifth Amendment right."

"On April 6, 2006, you owned a pair of glasses, correct? Those glasses that you're wearing today, how long have you owned those? How long have you been prescribed glasses? Did you use Pearle Vision in Conyers, for the purchase of your glasses or glasses frames? At the Pearle Vision in Conyers you obtained a pair of eyeglasses that had titanium type frames, correct? You and Dr. Schiess purchased twelve-gauge shotgun shells at Piedmont Outdoor Store, correct? When you were at the firing range, did you and Dr. Schiess use a twelve-gauge shotgun? You knew what kind of car Darlene Roberts drove, didn't you? You and Dr. Schiess were laying in wait until Darlene Roberts came home from work, weren't you? You saw Darlene Roberts driving her car toward her home, correct? You and Dr. Schiess stopped Darlene Roberts on the dirt road or the gravel road on the way to her home, correct?"

Attorney Davis was getting absolutely no response from his questions other than the assertion of Barbara's Fifth Amendment rights, so he stopped using as many questions and began placing most of his remarks to her in the form of statements.

"You and Dr. Schiess were present when farmworkers came by on an ATV. You and Dr. Schiess tried to bind Darlene Roberts's arms and placed plastic wrap over her head and around her neck. You and Dr. Schiess dragged Darlene Roberts from her car. You and your lover, Dr. Schiess, chased Darlene Roberts through the pasture after dragging her from her car, correct? You and Dr. Schiess, your lover, fired a firearm toward Darlene Roberts, fired a shotgun at Darlene Roberts more than one time. Darlene Roberts was struck by shotgun pellets from the shotgun that you and Dr. Schiess fired. Darlene Roberts was killed at the hands of you and Dr. Schiess. You suffered a black eye as a result of the events that occurred on April 6, 2006, while you were trying to commit the murder of Darlene Roberts. You still had the black eye when you attended your mother's funeral four days later. On April 7, 2006, you called

Pearle Vision in Conyers and reported that you only had the right arm and right lens of glasses and you needed to order a new pair of glasses. You gave a statement to law enforcement personnel implicating you and Dr. Schiess in the murder of Darlene Roberts. You and Dr. Schiess attempted to dispose of Darlene Roberts's body after you had committed murder, correct? You observed Robert John Schiess fire a firearm at Darlene Roberts. You observed Robert John Schiess shoot and kill Darlene Roberts."

The questioning kept on, with Davis issuing statements and Barbara continuing to answer with Fifth Amendment rights assertions.

"Prior to her death, Darlene Roberts never attempted to physically harm you. Prior to her death, you never witnessed Darlene Roberts threaten Robert John Schiess, or have any contact with him. Prior to her death, Darlene Roberts never threatened you. Neither you nor Robert John Schiess has an alibi regarding the death of Darlene Roberts. You were in the presence of Robert John Schiess on April 6, 2006, weren't you? And the two of you committed the killing and the murder of Darlene Roberts on that day, didn't you? On that day you and Robert John Schiess engaged in an attempt to kidnap Darlene Roberts, correct? On that day, or prior to that day, you stole road signs from Floyd County as part of your plot to kill Darlene Roberts. You and Robert John Schiess did use stolen road signs on April 6, 2006, in Cherokee County, Alabama. You told investigators that you were behind the truck as Darlene Roberts came driving up so she would not recognize you, correct? And you saw Dr. Schiess stop Darlene Roberts and get her out of the car, correct? And you told investigators that Dr. Schiess bound Darlene Roberts with Saran Wrap, correct? And Darlene Roberts got loose and ran, and you and Dr. Schiess chased her, correct? You told investigators Dr. Schiess actually got in the car and chased her in the car, correct?"

Greg Price had begun frequently objecting to questions that involved his client, Schiess, and Davis decided he had done enough for the time being. He stated for the record that was all he had at that time, and turned the cross-examination over to Price until his turn came to recross-examine the witness.

47

The questioning style of attorney Price was not quite as aggressive as Davis's had been. He was looking out for the interests of his client, Schiess, and his questions were focused more on Barbara's relationship with Vernon Roberts.

He began by asking Barbara if she knew Ron Kelly, a security guard for Temple-Inland, and asked if he had ever communicated with her in any manner. Then he asked if during the time period after the divorce, she had continued to have any communication with Vernon.

Barbara answered that she had communicated with her ex-husband by telephone, in writing, in person, or by e-mail.

Barbara said that she'd had frequent e-mails from Vernon, discussing all manner of topics, and said that she and Vernon were still dating at times following their divorce, even having a physical relationship beyond the time of his marriage to Darlene. She and Vernon had contacted each other by e-mail frequently during the time of that physical relationship, and had spoken often, both on cell phones and home phones.

"When would you have occasion to see Vernon?" Price asked.

"We met one time at the back gates on Mays Bridge Road, where the contractors and stuff would come in and out, and at that time we talked and stuff, and I gave him a mink coat to give to Darlene."

"Did you and he and Darlene ever socialize together?"

"Not really," Barbara said. "We would sometimes end up at the same place."

"During that time period that he was married to Darlene, was she aware of the fact of your physical relationship with Vernon?"

"Not total knowledge. I don't know how to answer that exactly."

"Did you and Darlene ever have any confrontations about the fact that you were sleeping with Vernon while she was married to him?" Price asked.

"Assert the Fifth Amendment right," Barbara answered.

"Was Vernon present during that confrontation?"

The Fifth Amendment right was invoked again.

"And, in fact, Vernon and Darlene had some serious issues about the fact that you and Vernon were sleeping together, is that correct?"

"Assert the Fifth Amendment right amendment," Barbara said, overstating the privilege.

"On April 5 and 6 of 2006, you had telephone communications with Vernon, is that correct?"

"Yes, sir."

"These telephone communications were done with a calling card, is that right? Do you know where you purchased that calling card?"

Barbara did not remember.

Price asked what Barbara and Vernon were talking about during those times, and Barbara said, "Different things on that day."

"Different things," Price repeated. "How many times did you call Vernon on the day of Darlene's death?"

"I'd have to be guessing," Barbara said, and Price told her that her best recollection would do.

"Four or five, something like that. He called me a couple of times, I'm not sure."

"And during that time period that he called you, do you remember what time of day or night it was that Vernon called you on the day of Darlene's death?"

Barbara said that she thought it was once in the morning, probably before nine o'clock, and once in the afternoon around the time he'd be getting off work, between four and five o'clock.

"Did you have a cell phone? Is there any reason why you used the calling card as opposed to the cell phone?" Price asked.

"Because he had asked me to," Barbara answered.

"Okay. Was that so that Darlene wouldn't find he was calling and there wouldn't be a record on the phone? Was using the calling card to mask the fact that you and Vernon were communicating with each other?"

"Yes, sir," Barbara said, "and from other employees that might be in his office at that time."

"Did Vernon ever communicate with you by telephone after Darlene's death?"

"I'm not certain, sir."

"Did you ever call him after Darlene's death?"

"Yes, sir."

"Did you call him using the calling card, or did you call him using your cell phone, or how did you call him?"

Barbara told him she had called Vernon both ways.

"Did you discuss the fact of Darlene's death with him? Can you tell me about that conversation?"

Barbara answered Price's question at length.

"The first call was right after my sister called me from Texas when we found out that Darlene was dead, and I called him and he was coming back from the funeral. And then, later that night, early in the morning—midnight, one o'clock, something like that—I called him to let him know that my mother had died and he had told me that if things would have been different, he'd have been at my mother's funeral, and then he asked me to pick up some flowers for her, and I asked him what he wanted to say on the card, and he said, 'Just put something that you know what I'd say,' and that was the first couple of times."

"Now, these conversations . . . Dr. Schiess was not aware of those conversations. He was not present during the time period that those conversations between you and Vernon occurred, is that correct?"

"He was nowhere around," Barbara said.

Stallings asked for another short break; then the deposition resumed.

"You'd indicated that you had been having e-mail contact with Mr. Vernon Roberts, and we know that there was an e-mail—based on your testimony—there was e-mail communication in April 2006," Price said. "Was there any communication in March 2006 via e-mail with Vernon?"

When Barbara answered that there had been, Price asked her approximately how often she would e-mail Vernon, and she said she would guess somewhere around eight times a month, from December 2005 through March 2006, going to Vernon's e-mail address at his office at Temple-Inland.

"Now, the police have asserted that you had issues, and I'm not talking about the allegation of murder," Price said, "but the police have indicated that you had issues with Vernon and Darlene to the extent that you would go onto their property and stalk them, is that correct?"

"Assert the Fifth Amendment right amendment," Barbara said.

"And, in fact, the police have accused and have evidence of you wearing a disguise and a mask and going onto Vernon and Darlene's property and committing acts of vandalism?"

Barbara invoked the Fifth Amendment once again.

"And you're aware of the fact that the police told you that Darlene said that if she died, that you would be the one that did it? Now, you, in fact, told people that Bob Schiess is innocent of these allegations, isn't that correct?"

"Assert the Fifth Amendment right amendment."

"Will you give me the names of the people that you wrote to or communicated to verbally that fact, that your opinion was that Bob Schiess was innocent of this charge?"

Stallings quickly interrupted for another short, off-the-record consultation with Barbara.

When the deposition resumed, Price asked several questions regarding Vernon's current wife, whom he had married six months after Darlene's death, inquired once again about the photo of Barbara's bruised eyes, wanted to know if Barbara and Darlene attended college together, and asked about the broken eyeglasses and Pearle Vision. All these questions drew the same response: the Fifth Amendment assertion.

Then Price jumped to other topics, which primarily got Barbara's stock answer.

"You've asserted to law enforcement that you knew that there was blood in Vernon's house after the murder. How did you know that? Did Vernon put that blood in the house? How did you know, and why did you say that you knew, there was blood in Vernon's house?

"On the day of Darlene's death, you've already told individuals that you wore a disguise on that date. Why did you wear a disguise? Describe it. Has Vernon ever worn a disguise, to your knowledge? Did you assist Vernon in putting dirty, bloody clothing in a trash can outside of Vernon's residence? Did you dispose of any of Darlene's property on the day of her death?"

Barbara asserted her Fifth Amendment right to everything.

Price then got into an area that Barbara was not hesitant to answer.

"Are you currently under the care of physicians at this time?" Price asked.

Barbara answered that she was under the care of Dr. Cecilia Kane and Dr. Steve Felton for bipolar depression, post-traumatic stress disorder, and nerve damage in her arms and both wrists. She told Price that she had been hospitalized and treated for mental-health issues at Windwood in Rome, Georgia, on five or six different occasions, from 1999 until the present.

Price asked for a couple of minutes off the record to organize his notes, then came back for a hard-hitting finish.

"Ms. Roberts, Vernon, in fact, told you in your communications with him that he could not afford another divorce, isn't that correct, speaking of him and Darlene?"

"Yes, sir."

"When did he tell you that?"

"A couple of different times. One time particularly was when we had the affair in October."

"He also told you that within several months of Darlene's death, isn't that correct?"

"Yes, sir. I think he said it would financially devastate him."

"And, in fact, didn't Vernon call and leave a recorded message for you telling you that he loved you?"

"Two or three of them."

"Do you know where those tapes are?"

"Steve Lanier's office."

Price then said, "That's all I have."

48

Attorney Davis began his recross-examination by asking Barbara if she had any contact with Schiess after their initial arrest, all of which were answered with the Fifth Amendment assertion.

"After you were arrested, you and Robert John Schiess posted a cash bond for each of you, which was one hundred twenty-five thousand dollars each, and Robert John Schiess made arrangements for those cash bonds to be paid on yours and his behalf, correct? You and Robert John Schiess have communicated since both of you have been charged with the murder of Darlene Roberts. In fact, you resided together after you were released on bond, correct?

"At one time Robert John Schiess and his family was providing you with payments for your counsel, for your attorneys, and then following your statements to the law enforcement, to the police, implicating Robert John Schiess, he withdrew the funding for your defense counsel, didn't he?"

Having had no answers other than the Fifth

Amendment assertion, Davis moved to another area of questioning.

"The calling card that you referenced earlier in your responses to Mr. Price—where is that calling card located?"

"In my purse," said Barbara.

"You still have it on your person here?"

"I don't know where it is, sir."

Barbara told Davis that the card had been in her purse the last time she saw it, but she had no idea where her purse was at that time, and she did not remember if the purse had been in her possession at the time of her arrest.

In another sudden switch of his line of questioning, Davis asked Barbara if Schiess had ever prescribed or provided medications to her. She immediately asserted her Fifth Amendment right, as she did when he asked if she was on any medications on April 6, 2006, or if she knew what the medical diagnosis for Schiess was, on or before that day.

When Davis asked Barbara what her injuries were in the wreck in Gwinnett County, she told him she broke her left arm and wrist, right foot, most of her ribs on both sides, had damage to her lungs, injured her neck, and had surgery on her neck and arm. Davis asked her if she knew what Schiess's injuries were in the wreck. Barbara said he had a blowout fracture of his right eye socket; he had fractured his left femur and consequently had a rod in the left femur from the hip to the knee; his right ankle was totally reconstructed; he also had some lung injuries. Both of them had been hospitalized for some time, she said, and had to rehabilitate for quite a while following their release from the hospital.

Davis wanted to know if she and Schiess were both taking pain medication following the accident.

"And he was prescribing them for you?"

"No, sir."

"Did you ever notice whether he prescribed any pain medication for himself?" Davis asked.

Barbara asserted her Fifth Amendment right.

At that point, after a long and tiring session, Davis stated that would be the end of the deposition. Stallings was asked if he wished to sign off on the deposition at that time, or read it first, and he reserved the right to read and sign the deposition when it was prepared. The session was then adjourned, and the parties returned to their respective offices and jail cell.

49

On May 29, 2008, Barbara signed the acknowledgment of a plea bargain offer from the Cherokee County district attorney offering her the
following terms:

For a plea of guilty, she would be sentenced to
a life sentence with a possibility of parole in ten
years, with time served. Deadline for acceptance
of the plea offer made by the state of Alabama expired at 5:00 P.M. on May 30, 2008.

Much to the chagrin and frustration of her
attorney, Barbara's answer to this offer read, *I,
Barbara Ann Roberts, do hereby decline the above offer
of the Cherokee County District Attorney.*

In a May 30 letter to the circuit clerk of Cherokee County and ADA Bob Johnston, Rodney
Stallings told them he had again met with his
client concerning their offer.

He told them that he appreciated all their efforts in offering a fair and reasonable settlement
in the case, but *unfortunately, my client is not in a
mental state to fully appreciate the significance of this*

plea, and he regrettably would have to decline their offer at that time.

On June 6, 2008, Rodney Stallings filed a motion to continue, asking for Barbara's trial, which was set for June 23, to be continued on several grounds. Foremost was his contention that he had been involved extensively with Barbara in settlement negotiations, and, he said, he had become aware that Barbara could not appreciate and understand the significance of her case, therefore causing delay, and comprehend the severity of the state's indictment of capital murder. Stallings asked for more time to *deal with the issue at hand.*

Stallings also stated that Barbara had been *hospitalized (committed) on three prior occasions for mental breakdowns generally caused by stressful situations or situations that the Defendant feels she cannot deal with.* Her treating physician had recently changed her medications dealing with her psychosis treatments, he said, and had reason to believe her prior medications were not effective in controlling her mental disorder. Her doctor was now hopeful her new medication would better control her mental disorder. The new medications were administered in early May, and both treating physicians had indicated that in order for the medication to be completely effective, the patient was usually required to have been taking them for a minimum of one month.

Stallings also pointed out that Barbara was being held in the Cherokee County Detention

Center on no bond, and she was not likely to be granted bond or be released, and therefore posed no threat to the victim's family, society, or herself.

The motion was subsequently denied, and the trial remained scheduled for the week of June 23, 2008.

On the same day the motion to continue had been filed, Stallings wrote a letter to District Attorney Mike O'Dell, Assistant District Attorney Bob Johnston, and Investigator Bo Jolly, thanking them for their time, patience, and consideration. They had made a plea bargain offer to his client, and Stallings told them that he was sorry that he could not at that time adequately prepare her to appreciate *the sincere and substantial benefit* of their offer to settle, partly due to other input and her mental state.

"I feel that it would be in her best interest to accept the offer and begin her sentence," he said, "but that decision will be hers to make."

On June 12, Barbara signed an acknowledgment that she had been offered another plea bargain, this one having the following terms:

For a plea of guilty, she would be sentenced to a life sentence with a possibility of parole in ten to fifteen years, being given credit with time served. The deadline for acceptance of the plea offer by the state of Alabama expired at 5:00 P.M. on June 16.

The plea was signed, *I, Barbara Ann Roberts, do hereby decline the above offer of the Cherokee County District Attorney.*

50

On June 12, a motion with an exhaustive title was submitted to the court on Barbara's behalf: "Motion to Suppress 'Statement of Admission' as Alleged by Agent Brent Thomas in His Words, Expressions, Assertions, Idioms, Sighs, Release, Movements Or Sarcastic Tone Purported to Be the Words, Expressions, Assertions, Idioms, Sighs, Release, Movements Or Sarcastic Tone of the Defendant, Barbara Ann Roberts."

The object of this motion was to suppress the statements that Barbara had allegedly made on April 26, 2006, as evidence against her in the prosecution's case-in-chief, as rebuttal evidence or as impeachment evidence, which the motion claimed was in violation of the Fourth, Fifth, Sixth, Eighth, and Fourteenth Amendments of the United States Constitution and Article 1 of the Alabama Constitution.

The facts listed in the motion were as follows: Barbara was charged with capital murder for theft of property, abduction, or attempted abduction and murder of Darlene Roberts on April 6, 2006.

Barbara was arrested in Conyers, Georgia, on April 19 and charged with the murder, and extradited to Cherokee County, Alabama, on April 21.

On April 26, Barbara met with Agent Brent Thomas and Investigator Mark Hicks. Agent Brent Thomas signed an interview sheet alleging words, expressions, assertions, idioms, sighs, release, movements, or sarcastic tone as purported to be Barbara's words. The motion went on to claim that the statement was, in fact, the words of Agent Thomas and not those of Barbara, and therefore were hearsay.

The officers told her, the motion said, that they knew she had committed a murder because they had videotapes, physical evidence, confessions, and eyewitness testimony that she had called her attorney, Steve Lanier, at her arrival at the Hartsfield-Jackson Atlanta International Airport, of which he had documentation to that effect, and Lanier advised her to proffer attorney-client privilege and advised her not to speak with anyone without his presence, and that he would call her the next day for details of the situation.

The argument presented in favor of the motion being granted were as follows:

Barbara was seized and interrogated on less than probable cause, in violation of her Fourth and Fourteenth Amendment rights. Accordingly, her statement was obtained after an illegal seizure and must be suppressed, along with all other fruits of the illegal seizure.

Barbara did not voluntarily answer questions

or voluntarily make a statement, but was instead coerced into responding to the police interrogation, the motion said. The circumstances surrounding the interrogation, the motion claimed, were coercive, and the police made material misrepresentations to the defendant. The motion said the totality of the circumstances showed that the statement was involuntary and taken in violation of federal and state constitutional guarantees, and that the state had failed to prove that Barbara's statement was voluntary.

Another claim in the motion was that Barbara had not adequately been advised of her Miranda rights, that she did not knowingly and intelligently waive her rights, and that the state had failed to carry its burden of proving that she had validly waived her rights.

For those reasons, the motion stated, Barbara's statement was obtained in violation of constitutional and state law.

51

As with almost all other similar court cases, the months prior to the capital murder trial of Barbara Ann Roberts were filled with a continual stream of motions—filed dozens at a time—having to do with everything from potential jurors to evidence to witnesses. In June, the stream of paperwork had become a veritable flood as time for the trial grew nearer. On June 13, a particularly large group of motions on Barbara's behalf was filed in the office of Circuit Clerk Dwayne Amos.

A "Motion for Personal Service on Potential Jurors Who Do Not Respond to Their Summons, and for the Court to Determine All Excusals" was presented to the court, asking that service of summons on jurors be determined so as to avoid any prejudice to her right to a fair trial. The motion asked that personal service be made upon any jurors who failed to respond to their summons mailed by the clerk, and that the court hear and determine any applications for excusal or to have jury service deferred only after notice to Barbara and Stallings. The case, the motion said, had received extraordinary news coverage in the Centre media, as well as throughout the state. There was widespread knowledge about the case in the community, and strongly held opinions about Barbara's guilt and the appropriateness of the death penalty in this case.

She was also entitled, the motion said, to have the jury selected in a manner that did not raise or leave any question as to how the pool from which the jury was struck had been assembled. It was of vital importance that the process leading to consideration of the death penalty be fair and reliable.

Another document, a "Motion to Require Disclosure of Any and All Information Concerning Prospective Jurors That May Be Favorable to the Defense," asked for a court order requiring the district attorney to disclose any information about prospective jurors that would be exculpatory to Barbara with regard to either guilt or punishment. Since it was to be a capital prosecution, said the motion, exacting standards must be met to assure that it was fair, and Barbara was clearly entitled to any and all information in the possession of the state that could prove favorable to her during trial.

Another motion filed on June 13 sought an order requiring the district attorney to reveal any connections of any sort with prospective jurors: a "Motion to Disclose the Past and Present Relationships, Associations and Ties Between the District Attorney and Prospective Jurors."

The motion asked the court, pursuant to the Fourth, Fifth, Sixth, Eighth, and Fourteenth Amendments to the United States Constitution, and Article 1 of the Alabama Constitution, for an order requiring the district attorney to reveal any and all relationships, associations, or ties with any prospective jurors, and to disclose any and all notes, memoranda, or records in the possession of the state concerning any relationships, associations, or ties between the office of the district attorney and those persons called for jury duty in this case.

In support of the motion, Stallings noted that the state, through the district attorney, had announced that it possibly intended to seek the death penalty, and Barbara was entitled by the Sixth, Eighth, and Fourteenth Amendments and the law of Alabama to be tried by impartial, fair-minded jurors.

52

The next motion in line was for individual sequestered voir dire. It was an attempt by Stallings to insure that prospective jury members did not have an opportunity to "compare notes" with one another, either before or after being questioned. Stallings asked that he be allowed to question those prospective jurors individually and apart from all the other jurors, to sequester those who had already been questioned from those who had not, until such time as the jury was selected, and to admonish prospective jurors not to talk with one another regarding the case. The motion asked for individual questioning of prospective jurors on the basis of the extensive and highly prejudicial publicity that had followed the case, and the severity of the penalty sought by the state. It said that such action was constitutionally required if Barbara was to receive a fair trial before an impartial jury.

Also filed was a "Motion for Disqualification from the Jury Venire of All Potential Jurors Who

Would Automatically Vote for the Death Penalty If They Found Ms. Roberts Guilty of Capital Murder."

This motion petitioned the court to disqualify from the jury pool all potential jurors who would automatically vote for a sentence of death if they found Barbara guilty of the intentional murder of Darlene Roberts. A number of Amendments were cited, both from the United States and Alabama Constitutions, and the motion said that as a matter of constitutional law, it was established that a potential juror was not fit to sit on a capital sentencing jury if that person would automatically vote for the death penalty in the event the defendant was found guilty of capital murder.

The next motion in the series was a "Motion to Disqualify All Potential Jurors Who Knew or Were Acquainted with the Victim or Her Family."

In the case of the murder of Darlene Roberts, this was somewhat more of a consideration than it might have been in other areas of the nation. Cherokee County, Alabama, was a rural area where people knew their neighbors, visited with their friends, and large extended families often were in very close, continual contact with each other. It was a distinct possibility in this case that many people who might be called for jury duty either knew, worked with, or were related to Darlene or Vernon Roberts, or their other family members and acquaintances. And it was almost a certainty that nearly everyone would have, at the very least, heard something about the case, either from others or from the media.

Rodney Stallings intended to be very careful

regarding jury selection for those reasons, as well as many others. The motion at hand requested a court order disqualifying from jury service all members of the jury pool who knew or were acquainted with Darlene, or with any member of her family. Individuals who had been exposed to highly prejudicial information regarding a capital defendant must be presumed biased for purposes of sitting on the capital sentencing jury, and thus should be excused from jury service, the motion said. Exacting standards must be met to assure that the jury was fair.

Due to other cases of his that were fairly high-profile and due for trial during the same week as Barbara's trial was scheduled—and with the intense, extreme amount of pressure generated by a capital murder defense—Rodney Stallings was beginning to feel overwhelmed. One of his other cases, in particular, had garnered a great deal of publicity; it had to do with the arrest of one of the county's well-known convenience store owners, and public opinion ran high regarding both guilt and innocence.

Stallings was working practically around the clock in an attempt to keep up with everything, much like a juggler with too many balls in the air at one time.

"People were telling me that I looked like the walking dead," Stallings said. "I wasn't sleeping or eating, and it was taking a real toll on me, and my family, and my staff."

53

On June 18, Stallings filed a second motion to continue, asking the court to continue Barbara's trial for several reasons from its date of June 23, 2008, to a later date. First he stated that he had four cases set for the week of June 23, 2008, in addition to Barbara's capital murder trial. The motions to continue in the four cases had been filed as the state's deadline for the plea offers in those cases had expired on Monday, June 16, at 12:00 P.M., and they were subsequently denied.

Stallings told the court that he had been completely inundated with Barbara's case. Due to the complexities and dire consequences associated with capital charges, he believed that an adequate defense could not be provided due to the need to prepare for the four other cases also set for trial during the June 23, 2008, docket. Therefore, he asked that the court grant the motion to continue the case to another available date.

It came as a devastating blow to Barbara's defense when the motion to continue was denied, and the trial, as well as the four other cases, were set to proceed as scheduled, with no additional time to prepare for any of them. Rodney Stallings had been under tremendous pressure before; now, with the motion to continue unexpectedly denied, and the trial looming, desperate times were going to call for desperate measures. He had fully expected the continuance to be granted, and now he would have to ramp up his preparations for the trial drastically.

In addition to the failed motion to continue, another large group of motions were filed on Barbara's behalf on June 18. One of those most important to the outcome of the trial was a "Motion in Limine to Preclude the State from Moving to Admit into Evidence Photographs Prejudicial to Ms. Roberts."

The photos in question, taken at the crime scene and at the autopsy, were incredibly shocking and gruesome, and Stallings feared the jury would be unduly swayed by the sight of them and, therefore, prejudiced against his client.

The motion asked the court to act pursuant to the Sixth, Eighth, and Fourteenth Amendments to the United States Constitution and Article 1 of the Alabama Constitution, and preclude the state from moving to admit into evidence any gruesome and highly prejudicial photographs of Darlene Roberts's body.

Gruesome and highly prejudicial photographs of the victim, Stallings said, would advance no evidentiary purpose and serve only to inflame the passions of the jury in violation of Ms. Roberts's rights guaranteed by the state and federal constitutions.

The state's photographic evidence depicted full-body and close-up head shots of the victim that were entirely gruesome, gory, and inflammatory. They served no evidentiary purpose, the motion said. Because it was a capital prosecution, exacting standards had to be met to assure that it was fair. The court must not permit the photographs to be introduced at Ms. Roberts's upcoming trial, Stallings said. The prejudicial effect of the photographs would clearly outweigh their probative value, and their admission would constitute irreversible error.

Stallings cited several prior court cases where photos of the same nature had been ruled inadmissible at trial. Even when dealing with noncapital cases, the court had ruled as inadmissible the introduction of photos during autopsy, since they did not portray wounds at the time they were inflicted.

The motion also said that the Alabama Legislature had mandated that no death sentence should be imposed under the influence of passion, prejudice, or any arbitrary factor. And at a capital trial, the avoidance of inflammatory appeals to the passions and prejudices of juries was constitutionally protected. The United States Supreme Court, the motion said, had repeatedly held that *because of the qualitative difference [between death and any other form of punishment], there is a corresponding difference in the need for reliability in the determination that death is the appropriate punishment in a specific case.*

As a matter of state law, the motion said, it was established that where the prejudicial effect of photographs outweighs the probative, they should not be admitted.

Another point in the motion stated that it was clear from the photographs introduced by the state as discovery that close-ups of the victim's head and the full-body shots of the corpse had very little to do with whether Ms. Roberts committed these acts, and even less to do with what penalty she should suffer if she was found guilty. Instead, the photographs were gratuitously gruesome and inflammatory. The purpose of the trial, the motion said, was to determine the truth about guilt or innocence. Ms. Roberts entered the court cloaked in a presumption of innocence. It was no answer to say that Ms. Roberts had only herself to blame for the gruesome nature of the photographs of a killing she wasn't even alleged to have committed personally. At that juncture in the trial, she was presumed innocent, and at the sentencing, if any, she was to be judged by a fair and impartial jury, not an inflamed panel.

The motion stated that under the law, the photographs must be excluded, even if they did have some evidentiary value in light of their highly prejudicial nature. A previous court case had established that a photograph must be excluded if there was no showing that *the probative value outweighs any prejudice.* In particular, the motion said, that rule applied to the admissibility of photographs that depicted gruesome scenes involving victims of violent crime. In interpreting that evidentiary role, the courts had stated that *in situations where the state has already made out its case and the photographs are merely cumulative in nature and were not "substantially necessary to show material facts or conditions" the probability was high that the probative value of those photographs would be outweighed by their prejudicial effect.*

If Barbara was convicted, Stallings said, the gruesome bloodiness of the photographs would have an enraging impact on the jury. What was relevant in a capital sentencing hearing, he said, was assessing the conduct, culpability, and character of the defendant. Instead of a sentencing hearing in which the jury was required to weigh aggravating and mitigating circumstance, thoughtfully consider Barbara's role in the offense, conscientiously judge her character and background, and finally decide whether she should be executed or sentenced to life imprisonment without parole, the jury would be overwhelmed by the gruesome photographs and would be motivated by passion and prejudice.

Because Stallings had seen the photographs of Darlene Roberts, he knew they would have a great negative impact on the jury. His motion was an attempt to suppress those photos and lessen the damage they were very likely to do to Barbara's case if they were shown during the trial. His efforts failed, however, and as Darlene's family members fled the courtroom to avoid such an upsetting sight, the jury would be shown the gruesome photos of Darlene Roberts lying facedown in the murky water of the farm pond, her horrific injuries plainly showing.

54

Another motion that was introduced on June 18 was clearly made in order to lessen the potential burden on Rodney Stallings during the trial. He filed a motion to adjourn at a reasonable time, asking that the trial adjourn each day without extending over into the evening hours.

The motion said that defense counsel anticipated that the trial could last at least two weeks. A traditional workday consisted of eight hours, and throughout the trial, each evening, Stallings would have to consult with Barbara concerning each day's developments and the strategy to be pursued on the next day. Stallings said he would have to research legal questions that arose during the trial, possibly make arrangements for witnesses' travel, and confer with them prior to their testimony. An excessive work schedule, he said, would prohibit Barbara from receiving effective representation.

If the proceedings, with or without the jury, lasted long into the evening, he said, the defense would have no time in which to prepare for the next day. While the long days and evening hearings would obviously affect all concerned, it was Barbara whose life was at stake, and who would suffer from the lack of care and attention that hurried proceedings would yield. Therefore, the motion asked that the court would be adjourned each day at a reasonable time.

A motion for adequate sequestration of jurors was filed asking that adequate sequestration of jurors prior to and during the trial be ordered by the court.

Since it was to be a capital prosecution, exacting standards should be met to assure that it was fair, the motion contended. There could be no more serious duty that a juror ever had to face than the decision between life and death in a capital case, the motion said. A decision by the Mississippi Supreme Court was cited, which said that a jury's verdict must be based upon the evidence and not affected by extraneous influences. The court, the decision said, had repeatedly recognized the gravity and immeasurable solemnity of a jury's deliberations during the sentencing phase of a capital murder trial. The importance of this deliberation might, at times, cause inconvenience and hardship; however, to allow distractions and outside influences to infect the jury's thoughts at such a critical juncture of the proceedings was to devalue human life.

Despite any suggestions to the contrary, the motion said, the jury must be sequestered at Barbara's capital trial. The publicity surrounding the case and the sensationalizing of the crime necessitated sequestration, and allowing the jurors to separate during the pendency of the capital case would result in the need for a new trial.

Sequestration should take place before the jurors were sworn, the motion stated, keeping those who had been questioned on voir dire separate from the others. The failure to follow this procedure could be fatal to any resulting verdict. Stallings cited a Louisiana case where the court noted that the purpose of sequestration was to insulate the jurors from outside influence or the possibility thereof, even unconscious; and in capital cases, especially, the sequestration was strictly enforced so that, upon a separation of a juror after she was sworn, a presumption of misconduct arose and irreversible error would be presumed. (This was in reference to a case where unsupervised telephone calls were made by jurors during a capital trial.)

The motion also noted that there were more subtle rules guiding what may and may not influence the decision of a juror, such as a ruling in a 1991 Alabama case that it was improper for a juror to read a dictionary during deliberations.

Some intolerable opportunities for prejudice seemed to occur in almost every capital case, the motion said, and the court should take careful measures to avoid them. For example, jurors in motels were sometimes exposed to television or radio programs that could be devastating. Capital verdicts had also been reversed where jurors relied on their Bibles in reaching a verdict.

In a case that could go over two or more

weekends, jurors sometimes went to church. Again, sometimes the preachers in church preached sermons that might favor one party or the other. It would be most unfortunate were this to cause the case to get reversed.

The motion also said that where and with whom jurors dine could also raise causes for concern. Sometimes jurors were taken to dining facilities that had a history of racial discrimination, or where the jurors might be exposed to local patrons with strong views about the case at hand. The jurors' badges identifying them as such might only spur the patrons to greater excess. Stallings cited a reversal in a Virginia case where jurors were having a meal and one of the patrons of the restaurant expressed the opinion that they should execute the defendant.

Those, Stallings said, were only a very few of the examples of what might happen in a trial, and the court should take excruciating care to avoid any possibility of jury taint by effectively sequestering all jurors prior to and during the trial, and set out the means of sequestration in open court.

55

On June 18, in order to put together a more accurate view of exactly what had happened at the farm pond near the home of Vernon and Darlene Roberts on April 6, 2006, Rodney Stallings filed a motion to allow the defendant to view the scene of the crime with her attorneys. It asked that a law enforcement official be allowed to take Barbara and her attorneys to the scene of the crime, at least one week prior to trial, and allow them to discuss the facts of the case in a manner whereby the law enforcement official would not hear the discussion. In support of the motion, Stallings listed a ruling from Washington State that said it was necessary that defense counsel view the crime scene in the presence of the defendant.

The facts of Barbara's case, the motion said, were so complicated that there was no way for her to explain adequately the situation to her attorneys in a manner whereby they could take pictures, take measurements, or otherwise properly investigate the scene of the alleged crime without her assistance. To deny her the right to do that would amount to a denial of due process of law and effective assistance of counsel as guaranteed by the Alabama and United States Constitutions. To allow the defendant to view the scene as requested would not prejudice the state's case in any manner, and would only serve to promote a fair and impartial trial.

A wide array of other motions were filed, most having to do with witnesses and evidence. A "Motion for Deposition of State Expert Witnesses and Request for Production of Documents" asked that the court grant Barbara's counsel leave to depose the expert witnesses that the state intended to call to testify and to direct the state to provide the curriculum vitae, certificates, qualifying documents, and all other background documentation necessary to assess adequately the qualifications of the state's expert witnesses. The motion also referenced an Alabama Supreme Court decision that held that *the hovering death penalty is the special circumstance justifying broader discovery in capital cases.*

A "Motion for Discovery of Institutional Records and Files Necessary to a Fair Trial" asked for the production of all requested documents from the state for inspection and copying. The "state" referred to any and all of the following organizations: the district attorneys for the Ninth Judicial District of Alabama; the Cherokee County, Alabama, Sheriff's Office; the DeKalb County, Alabama, Sheriff's Office; the Alabama Bureau of Investigation; the Georgia Bureau of Investigation; the Rockdale County, Georgia, Sheriff's Office. The "state" also meant all present and former agents, officers, investigators, consultants, employees, and staff members of organizations or officials named above.

The court asked in a motion for production of negatives, to direct the state to produce the negatives of all photographs taken by any prosecution agent in preparation for the case. In this instance, since digital photography has almost universally become the standard practice, the defense was furnished with discs containing all photos taken by the various agencies concerned.

Stallings also filed a motion to reveal the identity of informants and to reveal any deals, promises, or inducements. This motion was primarily directed at the testimony of jail inmate Tonya Regalado, and Stallings wanted to establish whether or not any rewards had been promised to her in return for her testimony.

Stallings asked for a court order directing the state to reveal the identity of all confidential informants, to reveal any promises or understandings (explicit or implicit) with any witness or informant, and to reveal whether any threats or inducements of any nature whatsoever had been made regarding any witness or informant.

Another motion, filed at the same time to inspect, examine, and test all physical evidence, asked for a court order compelling the state to produce certain items of physical evidence in its possession and control, collected by the state in the investigation of the murder of Darlene Roberts, for inspection and testing by experts designated by defense counsel.

56

While Rodney Stallings was busy filing motions, the state requested and received a court order for the transport of Tonya Regalado from the custody of the Department of Corrections to the Cherokee County Sheriff's Office for the trial, which was set for June 23, 2008, at 9:00 A.M. in the third-floor courtroom. The order directed the sheriff or one of his authorized deputies to transport Regalado from Tutwiler Prison to the Cherokee County Jail for the duration of the trial, then return her to prison after the trial's conclusion.

Regalado was expected to testify about conversations she and Barbara had while they were both in the Cherokee County Jail together. Regalado claimed that Barbara had told her details of Darlene Roberts's murder, with Barbara allegedly saying to her that it was she, not Schiess, who had shot Darlene, point-blank, at the pond.

Another inmate had given a written statement to the authorities about what Regalado had said to her about Barbara and their interaction at the Cherokee County Jail. That statement, which comprised hearsay evidence, would have provided proof of the relationship between the two women if it had been admissible as evidence.

The inmate stated that she was an inmate in the Cherokee County Jail, having been transferred there from the Etowah County Jail on October 2, 2008. While she was there in Etowah County, Tonya Regalado was brought in from August 4 to October 2. She had been temporarily transferred there from Tutwiler Prison.

We were sitting out in the day room talking, remembering that we had met once at a dope house, the inmate wrote.

During the dayroom conversation, the woman said that she told Regalado that she was going to have to be transferred to the Cherokee County Jail before she was released. Regalado told her, she said, that when she got there, there would be a lady, Barbara Roberts, who was doing life for murder.

Tonya said she had almost drove Barbara crazy singing this song, "One, two, I'm coming to get you."

Regalado told the inmate that Barbara had made her life hell at the Cherokee County Jail and was the reason Regalado was sent on to prison. Regalado went on to tell the woman that Barbara and her boyfriend had raped, tortured, beat, then shot to death another woman. The inmate claimed that Regalado was talking as if they enjoyed it, like Barbara was a monster. She never mentioned the man's name, the inmate said, only that he was Barbara's boyfriend.

She wrote that she really didn't know either Barbara or Regalado, only briefly. Regalado had been transferred to Etowah County on a county charge, and after court she told the woman that her sentence was to run concurrent and she still would be serving about fourteen months at Tutwiler.

From this inmate's statement, it was clear that there was no love lost between Tonya Regalado and Barbara Roberts. Had this letter been allowed as evidence, Regalado's testimony against Barbara might perhaps have been viewed differently.

57

The capital murder trial of Barbara Ann Roberts began, as scheduled, at 9:00 A.M. on June 23, 2008, in the Cherokee County Courthouse, with Circuit Judge David Rains presiding. In spite of the intense heat and the inadequate air-conditioning system in the old, outdated building, spectators filled the church pewlike seating in the courtroom to capacity, and many more left, disappointed, when they were unable to squeeze into the room. The case had created so much interest among the public that it had become one of the most anticipated trials in the county's recent history.

There were two reporters present during the trial who had generated the most public information about the case from the day the body of Darlene Roberts had been discovered. Scott Wright reported for the *Post*, a Cherokee County newspaper that had started several years before as a free-classified-ad paper distributed at no charge at locations all around the area. Thanks to its continuing improvements, which included adding well-reported local and, later, state and national news, editorials, numerous other regular features, and a very extensive paid-advertising section, the *Post* was still given away free to the tune of very many thousands of copies per week, and the public could still place free classified advertisements. For those reasons, the *Post* was an extremely popular paper, and its quality of coverage had grown commensurate with its popularity.

Kathy Roe did double duty in her reporting. She wrote for the *Cherokee County Herald,* the oldest newspaper in the county, and also for the *Rome News-Tribune* in Rome, Georgia, where there had been much interest in the case because of Darlene and Vernon Roberts's employment at Temple-Inland and their many other close connections to the Rome area. Like Scott, Kathy had much experience, and her reporting was trusted by the public to be fair and accurate.

Both reporters had followed the case very closely, were familiar with all the parties involved on both the defense and prosecution sides, and had been anticipating the start of what they both knew would be an intense, sensational trial. Their accounts of the proceedings would be posted on the Internet, and served as the main source of information on the trial for out-of-state residents who were unable to attend. Barbara's family, among others, relied on the Internet coverage for daily reports on the events of the trial.

An extensive list of exhibits had been prepared for the trial, along with another long list of witnesses who could be called to testify, and, if called, what their testimony would concern.

58

Among the items listed as exhibits were the incident/offense report of the crime and the arrest reports for Robert John Schiess III and Barbara Ann Roberts. The initial statement by Barbara following her arrest, along with her second and third interviews, were probably among the most crucial evidence that would be presented at the trial. The jury would have the opportunity to watch and listen to the videotaped interview with Barbara, when she had described the sexual activity during her affair with Vernon Roberts in a particularly graphic manner. That same videotaped interview included Barbara's moment of inappropriate laughter, which was described in court as a "maniacal outburst."

Two notes were entered as evidence at the trial as proof of the harassment that Vernon Roberts claimed that his ex-wife Barbara had heaped on him and Darlene, prior to Darlene's death. The harassment, he contended, had ranged from the notes to attempted arson to several forms of stalking and trespassing, and several friends and relatives stated that Darlene had lived in constant fear because of it. She had even gone so far as to say that if anything ever happened to her, it would be Barbara who would be responsible.

The notes had been written on lined notebook paper and appeared to have been prepared by using a plastic school ruler with stencils cut into it so that the letters of the alphabet could be traced. Many words had been misspelled, which could have been intentional.

One note read as follows:

> *DARLENE* (drawing of a heart) *VERNON*
> *YOU <u>THOUGHT</u> ENOUGH TIME*
> *HAD <u>PASTED</u>*
> *<u>NEVER</u>*
> *<u>IF</u> <u>YOU</u> WANT*
> *IT TO BE <u>FOREVER</u>*
> *I <u>CAN</u> SEE TO THAT*
> *<u>EASY</u> BE TOGETHER*
> *FOREVER, <u>ETURNITY</u>* (drawing of a
>   tombstone with RIP)
> *ALL EYES ARE ON YOUR*
> *EVER MOVE*

The second note was more ominous, since it made reference to several other family members. It was addressed to Darlene, also contained some misspelled words, and ended with a line that looked like an attempt to make the note appear to have been sent by someone from Darlene's past:

DARLENE
NO JOKE
KNOW WHERE
YOU VERNON
YOUR DARTHER
AND NOW WHERE
YOUR SISTER, SON
LIVE HAVE SOME WATCHING
ALL   YOU CHOSE
ONE OR ALL
YOU ARE MINE OR
NO ONES

These two notes were included in the discovery files and presented as evidence, but there was no apparent positive proof that Barbara herself had prepared or sent either note; nothing on the notes themselves indicated the identity of the sender.

The interview and statement of James Anthony Captain concerning conversations he'd had with both Barbara and Schiess were brought in as exhibits, as were the first and second interviews of Vernon Roberts following his wife's murder. The farmworker Jose Luis Richiez, who had observed Schiess and Barbara in the black pickup on the day of the murder, had been interviewed twice, and both those interviews were presented. Also on hand were the first and second interviews of Jason Alan Sammons and the interview of his friend Ellis McNeill Williams, who discovered the body of Darlene Roberts, and Todd Waits, who stopped to help Williams and Sammons.

The interviews of Charles Edward Young Sr.,

Ryan Kyle Tippens, Charles Edward Young Jr., and Leah Marie Stoker had all helped to place Barbara and Schiess near the scene of the murder; these were all included as exhibits.

Andrea Knight and Danielle Lyn Anderson, employees of Pearle Vision in Conyers, Georgia, had been interviewed regarding Barbara's broken eyeglasses, and their interviews were among the exhibits.

Heidi and Benji Langford, the daughter and son of Darlene Roberts, had given very lengthy interviews following their mother's death, and those interviews had provided some key information in the investigation and were included as exhibits.

The North Carolina State Bureau of Investigation had talked to the father of Robert John Schiess III, and that interview was also presented.

Quite a few other items were included on the exhibits list: a diagram of the murder scene on Cherokee County Road 941, which had been made by law enforcement, the photo lineup shown to witnesses, who identified Schiess and Barbara, as well as the photo of Barbara's bruised face and a receipt for in-line skates. The subpoena of Barbara's records from Pearle Vision, the membership information from Schiess's application to the South River Gun Club, and Schiess's rental agreement for the storage building, where the black Dodge Dakota pickup was hidden, were all listed as exhibits.

Schiess had downloaded a long list of "Frequently Asked Questions About Fingerprints" from the Internet, and that list was found in his possession at the time of his arrest. It was included, along with the Wal-Mart receipt from Darlene Roberts's final shopping trip, which was recovered from Darlene Roberts's vehicle. Photos were shown of prior vandalism to another of Darlene's vehicles, and the two harassment letters purportedly from Barbara to Darlene and Vernon were presented as exhibits.

Barbara's Cingular Wireless cell phone records had been subpoenaed as proof of her calls to Vernon and to others, both on the day of the murder and in the preceding months. Those records were included on the exhibits list. Also on the list was an assistance rendered report from the Georgia Bureau of Investigation, whose personnel had played a key role in the investigation and subsequent arrests, and a report from the Lee's Summit, Missouri, Police Department involving the shotgun located there, but it had proved not to have been the one used in the crime. That shotgun—the murder weapon—had never been located.

The last items on the exhibits list were forensic in nature and were reports on the evidence submitted to the Alabama Department of Forensic Sciences, the Lee's Summit Police Department ballistic test results, and the preliminary autopsy report on Darlene Roberts.

59

When testimony began in the trial, the witnesses all testified as expected, repeating the facts that they had previously given in their statements to the investigators. There were no surprises until prison inmate Tonya Regalado took the stand. She had been brought from Julia Tutwiler Prison For Women to testify against the woman she clearly disliked, judging by the statement from the other inmate who said Regalado taunted and annoyed Barbara during their time together in the Cherokee County Jail.

Regalado was serving prison time for forgery and drug possession, and she had an extensive rap sheet for numerous other offenses, according to the authorities.

Regalado claimed that she shared a cell with Barbara for around seven months in 2007, although Barbara later said that they had not been cellmates and had only spent time in the dayroom together. Regalado said she had no knowledge of the case other than what Barbara had told her.

According to Regalado, Barbara had told her that it was the kick from the final blast of the shotgun that had broken her glasses and bruised her face, not a blow from Schiess to stop her from "freaking out" at the crime scene. She and Barbara had talked about the murder several times, Regalado said, claiming that Barbara told her she did not realize the glasses had been knocked off her face and lost until she and Schiess fled the scene.

"She talked to everybody about it," Regalado claimed, but no other inmates had come forward to testify against Barbara.

According to Regalado, Barbara told her that Schiess had been furious when he found out that she'd had an affair with Vernon Roberts, saying that he "went ballistic."

When Regalado was asked if she had been offered any deals for a reduction in her sentence in exchange for her testimony, she told the court, "I had already been sentenced."

When Investigator Mark Hicks took the stand for questioning, he testified about the several versions of the crime that Barbara had told during her interviews. During the initial questioning session, Hicks said, Barbara had at first claimed she was not near the area on the evening of the shooting. Later, after being confronted with the broken eyeglasses traced to her, Barbara admitted that she was present at the shooting and had been a participant in what happened, but she did not say that she had fired the shotgun.

When the jury was shown Barbara's videotaped interview with Hicks, they heard her describe what she claimed had happened on the day of the murder, when she and Schiess stopped Darlene on the road under the pretense of having trouble with the truck. They also heard Barbara relating the graphic details of her affair with Vernon, and heard for themselves the episode of Barbara's burst of nervous, inappropriate laughter, which the prosecution termed "maniacal."

Barbara had claimed in her statements that Schiess had become enraged when he learned of the affair with Vernon, and had planned to get revenge on Vernon by confronting Darlene. Instead, she said, the plan had gone awry when Darlene escaped from Schiess's attempts to bind and gag her, and Barbara had claimed that Schiess had then gotten into Darlene's Nissan Murano, followed her to the pond, where she had attempted to hide, and had shot her. Then, Barbara said, Schiess had hit her in the face with the shotgun butt, breaking her glasses. The two then left the Murano and returned to their truck, and headed back to Georgia. Along the way, they discarded the unrecovered murder weapon; they threw the shotgun into the Etowah River as they crossed the bridge over it, Barbara claimed.

In opening statements to the jury, District Attorney Mike O'Dell and Assistant District Attorney Bob Johnston had described Barbara Roberts as being obsessed with her former husband, Vernon Roberts, to the point of planning to get rid of Darlene, whom she saw as an obstacle to reuniting with Vernon. O'Dell described Barbara's "obsessive rage," and said that "there was premeditation."

O'Dell told the jury that Barbara was a "master manipulator," describing Schiess as an "alcoholic, former neurosurgeon," who, he said, was "hopped-up on drugs." He claimed that Barbara had convinced her lover to help her in her plot to kill Darlene. The plan, O'Dell said, was to remove Darlene from the picture so that Barbara could once again be with Vernon, who was the actual object of her affection.

The two prosecutors outlined what they believed was Barbara's plan to kill Darlene. They said the plan involved the purchase of the Mossberg 500 shotgun and the membership in the South River Gun Club, where they "spent months" practicing target shooting. Then, because they knew Darlene's daily routine, they came at around 5:50 P.M., on April 6, 2006, to the dirt road near her home to lie in wait for her and stop her as she came home from work.

"They practiced, they planned, and then like a spider setting her web," O'Dell said, "she set the trap."

The prosecutors outlined the events leading up to Darlene's murder, saying that Darlene had been forced from her car as Barbara hid in the truck to keep from being recognized. But when Schiess began attempting to bind and gag Darlene, Barbara got out of the truck and held the shotgun. O'Dell said that it must have been at that moment that Darlene recognized Barbara, that she realized her life was in danger.

"Somehow she broke free from her restraints and ran," he said. "For a few brief moments, Darlene Roberts felt some freedom. But it didn't last long."

According to O'Dell, Barbara then chased after Darlene on foot, firing the shotgun. Expended shells were found between the roadside and the pond, confirming the sequence of events, he said.

"The first five shots all missed as she chased after her," he said.

Schiess then jumped into the Murano and followed the two women through the pasture to the pond, O'Dell said, damaging the undercarriage after driving through a field between the road and the small fishing pond, where Darlene had hidden in the weeds to seek shelter.

O'Dell then referred to Tonya Regalado's testimony about Barbara's alleged jailhouse confession. As Darlene lay partially hidden in the weeds along the edge of the pond, he said, Barbara "calmly and coolly pumped the shotgun," and fired the last three remaining shotgun shells into Darlene Roberts, hitting her twice in the back and once in the head, point-blank, "from a distance of five to seven feet," killing her instantly.

Darlene's autopsy report indicated that she had died from three shotgun wounds—one to the head, one to the upper back, and one to the middle back. In addition, X-ray examination revealed multiple "snowstorm" images of shotgun pellets covering the whole right side of the chest and scattered over the upper arms. Photos of Darlene's horribly mutilated body were shown to the jury, with Darlene's family fleeing the courtroom to keep from having to see them.

The jury had already been presented with the evidence of the broken piece of the shotgun butt that was recovered from Darlene's vehicle, and the broken glasses found at the crime scene, which had been proven to belong to Barbara. Those, plus the testimony of Tonya Regalado and Barbara's own statements during interviews, were proving to be an almost insurmountable amount of evidence that Rodney Stallings would have to try his best to refute.

60

A motion had been filed by the district attorney on February 13, 2007, to have a mental evaluation performed on Barbara Roberts. The prosecution wanted to determine her competency to stand trial and also to determine her mental status at the time of Darlene's murder. Dr. Doug McKeown was the expert who had performed the evaluation and also testified at the trial, where he described Barbara's mental-health history as "significant."

His forensic evaluation report noted that Barbara had experienced "psychiatric problems and difficulties associated with treatment for a primary bipolar disorder with panic attacks and post-traumatic stress disorder associated with her previous motor vehicle accident." He reported that she had been seen on an outpatient basis and had a history of six hospitalizations at Windwood Hospital and one hospitalization at Northwestern Hospital, with her last psychiatric hospitalization in July of 2006, during the time she was out of jail on bond.

Dr. McKeown concluded that Barbara had a "well-documented history of mental-health-related issues," and he referred to her reported history of auditory hallucinations beginning in early 2006. He also reported that his assessment was that Barbara appeared capable of assisting her defense counsel and also assuming the role of a defendant in a judicial proceeding. His opinion, he said, was that she would have maintained the ability for appreciating the nature and quality of her actions and behavior during the time frame associated with the crime.

Dr. Jason Junkins testified at the trial about Barbara's physical condition, and told the court that the doctor at the Cherokee-Etowah-DeKalb Mental Health Center had diagnosed her with "depression with psychotic features." He explained to the court that people suffering from a psychosis sometimes could lose touch with reality and experience visual or auditory hallucinations.

61

Rodney Stallings did not attempt to put his client on the witness stand during the trial, but he brought forward three character witnesses to testify that they believed that Barbara's religious beliefs were very sincere and felt that she could have a positive influence on others. Two of the three ladies had only known Barbara since her incarceration in the Cherokee County Jail, but they had visited with her often during her time there. Pamela O'Neal worked with the First Baptist Church jail ministry, and Amanda Yarbrough was affiliated with the jail ministry of the Church of God. They both testified on Barbara's behalf, based on their acquaintance since Barbara's arrest.

Rodney Stallings also called Elaine Jones, his legal assistant, as a character witness. She said that Barbara had not only shown strong religious convictions, but had also been concerned about Ms. Jones and her family. She and Barbara had known each other since first becoming acquainted following Barbara's arrest.

Stallings put great emphasis during the trial on the fact that there was no DNA evidence that linked Barbara to Darlene's murder, and the murder weapon had never been recovered. But during closing arguments, the strong statements and evidence and testimony cited by O'Dell and Johnston weighed heavily with the jurors.

Johnston said that Darlene would have realized her life was in danger the moment she saw Barbara's face. When Barbara and Schiess chased Darlene and shot her at the edge of the pond, "Darlene Roberts ran for her life. She was chased down like an animal. They chased down Darlene Roberts and shot her like an animal," he told the jury.

In his closing statement, O'Dell told the jurors, "This was designed to be the perfect crime."

In presenting his closing arguments, Stallings told the jury that there was nothing definitively placing Barbara at the crime scene at the time of the murder. He told the jury that the story of the death of Darlene Roberts was "a puzzle with many truths," only one side of which the prosecution chose to present in order to seek Barbara's conviction.

But O'Dell told the jury, "This puzzle fits. It's not one-sided, it's three-dimensional. And it's the truth."

62

Stallings had submitted a large list of "Defendant's 'Given' Charge to Jury," and when the trial was finished and the jury was to begin deliberating, it was carefully explained to them the various verdicts they could reach in a capital case involving murder, robbery, and kidnapping. The possible choices of charges could have resulted in a lengthy and complicated deliberation, but that was not to be. The case went to the jury on Friday evening, June 27. After slightly over two hours, the jury of five women and seven men returned guilty verdicts on three counts and convicted Barbara Ann Roberts of capital murder in the shooting death two years previously of her ex-husband's late wife, Martha Darlene Roberts.

The verdict saddened the defense, but came as no surprise. Inundated by all the evidence presented by the prosecution at the trial, Stallings had little possibility of countering it. There were only two possible sentences that could be pronounced in a capital murder case: the death penalty, or life in prison without possibility of parole. Since Barbara had earlier refused all offers of plea bargains, all Stallings could do now was hope for the latter sentence.

On Monday, June 30, the sentencing hearing was held. This time around, the jury deliberated for only about twenty minutes before recommending to Judge David Rains that Barbara be sentenced to death by lethal injection. O'Dell told the press that the vote had been eleven-to-one in favor of the death sentence.

The final sentencing order would be decided by Judge David Rains on August 29, 2008, and until that time, Barbara would have to live with her fate undecided, hoping the court would show mercy. Her codefendant, Robert John Schiess III, was expected to stand trial in November, but before Barbara's sentencing date, the case against him took a shocking turn in his favor.

63

On Wednesday, August 6, 2008, prosecutors met with Schiess, his defense team, and Circuit Judge David Rains in the same Cherokee County courtroom where Schiess had initially entered a plea of not guilty by reason of mental disease or defect. Now he was there because of a plea deal that had been worked out between the parties that allowed Schiess to change his plea voluntarily and enter a plea of guilty to the lesser charge of kidnapping.

When the judge asked Schiess if he was pleading guilty due to the fact that he was, indeed, guilty, Schiess answered in the affirmative.

As a result of the plea, Judge Rains then sentenced Schiess to twenty to ninety-nine years in the state prison, but the sentence was split, meaning the sentence was automatically reduced to three years. Schiess had already served more than 650 days in jail, which would be removed from the sentence. He would also have to pay

$549 in court costs. Instead of facing a jury trial, Schiess would likely walk out of prison a free man some time in mid-October 2009. He would be serving five years' probation following his release, which would be subject to the terms of probation for Cherokee County. Schiess requested that his probation be transferred to Missouri so that he could live there with his mother upon release.

Because of what the judge called "obvious disparity" in Barbara's capital murder conviction and the district attorney's decision not to prosecute Schiess, he called the decision to offer the plea bargain into question. District Attorney Mike O'Dell answered, "Your Honor, the state is satisfied that Barbara Roberts planned and committed the murder of Darlene Roberts. As we reviewed the evidence in preparation for both trials, we were convinced that Dr. Schiess was guilty of kidnapping, and that was a reasonable charge and conviction for him to receive in this case."

O'Dell said that the prosecutors, the defense team, and members of the victim's family had discussed the case at length. They were all in agreement, he said, that the evidence indicated that Barbara Ann Roberts was actually the mastermind behind Darlene Roberts's murder and kidnapping. They said they were satisfied to see Dr. Schiess receive the lesser kidnapping charge.

"We are satisfied that the person who planned and carried out the kidnapping and execution of

Darlene Roberts has been convicted of capital murder and is facing, at this point, either life without parole or the death sentence, based on what Judge Rains decides," he said. "The family is satisfied and ready to go on with their lives."

64

On August 29, 2008, Judge David Rains issued his sentencing order in the case of the *State of Alabama* v. *Barbara Ann Roberts*.

Judge Rains had enjoyed a long and distinguished career, and had a well-deserved reputation as a fair, thoughtful judge who gave very careful consideration of the cases he ruled on. He put a great deal of thought into the long, detailed sentencing orders he wrote in cases such as Barbara's, where he detailed all the facts and circumstances and explained his decision in each of them. In cases such as Barbara's, when a human life was literally in his hands, he took special care to arrive at a ruling that was just and appropriate for the situation as he saw it. The only sentencing choices available to him because of her capital murder conviction were either death by lethal injection or life in prison without the possibility of parole. Judge Rains put much time and careful thought into the lengthy sentencing order he issued, summarizing the case.

On November 2, 2006, the grand jury of Cherokee County, Alabama, had indicted the defendant, Barbara Ann Roberts, for three counts of capital murder.

Count One charged Barbara with intentionally causing the death of Darlene Roberts during the commission of robbery, first degree.

Count Two charged her with intentionally causing the death of Darlene Roberts during the commission of kidnapping, first degree, by abducting or attempting to abduct Darlene Roberts with intent to inflict injury upon her or to violate or abuse her sexually.

Count Three charged Barbara with intentionally causing the death of Darlene Roberts during the commission of kidnapping, first degree, by abducting or attempting to abduct Darlene Roberts with intent to terrorize her or Vernon Roberts.

At the same time, the grand jury, which returned this three-count indictment against Barbara, also returned a three-count indictment charging the same offenses against Robert John Schiess III.

On June 27, 2008, at Barbara's trial, the Cherokee County jury found her guilty of the lesser included charge of noncapital murder and guilty of the lesser included charge of robbery, first degree, under Count One. The jury also found Barbara guilty of capital murder under Count Two, and guilty of capital murder under Count Three. In accordance with the verdict of the jury, Barbara was adjudged guilty of capital murder under Count Two and Count Three of the indictment. She was also adjudged guilty of noncapital murder and robbery, first degree, under Count One.

After the jury's verdicts of guilty, they were convened again to recommend a sentence to be imposed for the capital murder conviction under Count Two and Count Three of the indictment. On a vote of eleven to one, the jury recommended that Barbara should be sentenced to death for the capital murder of Darlene Roberts.

Judge Rains ordered and received a presentence investigation report, and on August 29, 2008, he conducted an additional sentence hearing. At that sentencing hearing, the district attorney urged the court to uphold the jury's recommendation and sentence Barbara to death.

Rodney Stallings argued that the court should sentence Barbara to life in prison without the possibility of parole.

Judge Rains asked Barbara whether she had anything to say and whether there was any reason why sentencing should not be pronounced. As she had done during her arrest, questioning, and trial, Barbara had nothing to say in her own defense.

Judge Rains prepared a summary of the facts surrounding the murder of Darlene Roberts and Barbara's participation in it, in accordance with ALA. CODE 13A-5-47, which required that the court enter its written findings of the crime.

Darlene Roberts was murdered on April 6, 2006, found lying facedown in a farm pond near her home on County Road 941 in Cherokee

County, Alabama. She had been shot twice in the back and once in the head with a 12-gauge shotgun. All three of these killing shots were fired at very close range.

The investigators found a total of eight spent 12-gauge shells at the scene. Based on the victim's wounds, it was apparent that in addition to the three shots fired at close range, the victim was struck by pellets fired from a farther distance, allegedly while she ran from her assailants.

A broken pair of eyeglasses was found at the scene by the investigators as they searched for evidence. These eyeglasses were traced to Barbara Ann Roberts. Further investigation led to the arrest of Barbara and Schiess on April 19, 2006.

Barbara was interviewed by investigators three times after she was arrested. The first two interviews took place at the Rockdale County Sheriff's Office in Conyers, Georgia.

Notwithstanding the availability of video- and audio-recording equipment in the interviewing room, the first interview (April 19, 2006) was conducted without the equipment being activated, and the interviewing officer did not make written notes as he conducted the interview. His subsequent written account of what Barbara said was the only record of her first statement.

The second interview (April 20, 2006) took place in the same interview room, but with the audio and video equipment activated. The video and recording of this interview was transcribed so that a written text was also available.

The third interview (April 26, 2006) was conducted in the sheriff's office in Cherokee County,

Alabama. As in the case of the first interview, the investigator did not make notes, but following the interview, he made a written report of what he recalled Barbara saying.

In the three statements she made to investigators in April 2006, Barbara said that all three of the fatal shots were fired by Schiess. In one of those statements, she said that she did not know whether or not Schiess had killed Darlene because she could not see clearly. Schiess had broken her glasses by hitting her in the face with the butt of the shotgun when she began growing hysterical during the incident.

In July and August of 2007, Barbara's cellmate Tonya Regalado reported to personnel at the Cherokee County Jail that she had talked with Barbara about the murder of Darlene Roberts. Their conversation of July 18, 2007, Regalado claimed, was about Schiess's finding out that Barbara had had an affair with Vernon Roberts, and that was why she and Schiess went to Alabama— so that Schiess could get revenge on Vernon by having sex with Darlene.

Prosecutors did not ask Regalado during the trial about her reported second conversation with Barbara on August 20, 2007, but Regalado's written report of this conversation was made a part of the court file that Judge Rains reviewed. In this second written report, Regalado claimed that during this conversation Barbara told her that Schiess had found a video of her and Vernon having sex.

On August 22, 2007, Regalado reported a third conversation with Barbara. Regalado's testimony about this third talk is highly incriminating.

Among other things, she testified that Barbara admitted that she had shot Darlene twice, once in the neck and once in the back, and that Schiess also had shot Darlene twice. Regalado went on to say that Barbara claimed her eyeglasses were broken by the shotgun recoil.

In each of her statements to investigators, Barbara had laid the blame on Schiess. She told the officers that even though she and Vernon Roberts had been divorced for some time, she had an affair with him in October 2005, and that Schiess intended to kidnap Darlene Roberts in order to hurt Vernon the way that he believed Vernon had hurt him. This claim of a sexual motive for the murder fit the explanation given by Barbara to Regalado during their jailhouse conversations.

Judge Rains then presented his findings on weighing the aggravating and mitigating circumstances of the case.

The law, he said, provided that the punishment for the capital offenses Barbara had been convicted of was either life imprisonment without the possibility of parole or death. The law also required that the punishment that should be imposed depended on whether any aggravating circumstances existed beyond a reasonable doubt, and, if so, whether the aggravating circumstances outweighed the mitigating circumstances.

An aggravating circumstance, he explained, is a circumstance specified by ALA. CODE 143-A-5-49(1975). A mitigating circumstance is a circumstance specified by ALA. CODE 13-1-5-51(1975). Mitigating circumstances could also include any aspect of Barbara's character or background, any circumstances surrounding the offense, and any mitigating circumstances which Barbara's defense might offer in their appeal for a sentence of life imprisonment without parole instead of death. ALA. CODE 13A-5-52(1975).

The process of weighing the aggravating and mitigating circumstances in order to arrive at a fair and just sentence did not rely on numerical comparison. Instead, Judge Rains said, it meant that all the circumstances relevant to the sentence were assembled and considered to determine whether the proper sentence, in view of all the relevant circumstances, was life imprisonment without parole, or the death penalty.

If the evidence offered by the defense in mitigation was disputed, the state then had the burden of disproving the disputed mitigation evidence by a preponderance of the evidence.

Judge Rains then outlined his findings concerning whether or not aggravating circumstances existed in Barbara's case.

According to ALA. CODE 13A-5-47(d)(1975), the trial court would be required to make written findings concerning whether or not the aggravating circumstances enumerated in ALA. CODE 13A-5-49(1975) existed.

The judge said he found the following aggravating circumstances to exist:

1. The capital offense was committed while Barbara was engaged in, was an accomplice in, or was a party to an attempt to commit kidnapping or an attempted abduction of Darlene Roberts, while intending to harm her.

2. The capital offense was committed while Barbara was engaged in, was an accomplice in, or attempting to kidnap or abduct Darlene Roberts while intending to terrorize her.

In addition to those two aggravating circumstances, which the court found to exist beyond a reasonable doubt, the state urged the court to also find additional aggravating circumstance existed: that the capital offense in question was *especially heinous, atrocious or cruel compared to other Capital offenses.*

In the moments following Darlene's stop to assist an apparently stranded vehicle, she was bound, gagged, chased, shot, and killed. Those moments were without a doubt extremely torturous and terrifying for Darlene Roberts. She was the prey of her pursuers, and her murder was especially heinous, atrocious, and cruel as compared to other capital offenses. Accordingly, the court found this third aggravating circumstance was proven beyond any reasonable doubt.

In addition to those statutory aggravating circumstances the court set out, Judge Rains said, the court also considered the other statutory aggravating circumstances given in ALA. CODE 13A-5-49(1975) and found that none of those other aggravating circumstances existed in the case.

Findings Concerning the Existence or Non-Existence of Statutory Mitigating Circumstances

Judge Rains said that pursuant to Alabama Code 13A-5-47(d)(1975), the trial court was required to make written findings concerning the existence of mitigating circumstances given in ALA. Code 13A-5-51(1975).

He said that the court had considered whether or not the following statutory mitigating circumstances existed in the case:

1. Whether the defendant had any significant history of prior criminal activity.

In the jury's deliberation of a sentence they would recommend in this case, he said, there was no evidence that Barbara had any history of significant criminal activity. In addition, the presentence report prepared by the office of pardons and parole did not indicate she had any significant history of previous criminal activity.

Judge Rains said Barbara had no evidence of earlier crimes; therefore, he said that he found that particular mitigating circumstance did exist in her case.

2. Whether the capital offense was committed while the defendant was under the influence of extreme mental or emotional disturbance.

On February 13, 2007, the district attorney filed a Motion to have the judge order a mental evaluation to determine Barbara's competency to stand trial and to determine her mental state at the time that Darlene was killed. The evaluation was ordered by Circuit Judge Randall L. Cole on June 18, 2007.

In a report filed on September 4, 2007, Dr. Doug McKeown stated that Barbara had a significant history of psychiatric problems and trouble with treatment for a primary bipolar disorder. She also had difficulty with panic attacks and post-traumatic stress disorder due to a serious motor vehicle accident. She had been seen on an outpatient basis in Conyers, Georgia, and reported a history of approximately six hospitalizations at Windwood Hospital and one hospitalization at Northwestern Hospital. Her last psychiatric hospitalization was in July 2006.

The doctor reported that Barbara had a well-documented history of a bipolar disorder for which she continued to be treated. Depressive symptoms appeared to predominate with also some indications of post-traumatic stress disorder from her traffic accident. Some anxiety symptoms were also in evidence, he reported.

Diagnostically, he said, she demonstrated depressed-type bipolar disorder.

In making his assessment, Dr. McKeown referred to *medical records associated with previous hospitalizations for the Defendant*. He observed that Barbara had a *well documented history of mental health related issues*. . . . In his report Dr. McKeown made reference to Barbara's reported history of *auditory hallucinations*, beginning in early 2006. During the trial Dr. McKeown said that her mental-health history was "significant."

When Dr. Jason Junkins testified about Barbara's physical condition, he said that Dr. Grant, of the CED Mental Health Center, had diagnosed her with "depression with psychotic features." Dr. Junkins explained that a person suffering from a psychosis could lose touch with reality and experience visual or auditory hallucinations.

Judge Rains said that the mitigating factor that the court was required to consider was whether

Barbara was experiencing extreme mental or emotional disturbance at the time of the offense. This was, he said, an entirely different question from whether Barbara was sane or insane at the time of the murder.

Under ALA. CODE 13A-3-1(1975), the judge wrote, it was an affirmative defense to a prosecution for any crime that, at the time of the commission of the acts constituting the offense, the defendant, as a result of a severe mental disease or defect, was unable to appreciate the nature and quality or wrongfulness of his acts.

When Dr. McKeown rendered his report on Barbara's mental condition at the time of the offense, the report supported the affirmative defense of severe mental disease or defect.

For the purpose of sentencing, however, said the judge, the standard for review was completely different, and Dr. McKeown's report did not address the question of whether Barbara was under extreme emotional disturbance at the time that Darlene Roberts was murdered. While an extreme emotional disturbance was not a defense to the commission of the crime, it was a factor that would be considered in mitigation for sentencing purposes if extreme emotional disturbance was found to have been present at the time of the crime. In other words, the judge said, one can be sane and criminally responsible for his or her behavior, and nevertheless have acted under the influence of an extreme emotional disturbance.

Based on Barbara's significant history of psychiatric problems, including seven hospitalizations or commitments, the effects of a bipolar disorder, the significance of a history of auditory hallucinations, and her mental-health diagnosis of depression with psychotic features, the court found that the defendant had interjected the issue of whether she was under extreme mental or emotional disturbance at the time in question.

Judge Rains wrote that under ALA. CODE 13-5-45(g)(1975) when the factual existence of a mitigating circumstance interjected by the defendant was in dispute, the state had the burden of disproving the mitigating circumstance by a majority of the evidence. The court, he said, was not satisfied that mitigating factor had been disproved. Accordingly, he said, the court found that mitigating factor to exist in the case.

3. Whether the victim was a participant in the defendant's conduct or consented to it.

This court found that Darlene Roberts was not a participant in the defendant's conduct and found that Darlene Roberts did not consent to it. Accordingly, the court found this mitigating circumstance did not exist in the case.

4. Whether the defendant was an accomplice in the capital offense committed by another person and her participation was relatively minor.

Barbara Ann Roberts was an accomplice with Schiess, Judge Rains stated. While the court believed that Schiess had an influence on Barbara, her participation in the crime was not "relatively minor."

Barbara disguised herself so that Darlene would not recognize her when she stopped in the belief she was helping a stranded driver. Barbara was wearing a surgical mask, sunglasses, a baseball cap, with her hair tucked inside the cap, and a hooded sweatshirt with the hood pulled up over her head.

Whether her participation in Darlene's murder was as passive as she described it to the investigators in her statements, or if she was as responsible as her cellmate testified, Barbara's participation in this crime was not relatively minor.

The court, Judge Rains said, therefore found that this mitigating circumstance did not exist in this case.

5. Whether the defendant acted under extreme duress or under the substantial domination of another person.

In the sentencing order, Judge Rains wrote that the only living people who knew exactly what happened on County Road 941 in Cherokee County, Alabama, on April 6, 2006, were Barbara and Schiess. Neither of them had testified during the trial, and only Barbara had made any statements to law enforcement authorities.

In determining whether she was under extreme duress or under the dominant influence of Schiess on the day in question was a matter that the court would have to determine based on the evidence and the reasonable assumptions to be made from that evidence, the judge said.

Although there was no audio or video recording of Barbara's interview with investigators on April 19, 2006, he wrote, the officer's subsequent written account of that interview stated that Barbara first denied having any involvement in Darlene's murder. After being confronted with her broken eyeglasses, which the officers had found at the crime scene, she told them that she was afraid of Schiess, that he had an "anger management problem," that he was a heavy drinker, and that she was afraid of what he might do if he found out she had talked to the authorities.

In her April 19, 2006, statement, the judge said, Barbara described Schiess as the principal figure in the murder. According to Barbara, Schiess drove to a point near the home of Darlene Roberts, then stopped his truck and raised the hood to make it appear that his truck was disabled. He flagged Darlene Roberts in an attempt to get her to stop to give aid. Then he attempted to use surgical gauze and plastic ties to gag and subdue her. When she was able to escape and run for her life, Schiess drove into the field in pursuit. According to Barbara, "Schiess pointed the shotgun at Martha Darlene Roberts and shot her three times while she was laying facedown in the pond."

Based on the state's evidence presented at trial, Judge Rains said, the court concluded that it was Schiess who bought the shotgun, modified it for use as an especially deadly weapon, and joined a gun club in order to practice with it in preparation for the murder.

Barbara said to the investigators that at the time of the incident she was "really freaking out" and that in an attempt to "shut her up," Schiess hit her in the face with the butt of the shotgun, breaking her glasses.

Barbara wore a disguise, which was described elsewhere in the order. The mask, which she described, was apparently a surgical mask that had been provided by Schiess.

In her interview on April 20, 2006, Judge Rains said, Barbara made her final statement to the investigators. She again told them that Schiess had killed Darlene Roberts by shooting her with a shotgun at the edge of the pond, where her body was found.

After Darlene Roberts was murdered, the judge wrote, Schiess and Barbara returned to the public road where they had parked, and a passerby saw them standing near Schiess's black Dodge Dakota pickup. In his testimony the passerby described the woman he saw as having a red face. He said that she appeared to be crying. He testified that the woman's hair was "messed up," and he said he saw that the man pushed the woman into the truck.

In the forensic evaluation by Dr. Doug McKeown, Barbara's statements, the testimony of Dr. Jason Junkins, and other proof, she was described as being physically disabled. Her disability was apparently the result of a serious automobile accident that occurred in May 2004.

Dr. Junkins was the medical provider for inmates at the Cherokee County Detention Center. Based on his treatment of her medical needs during her incarceration, Dr. Junkins was of the opinion that Barbara, if acting alone, did not have the physical ability to abduct another adult.

Based on all the evidence in the case, Judge Rains said, including the defendant's living arrangements with Schiess, her medical problems that resulted from her 2004 automobile accident, her long history of psychiatric treatment, and her inability to work due to her disability, the court was satisfied that she was mentally, emotionally, physically, and financially dependent on Schiess.

This conclusion, the judge said, by no means excused Barbara's involvement in the tragic crime. Even from her own statements to the investigators, it was clear that she was not blameless. On the contrary, he said, taken as a whole, he had to conclude from her three statements to the investigators, she was much more than a mere bystander in the murder of Darlene Roberts.

During her many months of incarceration, Barbara was a cellmate with Tonya Regalado. Regalado testified that Barbara told her that when Schiess stopped Darlene on the road, he was drunk, and that when he tried to tie her up, she was able to get away from him. According to Regalado's testimony, Barbara said that she chased Darlene and shot at her, then said that she found her at the pond, where she fired and missed, then shot Darlene two times in the back. Regalado testified that Barbara told her that Schiess then also shot Darlene twice.

In Barbara's statements to the investigators, she implicated Schiess as the primary actor. On the other hand, Regalado testified, Barbara told her that both she and Schiess had shot Darlene. Judge Rains said that he believed Regalado's testimony about her conversations with Barbara was far more incriminating than any of the three statements that Barbara herself had made to the officers.

In Barbara's statements to the investigating officers, and in Regalado's testimony and written statements about her conversations with Barbara, she claimed that she and Vernon Roberts were having a sexual affair, which enraged Schiess when he learned of it, and that Darlene Roberts had been murdered for sexual revenge.

In determining the weight to give an inmate's conversations with a cellmate, Judge Rains said, he had to weigh whether the inmate's claims to be a killer, and to be the object of men's sexual desire, was a boastful effort by the inmate to elevate her status in the jail population. While the court was not willing to disregard the incrimination shown by the Regalado testimony, neither was the court willing to disregard the consistency of Barbara's several claims that Schiess had acted out of jealousy or sexual revenge.

Based on the evidence, and the reasonable inferences therefrom, Judge Rains said that he was satisfied that Schiess had a high degree of culpability. The court, he said, was also satisfied that Barbara's mental, emotional, physical, and financial dependence on Schiess made her vulnerable to his manipulations. While she was an active participant in the murder of Darlene Roberts, the court was satisfied that Barbara acted under the considerable domination of Schiess.

On the basis of these findings, the judge said, the court found that this mitigating factor did exist in the case.

6. *Whether the capacity of the defendant to appreciate the criminality of her conduct or to conform her conduct to the requirements of law was substantially impaired.*

Subject to the findings of the court as stated herein, Judge Rains said the court had found that

Barbara's capacity to understand the criminality of her conduct or to control her conduct to meet the requirements of law was not substantially impaired.

Accordingly, he said, the court did not find this mitigating factor to exist in the case.

7. *The age of the defendant at the time of the crime.*

Barbara Ann Comeaux Roberts was born on April 18, 1956. She was fifty years old at the time of the murder of Darlene Roberts. Her age, the judge said, was not a mitigating factor in this case.

Findings Concerning the Existence or Non-Existence of Non-Statutory Mitigating Circumstances

In this section of his sentencing order, Judge Rains wrote that under ALA. CODE 13A-5-52 (1975) in addition to the statutory mitigating circumstances specified hereinabove, mitigating circumstances should include any aspect of a defendant's character or record, and any of the circumstances of the offense that the defendant offered as a basis for a sentence of life imprisonment without parole instead of death, and any other relevant mitigating circumstance that the defendant offered as a basis for a sentence of life imprisonment without parole instead of death.

In her attempts to justify overruling the jury's recommendation of the death penalty, Barbara offered the testimony of Ms. Pamela O'Neal, who worked with the First Baptist Church jail ministry, and Ms. Amanda Yarbrough, who worked with the jail ministry of the Church of God. Both of the women had only known Barbara since she had been incarcerated in the Cherokee County Jail. Both of them told Judge Rains that they felt that Barbara was sincere in her religious beliefs and that she could have a positive influence on others.

Elaine Jones, the legal assistant in Rodney Stallings's law firm, testified about her acquaintance with Barbara since first coming to know her following Barbara's arrest. She, too, spoke of her religious beliefs and her concern for Ms. Jones and her family.

Judge Rains said that the court found that the testimony of Ms. O'Neal, Ms. Yarbrough, and Ms. Jones did not support a finding of nonstatutory mitigation.

Findings Concerning the Existence or Non-Existence of Other Mitigating Circumstance

Judge Rains said that the state's case against Barbara was considerably dependent on the statements that she, herself, had made. On the other hand, Schiess had made no statements to anyone, at any time. Barbara's incriminating statements were admissible in evidence against her, the judge said, but under Alabama's rules of evidence, they were not admissible against Schiess. Accordingly, unlike the case against Barbara, the prosecution had no self-incriminating statements that they could use for the prosecution of Schiess. Nevertheless, the court was satisfied that Schiess had a high degree of culpability in the murder of Darlene Roberts. Even without any incriminating statements by Schiess, his involvement in the crime could not be ignored.

The case against Barbara relied heavily on the incriminating testimony of Barbara's cellmate, Tonya Regalado, who was a convicted felon.

The testimony of a jailhouse informant is often suspect, the judge wrote. *The testimony of a convicted felon is often suspect. Without the testimony of Rega-lado, the evidence points more toward Schiess.*

Judge Rains stated that on August 6, 2008, Schiess entered a plea of guilty to kidnapping, first degree, as a lesser included charge within Count Two of the indictment against him. All other charges, the judge wrote, including the charges of capital murder, were dismissed:

The sentence imposed pursuant to the plea agreement was twenty years in the state penitentiary. Pursuant to the Alabama Split Sentence Act, and in accordance with the plea agreement, Schiess was ordered to serve three years in the state penitentiary with jail credit for 652 days of confinement served up until the day of his plea, followed by five years on probation.

Judge Rains wrote that the only sentence alternatives to the court in Barbara's case were life in the state penitentiary without the possibility of parole, or death.

The disparity between the sentencing options available in this case and the sentence received by Schiess is significant, the judge noted.

When the Jury recommended that the Court impose a sentence of death, the jury was not aware of this disparate result.

Considering the culpability of Schiess, the Defendant's dependence on him, and the Defendant's expressed fear of him, the Court finds this sentencing disparity to be a mitigating factor.

Conclusion

In his conclusion Judge Rains wrote that the court had carefully considered the aggravating circumstances that had been proven to the satisfaction of the court beyond a reasonable doubt, and the recommendation of the jury:

The Court has also considered the mitigating circumstances as set out herein. The aggravating circumstances do not outweigh the mitigating circumstances.

Sentence

Judge Rains then presented his sentence:

It is hereby Ordered, Adjudged and Decreed that the Defendant shall be, and is hereby, sentenced to LIFE IN THE STATE PENITENTIARY WITHOUT THE POSSIBILITY OF PAROLE for the CAPITAL MURDER of Darlene Roberts. The Defendant is further sentenced to LIFE IN THE STATE PENITENTIARY for the noncapital murder of Darlene Roberts and LIFE IN THE STATE PENITENTIARY for Robbery First Degree. Each of these sentences shall run concurrently each with the other.

He advised Barbara of her right to appeal. If she wished to appeal, he wrote, she must do so by giving notice of appeal within forty-two days from the date of the sentencing order. If she was an indigent and could not afford a lawyer to represent her on appeal, the court would appoint a lawyer for her and provide a free transcript of all proceedings in the case:

The Defendant will receive credit for the time during which she has been incarcerated on the present charge.
DONE this 29th Day of August, 2008,
David A. Rains, Circuit Judge

Instead of the death penalty, as recommended by the jury, Judge Rains had, after much thoughtful deliberation, decided to sentence Barbara to life in prison without parole. There was much relief on the part of the defense, but Barbara's story was far from finished. The appeals process was just beginning, and it would be a long and complicated one.

65

Since Barbara Roberts was now categorized as being indigent, Judge David Rains notified a young Fort Payne, Alabama, attorney with an excellent reputation, Angela Cochran Morgan, that she was being appointed as Barbara's attorney of record. Morgan would be handling Barbara's appeals process, and she immediately notified District Attorney Mike O'Dell and Assistant District Attorney Bob Johnston of that appointment by filing an Entry of Appearance. Her first action on Barbara's behalf was to file a motion to delay the transfer of the defendant to the state penitentiary pending appeal, in the hope that Judge Rains would allow the motion and give her time to obtain a trial transcript and confer with Barbara after reviewing it. Judge Rains consulted Cherokee County sheriff Jeff Shaver, who told the judge that he did not object to Barbara remaining in the Cherokee County Jail for the time being.

Judge Rains issued a court order that allowed Barbara to remain in the Cherokee County Jail pending further orders of the court, issued on September 18, 2008. Instead of an immediate transfer to Julia Tutwiler Prison for Women, Barbara would stay in jail in Cherokee County for a short time while she and Morgan began the work on her first appeal.

Angela Cochran Morgan lost no time in beginning the paperwork essential to the requirements of the appeals process. She immediately filed a motion for a new trial, serving copies to the court and to the district attorney's office on September 29. Twelve points were included in the motion, which moved the court to set aside the verdict in the initial case and to grant Barbara a new trial on those grounds. They were as follows:

1. The verdict was contrary to law.
2. The verdict was contrary to the weight of the evidence.
3. The defendant was denied a fair and impartial trial.
4. The court erred in refusing to continue the trial of this matter, where the defendant was incompetent to assist her trial counsel in the preparation of her defense, and to understand fully and consider any plea offers made by the state.
5. The court erred in admitting into evidence statements of the defendant.

6. The court erred in allowing the testimony of witness Tonya Regalado.

7. The court erred in allowing the admission of evidence gathered at the scene of the crime where the crime scene was not properly secured.

8. For much of the defendant's incarceration related to this case, she failed to receive adequate psychiatric care, which affected the outcome of this case.

9. The court erred in failing to find the defendant not guilty by reason of mental disease or defect.

10. The defendant did not receive effective assistance of counsel at trial, as guaranteed her by the Sixth and Fourteenth Amendments to the United States Constitution and by Article 1, Section 6, of the Alabama Constitution of 1901. Without limiting the foregoing, the defendant set forth the following areas of ineffectiveness:

   a. trial counsel failed to fully review discovery information provided by the state with the defendant prior to trial;
   b. trial counsel was not adequately prepared for trial because he had expected the trial to be continued;
   c. trial counsel failed to contact, interview, and/or subpoena a number of witnesses whose testimony could have led to the

defendant's acquittal on one or more of
the charges in this case;

d. trial counsel failed to obtain and offer
at trial various evidence that could have
led to the defendant's acquittal on one
or more of the charges in this case;

e. trial counsel failed to obtain an independent psychiatric evaluation of the
defendant by a certified forensic psychiatrist and to offer evidence of such
evaluation at trial;

f. trial counsel failed to offer evidence at
trial of the defendant's medical problems, which evidence could have led to
the defendant's acquittal on one or
more of the charges in this case.

11. Such other, further, and different grounds
as this honorable court might find to
grant this motion.

12. The defendant reserved the right to
supplement and amend this motion for
new trial after the undersigned counsel had reviewed the entire transcript of
the trial proceedings in this case.

Morgan added a postscript to the motion
saying that she was the attorney who had been
appointed by the court to represent Barbara
following the pronouncing of her sentence;
she had not, she said, represented Barbara at
the trial.

She acknowledged that the court had made

every effort to provide her with a transcript of the trial proceedings to use in the preparation of posttrial motions, but said that the court reporter had been unable to complete the lengthy transcript by the thirty-day deadline for filing postjudgment motions set out in Rules 20 and 24 of the Alabama Rules of Criminal Procedure.

Up to that time, Morgan said, she had been able to review only some of the pretrial hearings and an equally incomplete record of the jury organization. Until the remainder of the transcript could be delivered to her, she said, she had been forced to rely on the amount of the total transcript she had received, the court file, information obtained from Barbara, and limited information she had received from trial counsel Rodney Stallings in drafting the motion. Ms. Morgan stated that she expected to have the complete transcript before the motion was set for hearing.

On the same day, Ms. Morgan filed a motion for judgment of acquittal after verdict or judgment of conviction. This moved the court to set aside the verdict and any judgment of conviction and any sentence pronounced in Barbara's case and to enter a judgment of acquittal on the grounds that the evidence presented in this case was insufficient to support a finding that Barbara was guilty beyond a reasonable doubt, and any other, further, or different grounds as the court might have to grant the motion.

With the prompt and efficient filing of such

motions and her expressed desire for a thorough review of the materials and evidence in the case, it was apparent that Angela Cochran Morgan was taking her responsibility as Barbara's court-appointed counsel very seriously.

66

In late September of 2008, Barbara again wrote to Judge Randall Cole and Judge David Rains. This time, however, the improvement in the composition, grammar, and consistency of her letter was apparent. Her train of thought remained steady, and she began by acknowledging the judges *for finding and talking to Ms. Angela Cochran Morgan to help me with my case. Thank you.*

Barbara next asked the judges to allow her to have another trial.

For the longest time, I was not in a good mental frame of mind to help in my own defense, she wrote. After a year of requesting the jail to arrange for her to be seen by a psychiatrist, she was seen for the first time around a month prior to the start of her trial, she said. The doctor had told her that it would take a few months for her to notice improvement from her changed medication. She'd had a second visit from the doctor in early September, and the medication was adjusted again, and she was starting to do much better, she said.

Barbara claimed that Stallings did not start preparing for her trial until around the time of the jury selection.

He was so sure that my trial would be delayed again and possibly take place after Dr. Robert Schiess's trial, she wrote. *As we both know, this did not happen.*

She had wanted to tell that to the judge on her sentencing date, she said, *but Rodney advised me to say nothing.*

Barbara then went on to list her own version of many of the other things in the trial that she thought had gone wrong.

The people who taught the shooting lessons that Barbara had attended had known she could not fire a shotgun, she said, and that information was not presented at trial, although Stallings had a letter from them to that effect. At the shooting range at the South River Gun Club, visitors had to sign in whether they were shooting or not, just to enter the gun range area. Barbara said she had only gone once.

Tonya Regalado had changed the statements she had made to investigators, giving conflicting information in the first and second versions of her story. Regalado, Barbara claimed, had over two hundred felonies on her record, and Regalado reported to the jail that attorney Stallings had threatened her life.

Stallings had been asked by Barbara to get the chief jailer to testify about why Regalado had to go on to prison instead of staying at Cherokee County Jail to serve her sentence. Another woman Barbara met in jail had known Regalado most of her life, and could testify about some of

Regalado's alleged crimes that, the woman told Barbara, had gone unpunished.

Regalado claimed that Barbara was her cellmate, but Barbara said that they were never in a "cell" together, since that was not how the jail was arranged. Regalado blamed Barbara for Regalado's being sent on to the prison, and she had allegedly told many of the other women at the Cherokee County Jail that she was going to make sure Barbara got life or the death penalty.

Regalado had threatened Barbara's life, Barbara claimed, by saying that Barbara was going to Tutwiler, and when she got there, Tonya was going to kill her and "stick a pin" in her neck.

Barbara was held without her medications from the time she was arrested until the time she left jail on bond. Since she was bipolar, she claimed, this lack of medication caused her severe decompensation problems. The doctor she was seeing in Conyers, Georgia, could testify as to how she would act without her medication, Barbara said, and he had written a letter saying he didn't see how she could have planned and carried out a murder.

One of the investigating officers, Barbara claimed, had "come up" with stories to bring the charges against her to capital murder after being told of and shown the bruises on her legs from a beating she allegedly suffered while in jail.

The weather reports from the *Rome News-Tribune* and pictures in the newspapers could confirm that there was severe weather in the area on the night of the murder and the following day. This, Barbara claimed, would have compromised the crime scene, but she said the prosecution had stated on several occasions about the sunshine and good weather at the crime scene at that time.

The crime scene was never secured, Barbara claimed, and photos from the *Rome News-Tribune* showed trucks inside the crime scene. Barbara also alleged that a security guard from Temple-Inland, who, she claimed, was a former FBI agent, had been allowed to come onto the scene and help with the investigation.

Her defense, Barbara said, had failed to enter the report from her surgeries and her nerve conduction studies outlining the nerve damage in her neck, shoulders, and hand.

From the home of Vernon and Darlene Roberts, Barbara said, all of County Road 941 could be seen, from the turn onto the road, all the way to the house. *It would have been close to impossible for [Vernon] not to see Darlene's car on the road or in the field,* she wrote. *I wanted the jury to go out to the crime scene to see it for themselves.*

When the Nissan Murano was found at the crime scene, Barbara claimed, witness Jason Sammons reported that the windows on the car were down and they put their hands in the windows. When they came back to the scene, the windows were up, Barbara said, and there were no keys. The car had electric windows, she said, and the garage door opener was not in the car, either.

Barbara claimed that her ex-husband had lied on the witness stand about several things, including his claim that he had paid her medical expenses from her serious auto accident. *He did not pay a cent,* Barbara wrote. *I bet he has no canceled checks or receipts.*

If Darlene had defense wounds, Barbara wondered, wouldn't they have been on her hand, and not on her arms? The hair found on the butt pad of the shotgun, Barbara claimed, was tested, and those tests showed that it was not hers, nor was it that of Schiess. She also thought the gun analysis on the shotgun shells had shown that two guns were used. Witness Jason Sammons, Barbara claimed, had reported two gunshots were heard after about a ten-minute wait after the initial shot or shots were heard.

Every time Barbara saw Agent Brent Thomas and Investigator Mark Hicks, she wrote, they asked her if she was okay because they were *afraid for my safety and life from Mr. Schiess,* and at one time asked her if she needed to go into protective housing.

Attorney Steve Lanier's daughter had made copies of Barbara's answering machine recordings from Vernon's calls, she said. Barbara had not made them.

One of the investigators had claimed Barbara was lying about being in West Rome instead of Conyers to see a banker, she said. The first recorded message on the answering machine tape made by Lanier's daughter was from a woman named Tiffany, from Housing in Rome, speaking of Barbara's appointment with the banker.

If Barbara's medication had been withheld after she asked about them, but was told no, did that make her confessions coerced? she asked.

I am praying that you will see it in your heart to allow me another trial with this new lawyer, Barbara concluded, *and allow me to stay in Cherokee County.*

Barbara had covered a long string of questions, allegations, and other statements in this letter, but it was far more cohesive and better thought-out than any of her previous efforts at communicating with the court. It was evident that her condition had, in fact, improved to an extent, and she would be far better able to assist her new attorney with her defense.

67

Because of the delays in obtaining a complete trial transcript and other necessary materials, the defense and the prosecution filed a joint stipulation for extension of time to rule on posttrial motions, in which both parties had agreed to extend for an additional thirty days the court's time for ruling on the defendant's pending motion for acquittal or for a new trial, which was filed on September 29. Before that time expired, a second joint stipulation was filed, extending the deadline for the court's time for ruling beyond November 27, 2008, up to and including December 27, 2008. And after that, a third joint stipulation was filed, giving an additional forty-five days that extended the deadline beyond December 27, 2008, up to and including February 10, 2009.

When a fourth joint stipulation for extension of time to rule on posttrial motions was filed on February 10, it extended the court's deadline beyond February 10, up to and including April 30. But that would be the final extension.

* * *

The first appeal hearing for Barbara Roberts was held on Wednesday, March 18, 2009, at the Cherokee County Courthouse. The parties present for the hearing had gathered in the main courtroom that morning, but there were many other people with business not related to Barbara's hearing crowded into the large room. Courthouse personnel quickly realized that the courtroom had been double-booked accidentally that day. People who were in attendance for Barbara's appeal were summoned to a smaller courtroom, which was just large enough for Barbara and her attorney, Angela Cochran Morgan, DA Mike O'Dell, ADA Bob Johnston, Officer Bo Jolly, Chief Deputy Tim Hays and three other law enforcement officers, two court staff, and Judge David A. Rains.

A motion for a new trial had been filed on September 29, 2008, and also another motion for acquittal.

The first issue presented by Morgan concerned the several plea offers Barbara had been offered during the course of her case.

"Ms. Roberts could not have had meaningful communication with her attorneys about plea offers due to the medications she was on at the time," Morgan said. "The trial should have been continued due to that."

The next item addressed by Morgan was the claim that the statements by Barbara on April 19, 20, and 26, 2006, that had been admitted into the trial, were not properly documented.

"The statement made on April nineteenth was not signed by Ms. Roberts, and ABI Agent Brent Thomas asked for it not to be recorded," Morgan said. "The statement on the twenty-sixth, made at the Cherokee County Jail, was not recorded, either. The one made on April twentieth was recorded, but not much information [on her right to an attorney to be present] was given to Ms. Roberts prior to signing the statement."

ADA Bob Johnston then addressed Morgan's statements.

"The motion to continue was filed without enough reason to justify its being granted," he said. "Mental evaluations showed Barbara Roberts was competent to stand trial and could assist Rodney Stallings during the trial. There was no reason to postpone the trial.

"As to the admission of Barbara Roberts's statements, she was willing to talk without an attorney present, and even requested interviews."

Morgan then claimed that the court had erred in allowing the testimony of Tonya Regalado during the trial, and Johnston countered by saying that Tonya Regalado's statement was not the only one of its kind.

"The court allowed the glasses—found too long after the crime to be allowed," Morgan stated. "The scene was unsecured for twenty-four hours before the glasses were found."

"Other evidence introduced at the trial tied the glasses to the murder," Johnston answered.

Morgan then moved on to a topic she hoped to pursue more successfully.

"The most important issue here is that the defendant did not receive effective assistance at the trial. Rodney Stallings didn't provide adequate evidence to continue the case. He told the court that Ms. Roberts didn't fully understand the settlement offers [she had received earlier on in the case], and he failed to have doctors present at the June hearing to verify her mental state. He only provided an unsigned and undated letter from Dr. Junkins.

"Rodney Stallings told the court in June that due to problems with her medications, he could not have a meaningful conversation with Ms. Roberts about plea agreements."

Barbara had been sitting, listening, restless in her seat. She had lost considerable weight during her time at Tutwiler Prison. She seemed frail and anxious.

"There was no last-minute plea offer," Johnston told the court. "Ms. Roberts has not shown any remorse for the crime, and her obstinance has caused her not to accept the offers that had been made for one and a half years previously. It's easy now to complain about her representation."

Johnston cited several appeals cases involving representation during criminal trials, and told the court that being granted an appeal "requires showing that counsel made serious errors that deprived the defendant of a fair trial. The defendant must prove failure of the attorney."

Johnston then pointed out that there was no evidence that Rodney Stallings didn't provide Barbara with effective representation. He said that claims of performance prejudices must show reasonable probability that results of the trial would have been different if representation had been handled differently.

"The defendant's glasses were found at the scene and led to her. Her statements showed that she was there," Johnston said. "It was not Rodney Stallings's fault that the glasses were left there. Now, only in hindsight, she wants to complain about Rodney."

Judge Rains asked Johnston for a copy of a letter written by Barbara, praising Stallings and saying how much his representation meant to her.

"She has written other letters complaining about Rodney Stallings," Morgan countered. "She felt like he was family, but since then, her opinion has changed. I feel like, after reading the transcript, the argument has to be raised. She was not competent to help him prepare for the trial. Mr. Stallings did not provide evidence for a continuance. The doctor testified at the trial that her competency could have changed, but Mr. Stallings didn't request a reevaluation of her mental state."

Johnston told the court that Barbara was in full assistance of Stallings during the trial.

"Mr. Stallings failed to pursue an insanity plea," Morgan argued. "A psychiatric evaluation was performed, but Mr. Stallings hadn't received it at the time of the trial. Ms. Roberts paid five thousand dollars for another psychiatrist to evaluate her, and no such evaluation was performed. An independent examiner should have been hired with the five thousand dollars. Rodney Stallings should have requested a reassessment of Ms. Roberts' mental condition."

Johnston told the court that Barbara was lucid during the proceedings, and recalled evidence.

"Rodney Stallings was not adequately prepared for the trial because he thought a continuance would be granted," Morgan countered. "He didn't start preparing until the continuance was denied. He introduced several exhibits without enough explanation. His defense strategies were the 'spaghetti effect,' where you throw enough of it at the wall and some of it will eventually stick. His defenses seemed desperate, first claiming that Vernon Roberts did it, then claiming that Barbara Roberts was physically unable to do it. There was no evidence on Vernon Roberts's involvement. By throwing him in, it becomes 'spaghetti.'"

"Rodney Stallings did what many do," Johnston answered, "with a guilty client on his hands. He claimed her codefendant was more culpable and was behind it all."

Morgan then switched to the issue of her client's physical problems, saying that Stallings had failed to provide the jury with enough proof of Barbara's physical disabilities and weaknesses.

"I don't believe the jury would have recommended the death penalty if they didn't believe Ms. Roberts pulled the trigger. She had said she couldn't hold or fire the shotgun because of her disability.

"Dr. Junkins had said that, according to her disabilities, her type of injuries would cause loss of upper-body strength. If an assessment had been properly performed, the outcome of the trial would have been different.

"I shot my husband's shotgun over the weekend, to see how it felt. It wasn't easy. If Rodney Stallings had offered evidence, he could have shown Schiess could have done the shooting. The gun was a pump-action, and it was hard to do."

Morgan told the court that Barbara had only come to the South River Gun Club with Schiess on one occasion. The green plastic, the gauze, and the cable found in the truck tied Schiess to the murder, she said. And the witness Richiez had testified that Barbara's face was red, she appeared to be crying, and he had seen Schiess push her into the truck.

Morgan also reminded the court that Investigator Mark Hicks had been informed by the FBI of Schiess's money transfer of $1.8 million to a Swiss bank account, and Jim Captain had testified that Schiess talked to him several times after the murder about various suspicious topics.

"All the facts pointing to Schiess were not presented to the jury. At best, the defense was a halfhearted effort," said Morgan. "Ms. Roberts had the right to a better defense."

Johnston told the court, "Everything we just heard was presented to the jury. [As for Ms. Roberts's ability to fire a shotgun], adrenaline powers people to do what they could not ordinarily do."

* * *

Judge Rains then addressed Ms. Morgan: "You said you believed the jury concluded Ms. Roberts pulled the trigger because of the eleven to one vote for the death penalty, and that result came about because of Mr. Stallings's poor representation. If Mr. Stallings was ineffective, isn't the fact that Ms. Roberts was sentenced to life without parole contradictory?"

Morgan respectfully pointed out to Judge Rains that if Barbara had not been convicted of capital murder, she could have received a lesser sentence.

Judge Rains then spoke directly to Barbara.

"The court clerk received on March ninth a letter from you requesting a copy of the court file and transcript, and a motion for discovery. The entire record was made available to your attorney. It is my judgment that by providing it to the attorney, I will not ask the clerk's office to prepare a separate, complete record for you."

Barbara told Judge Rains that the authorities at the prison had told her that was how she had to obtain the information, and told her that it had to be sent from the court and not from the attorney.

"Don't expect me to grant a request for the shipment of such a large amount of records to the prison," Judge Rains told Barbara. "It places an unreasonable burden on the court reporter to request a second copy."

* * *

At that point, the conclusion of the hearing, Bob Johnston ended his remarks by saying that the only way to grant a motion for a new trial would be proof of fault on the part of Rodney Stallings, "and that does not exist."

On March 29, Judge David Rains issued a court order:

The defendant's motions for a new trial and for judgment of acquittal after verdict or judgment of conviction were heard on March 18, 2009. In consideration thereof, the defendant's motions were hereby denied.

68

In Alabama, everyone convicted of a crime has the right to appeal his case and ask a higher court to review the decisions made by his trial court.

Appeals courts differ from trial courts in that, while trial courts are concerned about the facts of the case at hand, appeals courts deal with the legal matters behind those facts. There is a heavy emphasis on reviewing and discussing the arguments prepared by both sides.

Defendants must act quickly to file their appeals after their trials; Alabama state courts require filing of a notice of appeal to take place within forty-two days of sentencing. And defendants must also be able to show reasonable grounds for an appeal. Several of the better grounds for an appeal included points that related to Barbara's situation and that had already been mentioned, either by Barbara in her last letter to the judges, or by her defense counsel. Those points included her argument that evidence that should have been withheld, according to her, had been admitted at trial;

she had received ineffective representation; and that at several points during the course of her case, particularly for the first year or more following her arrest, she was not mentally stable enough to assist with her defense.

Barbara's case was to be appealed to the Alabama Court of Criminal Appeals, which hears all appeals of felony and misdemeanor cases in the state, and also hears violation of city ordinance cases and postconviction writs. If that court's decision was appealed, it could be then appealed to the Supreme Court of Alabama. If it was determined that the grounds for appeal involved civil rights or federal law, it might then be taken to the United States Supreme Court.

There were other types of postconviction relief that could be sought by petitioning the trial court; appellate lawyers could petition for state collateral review, or a Rule 32 Petition. If denied by the trial court, that decision could be taken to the Alabama Court of Criminal Appeals and then to the Alabama Supreme Court.

The appeals process was acknowledged to be more academic and technical than trial law, involving a lot of legal theory and requirements, and Barbara Roberts was pinning her hopes on her new attorney. It would take time, skill, knowledge, and patience to prepare a successful appeal.

On May 4, 2009, Angela Cochran Morgan began filing the necessary forms with the Alabama Court of Criminal Appeals to present Barbara Roberts's case for hearing. In the docketing statement, when asked the nature of the case, she summarized it quite concisely.

Morgan told how, on April 6, 2006, Darlene Roberts, the wife of Barbara Roberts's ex-husband, died of gunshot wounds inflicted at a pond near her home in Cherokee County, Alabama. Morgan's client, Barbara Roberts, and Barbara's boyfriend, Dr. Robert Schiess, had been placed near the scene of the murder by eyewitness testimony and physical evidence. A passerby testified that Barbara appeared to be upset and crying and was pushed into a truck by Schiess. Three statements given by Barbara had been admitted at trial, as well as testimony of Tonya Regalado, who testified regarding alleged statements made by Barbara in jail. Morgan stated that Barbara suffered from bipolar disorder, and her medication was either not taken or not properly adjusted during her statements to police and during her time in jail. Barbara also suffered from physical disabilities that would have made it extremely difficult—if not impossible—for her to shoot the type of gun used in the murder.

In stating the issues on appeal, Ms. Morgan listed nine key points: (1) the verdict was contrary to the weight of the evidence; (2) the trial court was in error when they refused to continue the trial, at which time Barbara had been incompetent to assist Rodney Stallings in the preparation of her defense, and was unable to understand fully and consider the plea offers made by the state; (3) the trial court was mistaken when they admitted into evidence the unrecorded statements of the defendant; (4) the trial court was also in error in allowing the testimony of witness Tonya Regalado; (5) the trial court acted incorrectly by allowing the admission of evidence gathered at the scene of the crime when the crime scene had not been properly secured; (6) for much of the time Barbara was held in jail prior to the trial, she failed to receive the psychiatric care she needed, which affected the outcome of the case; (7) the trial court should have found Barbara not guilty by reason of mental disease or defect; (8) Barbara did not receive effective assistance of her attorney at the time of the trial; and (9) the evidence presented in the case was not substantial enough to support a finding beyond a reasonable doubt that Barbara was guilty of the murder of Darlene Roberts.

At last writing, the Alabama Court of Criminal Appeals had not yet addressed Barbara Roberts's appeal.

69

Of all the reasons offered to the Alabama Court of Criminal Appeals by Angela Cochran Morgan to justify a new trial for her client, those that were most compelling were the ones that have to do with Barbara Roberts's mental state—both at the time of the crime and in the following months and years. Having been diagnosed with bipolar disorder for many years, then with major depression, and with post-traumatic stress disorder following her near-fatal traffic accident, her mental condition could have been affected by overmedication prior to the crime, as well as a lack of medication following her arrest.

There are no means, after the fact, to determine Barbara's competence at any stage of the proceedings. A look at the causes, symptoms, treatment, and complications of those conditions she suffered with might bring some further understanding of her mental-health issues.

Barbara's primary diagnosis of bipolar disorder was said by the forensic psychologist who testified at her trial to be a predominantly depressed type. A closer look at bipolar disorder could bring a clearer understanding of Barbara's mental processes—both at the time of Darlene Roberts's death and in the years preceding, as well as those that followed.

70

When the life and actions of Barbara Roberts were studied, it became obvious that her bipolar disorder had been at the root of most of her difficulties in life. It caused a steady destabilization in her mental health from the time her family first noticed its gradual onset, when Barbara was in her early twenties. Although she sought treatment, there were also many times when that treatment was irregular or insufficient.

Bipolar disorder is a serious mental illness that can affect anyone of any age, race, gender, or socioeconomic group. It is less common in children and teens, but it is estimated that around 5.7 million adults in America are living with the disease. Many remain undiagnosed, and they and their loved ones suffer needlessly because of their lack of treatment.

Although bipolar disorder cannot be prevented, regular medical treatment and continual monitoring of the disease can allow those affected with it to keep the illness under control. They can lead satisfying, productive lives. There are two phases of bipolar disorder, which consist of mood swings back and forth between those two phases. In some cases, particularly in women, the primary phase is bipolar depression, also referred to as major depression. Sufferers experience a very depressed mood characterized by low energy levels, low self-esteem, slow speech, fatigue, poor coordination, suicidal thoughts and feelings, poor concentration, sadness, loneliness, helplessness, guilt, chronic pain without a known cause, anxiety, and insomnia or oversleeping.

In the other phase of bipolar disorder, called bipolar mania or hypomania, sufferers experience an unusual level of energy, excessive talk, impulsiveness, a reckless pursuit of gratification, periods of irritability countered by episodes of euphoria, racing thoughts, poor judgment, an inability to concentrate, and inflated self-esteem. Sufferers in this phase can sometimes progress from the first signs of mania to a full-blown case of manic psychosis in only a matter of a few hours, and the results can be devastating to families.

Those in the manic phase can pile up huge debts, drive recklessly, engage in substance abuse and extramarital affairs, encounter legal problems, and engage in other behaviors that can break down relationships. Early intervention when entering the manic phase can sometimes help control the escalation of the problem.

71

When dealing with a friend or family member suspected of having bipolar disorder, it is particularly important to recognize any symptoms of possible drug abuse, a common problem for persons with the disorder. There is a great deal of self-medication by some patients with bipolar disorder, and drug abuse by bipolar sufferers—particularly in men—can indicate a strong predisposition toward suicide in many cases.

It is also possible for those with the illness to have a condition known as mixed-state bipolar disorder, where symptoms of depression and mania can occur together, with patients experiencing symptoms of both phases simultaneously. This condition can sometimes confuse an accurate diagnosis and can be mistaken for other disorders.

Severe cases of either phase of bipolar disorder can lead to a detachment from reality known as psychosis, which can include delusions and hallucinations, with the patient hearing voices or seeing things that aren't there.

There has been research that indicates that bipolar disorder may very well have genetic links, as it often runs in families, but medical authorities still don't completely understand what causes the illness to strike unexpectedly when there has been no early indication of problems. In addition to a possible genetic connection, other risk factors for developing the disorder include drug abuse and highly stressful periods of life. Although it can affect children as young as six years old, it is more common in teenagers and young adults, and its onset usually begins between the ages of fifteen and thirty.

Bipolar disorder can be easily misdiagnosed as attention-deficit/hyperactivity disorder (ADHD) in children and teens. It is characterized by dropping grades, quitting activities, refusal to participate, poor attention and concentration, and boredom.

This would indicate that Barbara Roberts did not begin to suffer from the onset of bipolar disorder to a recognizable degree until the years following her graduation from high school, since she finished at the top of her class, was liked by her teachers, then shouldered the responsibility of working to pay for her own college classes and for her dance lessons, and remained a high achiever with definite goals and ambitions. Her family indicated that they began to realize Barbara had problems beyond what they could help her with, and urged her to seek treatment, when she was in her twenties.

Barbara did choose to see a mental-health professional and was prescribed medication, but her family reported that she stopped treatment because of having a bad reaction to the drug. She continued other treatment, off and on, for several years, but she voluntarily sought hospitalization frequently after moving to Alabama, when she began to have serious troubles in her marriage. Hospitalization for psychiatric treatment helped her stabilize her deep depression, but since her situation remained unchanged in her marriage, she was readmitted, at her own request, again and again, with little lasting change.

72

Following the auto accident that almost took the lives of Barbara and Robert John Schiess III, they both were diagnosed with post-traumatic stress disorder, an anxiety disorder that is triggered by experiencing or witnessing an event that has caused extreme fear or horror. Primarily known as a disorder affecting combat veterans, it can also occur following accidents like Barbara's, or other traumatic events, such as serious injury, shock, or violent assault. Most people involved in such events have a time when they have difficulty adjusting and coping, but those who develop PTSD can continue to have problems for months or even years, sometimes resulting in serious disruptions to their lives.

There is still much research under way on the causes of post-traumatic stress disorder, but when a person develops the mental illness, it is believed to stem from a combination of a predisposition to anxiety and depression, temperament, life experiences, and brain chemistry in response to stress.

Like bipolar disorder, PTSD can cause a higher risk of the sufferer having other problems, such as drug abuse, depression, alcohol abuse, panic attacks, and thoughts of suicide. Researchers are also beginning to believe there may be a link, in some patients, between PTSD and chronic pain, bone, and joint problems, as well as diseases such as rheumatoid arthritis.

Barbara Roberts may have suffered an increase in her chronic neck, back, and arm pain, caused by the accident and her multiple subsequent surgeries, because of the PTSD and its possible physical effects. There is continuing research in the area of PTSD and physical-health problems, and it could be possible that Barbara had suffered physical pain that was being exacerbated by her PTSD.

73

Thus far, Barbara's diagnosed mental illnesses and her physical problems showed the possibility of a distinct overlap of symptoms and causes. But one of her most telling emotional problems—her obsession with Vernon Roberts—could also be connected to her bipolar disorder in some areas.

Obsessive love is believed by some authorities to be triggered primarily by rejection. It can be identified by an all-consuming preoccupation with a lover, a longing to be together with the target of the obsession, being rejected by the desired one, and engaging in self-defeating behavior because of the rejection. Barbara's alleged episodes of stalking Vernon and Darlene, vandalizing vehicles—and other instances of harassment—seemed to fit these descriptions.

Obsessive love comes in several identified forms or stages, including love addiction, relationship addiction, and codependency. In love addiction, for example, a person is involved with the object of his obsession in a dependent, unhealthy way. Relationship addiction is where the addiction is to a relationship, such as a marriage, that the person is not willing to relinquish. In the codependency stage, the obsessed is completely dependent on the object of his obsession for the physical and emotional validation of himself. These stages can be experienced separately, successively, or all at the same time.

According to researchers, there are several factors that create a breeding ground for the development of obsessive love. They include feelings of being different—whether real or imagined—feelings of vulnerability, and, literally, boredom. Some psychiatrists and researchers have theorized that children who have not been shown enough healthy love and affection during their early years may go on in later life to develop an obsessive relationship. They also list dependent personality types as being a greater risk for developing relationship addictions.

As it has been documented, obsessive love can lead to stalking, and to crimes such as rape and murder. Those who are obsessed by another person can also engage in self-destructive behavior, substance abuse, and suicide. There is no doubt that Barbara Roberts was obsessed with her ex-husband, Vernon, but how far did that obsession go, and to what degree did it influence the events of April 6, 2006?

When Barbara and Vernon first met, there was apparently an instant romantic attraction on Barbara's part, helped along, no doubt, by Vernon's charm and good looks, and also by what she perceived as his need for her understanding, support, and help. She must have felt an immediate urge to rush into a relationship with him, and she helped him to get his financial life back into order.

After several fairly uneventful years of marriage, problems arose after the move from Texas to Alabama, and Barbara began to feel very insecure when Vernon subsequently began talking about separation and divorce. It was at this time that she began to seek mental hospitalizations and began to feel overwhelmingly depressed. The loss of the relationship caused a corresponding loss of self-esteem and feelings of self-hatred. After the divorce Barbara remained in denial that her marriage was over and believed that she and Vernon would get back together again. Those beliefs, when compounded with the symptoms of her bipolar disorder and PTSD, evidently resulted in a terrible tragedy that has all but destroyed many families.

Corrected medication, regular therapy, and consistent treatment since her incarceration seem to have changed Barbara Roberts somewhat. She apparently has experienced a degree of improvement in her mental state. But despite any such improvement she may have made in recent years, the past cannot, and will not, be changed. Even though she has expressed an extreme degree of remorse and regret for her part in the death of Martha Darlene Roberts, Barbara has paid for the tragic results of her earlier actions with the lifelong surrender of her freedom.

74

There had been very little contact between Barbara and any of her family members from the time of her mother's funeral. The tragedy of their mother's death had finalized the increasing estrangement between Barbara and some of her siblings, and she had gone through the time of her arrest, indictment, trial, and sentencing alone. But even though she might have been unaware of it, some of the members of her family had followed the events, and had been very concerned about her.

There were so many things that Barbara's family, especially her sisters, loved about her. They recollected her to be intelligent, kind-hearted, and talented. They remembered family camping trips with a used army tent and a homemade trailer, trips to the lake, picking blackberries, and chasing chickens.

One sister, who looked up to Barbara and wanted to be like her, spoke of Barbara's beautiful singing voice, her graceful dancing, the ease with which she learned in school, and her desire to make something of herself.

"I tried so hard to be more like her," she said of Barbara. "This was not how things were supposed to turn out." The only emotion she felt for her sister—even after all the heartbreak experienced since April 6, 2006—was love.

"I pray it offers you support," she said. "I love you, Barbara."

Edie Comeaux, one of Barbara's younger sisters, wrote a very touching letter to be included in this book. She took the opportunity to let readers know her feelings for her sister and how the events of April 6, 2006—and all that had followed—had affected her family. Eloquent and heartfelt, the letter will strike a familiar note with anyone whose family has been marked by similar tragedy:

> As an adult I always considered myself to be a conservative individual with an open mind. This self image tumbled down around me in April 2006, and remains scattered around my feet today. I realized I am a person with prejudice.
>
> My misconceptions of people are not based on race, creed, national origin, sexual preferences or economic status. Instead I possessed a very narrow view of the individuals in our prison systems. I formerly believed everyone in prison was there after a life of crime. I pictured the inmates from broken homes, poverty

*and a generational lack of education. Mean
and angry people who looked like the boogie
man of my childhood fears. I never pictured
one of my own family members as one, certainly not my own sister.*

*Nonetheless, Barbara Roberts is incarcer-
ated and will remain so for the rest of her life.
After the jury's recommendation of the Death
Penalty, a judge gave my sister Life without
the Possibility of Parole. Found guilty of capital murder, kidnapping with intent to harm,
robbery and a variety of other offenses.*

*My sister, my parents' child, my son's aunt,
had participated in the brutal murder of
Martha Darlene Roberts, whether or not it
was her finger that pulled the trigger. She participated in the planning, stood beside and
watched, assisted in hiding evidence and then
continued on with her life.*

*A life was taken, and it makes me physi-
cally ill to think of it even today. Knowing
that within days of this being done, two mur-
derers attended my mother's funeral and witnessed the mourning. Acting as if nothing
had happened, they shared meals, made small
talk, and continued to live their lives as
though it was totally unchanged. To me, this
is the behavior of a monster, not that of a
fellow human being.*

*Our mother died the day we found out
about the murder, before we knew Barbara
and Robert John Schiess were suspects. She
died from a broken heart, praying that her
child was not involved. Barbara had been*

married to Darlene's current husband. The divorce was not her idea. Barbara remains obsessed with her ex-husband. She has created in her own mind a much different picture of our childhood and her marriage than what actually existed. She was never happy in her marriage, or in her life. She is emotionally damaged in so many ways.

As much as I wanted to be present for the trial, I could not even begin to prepare myself to hear and see evidence against my sister. I could not bring myself to sit in the same room with her, her ex-husband and Darlene's family. I experienced a paralyzing ache knowing my loved one caused such pain for the survivors.

Readers of this book, please know that our parents were loving, kind and generous people. They worked hard to provide for the family and just as diligently to let us know we were loved. We were raised to believe in God, to love one another and treat others the way we would want to be treated. Darlene's murder is not a reflection of my parents. Barbara committed this crime just before her fiftieth birthday. The life she led as an adult, the people she chose to love, influenced her actions. I fully believe that another remains unpunished for his involvement in the crime, and yet another got by with a slap on the wrist.

I have forgiven my sister for her involvement in this brutal crime. She remains constantly on my mind and in my heart. I pray

for her to find peace. My prayers are also with the family of this and all victims. I also pray for the family members of the criminals, for I know their pain.
—Edie Comeaux, September 2009

75

On the afternoon of Tuesday, October 27, 2009, the suit for wrongful death, brought by Vernon Roberts against Barbara Ann Roberts and Robert John Schiess III, initiated in February 2007, finally came to trial. It was filed in the United States District Court, Northern District of Georgia, Rome Division, and was held in the courtroom of Judge Harold L. Murphy.

On the first day of testimony, some of the witnesses and the officers who were involved in the early days of the investigation of Darlene's murder took the stand to review and restate what happened on the late afternoon in April 6, 2006, when Darlene's body was discovered floating in the farm pond near her home just over the Alabama state line in Cherokee County.

The lead investigator in the case, Cherokee County Sheriff's Office investigator Michael "Bo" Jolly, described the scene of the crime, a pasture off County Road 941, where two neighbors rode their John Deere Gator down into the pasture to check on what they thought was an abandoned vehicle. The Nissan Murano, which had been left sitting in a small patch of willow sprouts and weeds, belonged to Darlene Roberts, whose horribly wounded body the two men discovered in the shallow water at the edge of the pond.

When Jolly arrived at the scene, many other officers were already there, and the area had been secured. Jolly testified about the evidence found that evening and in the coming days: spent shotgun shell casings, green plastic wrap, surgical gauze, and a broken pair of eyeglasses, which were found to belong to Barbara Ann Roberts.

Jolly told the court that Darlene was believed to be on her way home to Cherokee County from her job at Temple-Inland in Rome, and she had stopped by the Rome Wal-Mart, where a security tape showed her shopping for groceries during what would come to be the last hours of her life.

When testimony resumed on the following morning, Jolly returned to the witness stand to complete his testimony concerning the investigation and the facts of the case, and other remaining witnesses presented restatements of the evidence they had given during their testimony at Barbara's criminal trial.

The judge had already established that a great deal of the testimony from Barbara's case would not be admissible as evidence in the civil case. He said that he could not allow testimony about anything that was said by Barbara that implicated Schiess in the crime because it was hearsay and was therefore not admissible. That ruled out a great deal of information because of Barbara's extensive statements about the crime and Schiess's involvement in it, but there still existed what Vernon's attorneys believed would be ample findings against him.

After the evidence and the investigators' testimony was finished, attorney Gregory Price, representing Schiess, went back over the statements that had been presented and attempted to find as many holes as possible in what had been heard so far. He continued examining details of the statements until he was able to verify through the testimony that had been heard that none of Schiess's DNA had been found at the crime scene.

Then a video deposition given by Schiess was played for the court. It was much like the one Barbara had given, except that Schiess provided far less information than Barbara had during her deposition. In fact, he asserted his Fifth Amendment rights almost exclusively.

In an attempt to counteract this refusal to make any statements whatsoever, Vernon Roberts's attorney, Andy Davis, questioned Schiess in much the same manner that he had questioned Barbara, relying on his questions to present information to the jury whether or not Schiess chose to answer. Davis managed to put together a compelling story of the relationship between Barbara and Schiess, what happened at the time of Darlene's death, and what Schiess's involvement might have been.

Throughout all the questioning, Schiess continually cited his Fifth Amendment right to not incriminate himself.

"I assert my privileges," he would say, or "I assert my rights."

Davis asked Schiess about the events of April 6, 2006, attempting to question him about the trip to Cherokee County when he and Barbara allegedly carried two stolen Floyd County traffic barriers to use if they needed to block the road in order to stop Darlene.

Schiess answered with the assertion of his privileges.

When Davis asked if Schiess had attempted to bind Darlene with the green plastic stretch wrap found at the scene and in his apartment, Schiess asserted his rights. And when Davis described Darlene breaking free and running for her life, he asked Schiess if he had shot her at the pond. Schiess again invoked the Fifth Amendment.

Davis then described the arrest and indictment of Schiess and Barbara, and claimed that Schiess had paid Barbara's bail and legal expenses, then later stopped helping her financially after learning that she had given several statements to the police that had incriminated him.

Schiess again asserted his privileges. He would do so continually during his video deposition, answering no questions, making no admissions, and providing no information, not even his address, just as he had during the entire course of the case against him.

Throughout the video deposition of Schiess by attorney Andy Davis, the questions were carefully designed to present the jurors with the information that Davis wanted them to hear, knowing full well that Schiess was highly unlikely to provide any answers at all. But the questions themselves very successfully served to raise the specter of guilt.

As the trial proceeded, it was soon Barbara's turn to have her video deposition shown in court. Up to a point, her testimony was far more forthcoming than Schiess's had been. She answered quite a few more questions than Schiess had when the deposition began, but soon began to rely on the assertions of her Fifth Amendment right.

When Davis asked about her relationship with Schiess, Barbara stated they were dating at the time of the murder, and while she did not say they were living together, she did say they often stayed at each other's houses.

When asked several questions about Schiess's financial matters, Barbara said she had no knowledge of anything other than a checking account of hers that he would occasionally make deposits into. She denied having any knowledge of his personal finances, property he owned, stocks he had acquired, brokers or financial advisors he used, or any other matters concerning money.

Federal Court judge Harold L. Murphy had, on several occasions, advised the jury that they could make some assumptions when the defendants invoked their Fifth Amendment right, but only about the defendant who was speaking, not about the other defendant. He instructed the jury that, in the course of their duties, they did

not have the right to draw negative conclusions
about one of the defendants because of statements made by the other defendant.

Many of Barbara's statements made to investigators that implicated Schiess had been ruled inadmissible as hearsay, and attorney Gregory Price
again called them into question. He said to Barbara that she had told people Schiess was not
guilty of some of the things she had earlier
blamed him for, but she answered by asserting
her rights.

During almost her entire time of being questioned at her video deposition, Barbara had been
ill at ease, agitated, repetitive, and fidgety—much
the same way she had behaved during her video
interrogation session with Cherokee County
sheriff's investigator Mark Hicks a few days after
her arrest. But at that time, she did not invoke
her right not to answer any questions at all. In
fact, she seemed eager to talk to Hicks and told
him in detail about the crime.

Mark Hicks took the witness stand and told the
jury about Barbara's statements that Darlene had
managed to free herself following the ambush on
the dirt road. She said that Darlene then ran
around the edge of the pasture and down to the
pond, where she tried to hide in the weeds at the
water's edge.

Then, Barbara told Hicks, Darlene had been
shot three times at close range with a shotgun.

Hicks testified that Barbara had also provided
many other details about the murder scene,

including the fact that the black Dodge Dakota truck had been parked by the side of the road, with its hood up, to lure Darlene to stop. The investigators had learned, prior to the arrests of Barbara and Schiess, that Schiess was the owner of a black Dodge Dakota pickup. After she was arrested, Barbara told the officers where they would find the truck, hidden in a storage unit.

Hicks also told the courtroom what Darlene's final words were, according to Barbara. Before breaking free and running for her life, Darlene had told her captors, "Let me go. I live nine miles away. I don't know who you are from Adam. You have plenty of time to get away."

Barbara had made several lengthy statements to the authorities and had answered at length some of the questions in her video deposition, but as he had done from the time of his arrest, Schiess never made a statement of any kind to anyone, either in person or on videotape.

When closing arguments in the case began the following day, Andy Davis laid much of the blame for Darlene Roberts's death on Schiess. Gregory Price had argued that the civil case was being conducted like a murder trial, and he said that his client, Schiess, had acknowledged his part in the crime when he entered a kidnapping charge, but claimed again that Schiess did not kill Darlene. But Davis countered by telling the jury that the murder was a direct result of Schiess's acknowledged kidnapping, saying that the criminal case had begun with the kidnapping—and that if Schiess had not kidnapped Darlene, she would not have died.

Before the jury left the courtroom to begin their deliberations, Judge Harold L. Murphy had instructed them that if they were to award damages, it would be up to them to come up with what they felt was an appropriate amount. During their deliberations, the jurors had only one question for the court, and that was whether or not there was a limit to the amount of punitive damages they could award under the law.

Judge Murphy told them no, there was not a limit.

When the jury returned with a verdict, they awarded $30 million to the estate of Darlene Roberts. Darlene's family and friends hugged and tearfully congratulated each other, and Vernon told the media that he was glad the case had gone in favor of the estate.

"We can now get closure in our lives as a family," he said.

Attorney Andy Davis told the press that the outcome of the case was a great thing for the family, but it could never compensate for the loss of their loved one.

"They lived through some horrific events," he said. "Hopefully, this sends a message that we won't tolerate senseless killings."

Some of the jurors made statements following

the trial, saying that the sum they had arrived on was "an abstract sum" to be split between Barbara and Schiess. They said that it was impossible to put a price on a human life, and said that the failure of the two defendants to testify in person during the trial contributed to their decision. They mentioned Schiess in particular, noting that he had not answered a single question during his deposition.

Another point mentioned by the jurors was their inability to hear any of the hearsay evidence that Barbara had given concerning Schiess's involvement in the murder. Much of the evidence against Schiess was given by her immediately following their arrests when she outlined for the investigators how the crime had been planned and carried out. The jury had not been allowed to hear statements she had made concerning Schiess—only those that concerned her own actions during the crime. Those statements, plus the evidence from the criminal investigation and the testimony of the officers who worked the case so thoroughly, provided the jury with the information they needed to reach their verdict.

Now Vernon Roberts and his attorneys faced yet another difficult task as they planned to set out on attempts to collect the judgment they had been awarded.

76

Since the time when Barbara Roberts had given her video deposition, before her criminal trial was even held, she had not been kept apprised of developments in the civil suit. It was, naturally, not at the forefront of her priorities, since her very life was on the line with a capital murder charge hanging over her head.

Since she was not present for the civil trial, and had no legal representation there, she was unaware of the jury's verdict until another inmate at Tutwiler Prison informed her that she was now $15 million in debt. This came as a crushing blow to Barbara, who had not heard any news about the outcome of the suit until that time. She felt helpless and "out of the loop" when it came to her legal affairs. She could do nothing but wait until she was given whatever information that came her way.

Meanwhile, the civil trial had stirred up all sorts of emotions among the readers of the *Rome News-Tribune* who had followed the case so closely from the time of Darlene's murder through Barbara's trial and Schiess's guilty plea. Feelings had run very high among the community, and large numbers of people could count Darlene, Vernon, and their family, friends, or coworkers among their acquaintances. It seemed everyone had an opinion on the case, and was more than ready to weigh in with thoughts on the outcome of the civil trial, as opposed to the criminal cases. The comments posted by readers following the online articles reflected the wide variety of those opinions.

The posting began shortly after the verdict was released, beginning with someone who obviously did not feel things were as they might have seemed.

If only Vernon Roberts getting $30 million was truly justice, the first post read. The writer went on to say that if true justice would have been done, both [Vernon and Schiess] would have been held responsible for such a tragedy, not just a mentally ill woman on disability. The writer pointed out that Schiess would be getting out of prison in less than a month, Vernon would be rich—were he able to collect on his judgment—and Barbara was in prison for life. Does this sound like justice? the writer asked.

The post went on to describe Vernon's marriage to his fourth wife, only months after his third wife was murdered by his second wife, whom, the writer claimed, Vernon had been having an affair with. The writer said he had prayed for justice and would have to rely on God for the ultimate justice. When they meet Him on their judgment day, they will not be able to buy or charm their way out of HIS wrath!

A supporter from the opposition immediately fired back: The Roberts were my neighbors, and your comment sucks!

The post went on to say that Vernon would probably never see a dime of money, so he would likely never be a millionaire. And, as to his marriages, So what if he married again! So what how many times he has been married?

Barbara deserved every day she would be spending in prison, the writer said, and claimed Barbara was the mastermind of the whole plot. And to the writer of the previous post: You apparently are one of her relatives or someone Vernon jilted. Get a life.

Obviously, it did not occur to the writer that painting Vernon in the light of someone who had possibly "jilted" women might not necessarily be seen as a good character reference for him.

The following morning, another person posted a long opinion and an answer to the other comments that had been posted previously.

I see from your comments you don't know what really happened, said the writer. Barbara was not mental, the writer said, she was evil, and had stalked Darlene for a long time.

Even her family would not back her, the post said, because she was so evil. It went on to say that when Irene Comeaux had learned of Darlene's murder, she suffered a fatal heart attack because she knew Barbara had killed Darlene. No one from

Barbara's family had attended her murder trial: her family had her number.

Another post stated that Vernon was not having an affair with Barbara, and said the judgment was to be awarded both to Vernon and to Darlene's two children, with Vernon receiving $15 million and Darlene's son and daughter receiving $7 million each.

Vernon does not get it all, the writer said.

Claiming to be a relative of Darlene's, the writer said that no amount of money could replace her, and that Darlene had asked her sister to please take care of Vernon if anything were to happen to her. And, the writer claimed, Darlene's sister was the person who introduced Vernon to wife number four, and he did not know her until after Darlene had been murdered. And as for the money: Vernon doesn't really need it, but Darlene's children certainly do. Darlene would be pleased with the monetary judgment, the writer said, because it would insure that her children and grandchildren would be taken care of IF it ever comes through.

The next posting answered, Heard from Darlene's co-workers that she was indeed a fine person, but they didn't feel the same about Vernon.

It was true, the writer said, that Barbara's family didn't support her, but it was not true that they testified on behalf of Vernon at the trial. The writer was glad to hear that Darlene's children had been awarded part of the settlement.

As badly as Vernon talks about her and her kids, I know he wouldn't have been generous with them, the writer ended.

Another person wrote a very long post on behalf of Schiess, saying that they had prayed for justice and truth for three years: Dr. Robert Schiess is the kindest man I have ever known. He had spent his life dedicated to his patients and his family, and had paid on two occasions for his surgical staff to go to San Salvador to aid poverty-stricken children in need of care. He also cared for an elderly patient in his home because she had nowhere else to go, the writer claimed.

He is not a perfect man, but would never have hurt anyone.

According to the post, Schiess had just started to date Barbara when they were hit by an uninsured drunk driver, leaving him with a severe head injury and damaged legs. Barbara was also seriously injured, and the writer said that Schiess was horrified that she had no family who came to help her. He paid for Barbara's recovery, which, like his own, was very long and painful, and was forced to close his medical practice.

He became severely depressed when all he had worked for was taken away by the accident.

The writer claimed Schiess had told them repeatedly that he cared for Barbara and only wanted for her to be okay. But it was the writer's belief that Barbara was a sociopath who lied easily and frequently.

Robert Schiess was set up, the post stated. It went on to claim that Schiess had spent hundreds of thousands of dollars, "his retirement," on lawyers, who told the writer not to speak to the press, since they had already decided Schiess was guilty and would twist whatever was said in his support.

Others who read the post doubted seriously that Schiess's retirement was in jeopardy, since he had transferred nearly $2 million into a Swiss bank account.

We were repeatedly told, the writer said, that this was not about truth and justice but based on the law. The post went on to claim that Schiess had been told in both the criminal and civil cases that he should assert his Fifth Amendment rights.

The writer also said that evidence had been discovered and should have been used in the trials, but, allegedly, it had been misplaced and overlooked. Schiess had received an anonymous letter while he was jailed, seeming to have been written by someone who knew a great deal about the situation.

We appreciate the courage it took to write it, the post said, we were advised that the information could not be used.

In the civil trial, the writer continued, the jurors had only seen the shell of a man who had devoted his life to helping others. Schiess did not see what happened and did not know most of the details until the civil trial, the writer claimed; he had been lied to repeatedly by Barbara Roberts. What happened was horrible, the post ended; it had devastated so many lives, and ended Darlene's.

We will continue to pray for truth, justice, and healing for all.

The posting of comments on the civil trial finally ended, a couple of days later, with one final statement:

Well, I have met Vernon before, and he reminds me

of a snake oil salesman. I have never met anyone so full of himself.

The writer said that Vernon did not deserve one dime, and claimed he was a suspect in the murder until he "charmed his way out of it." Vernon's fourth wife had been riding around in Vernon's Corvette three days after Darlene's funeral, the writer claimed, and alleged that the woman had given up custody of her nine-year-old son to move to Florida with Vernon.

But you are right, the post ended, when Judgment Day comes you won't be able to charm your way out of things then. I feel very sorry for the family, and I'm praying for them every day.

Even after the conclusion of the civil trial, it seemed that there was still a very high level of emotion involved on all sides of the case. Those strong feelings were not likely to change soon, not in a community where so many people knew so much about all of those involved in the case of Darlene Roberts's murder. Years after its resolution, there will still be friends, relatives, and acquaintances of all the parties who will be ready to argue their opinions on who was guilty and who was not, who received due punishment and who did not, and who did or did not speak the truth . . . if they spoke at all.

The only point that will never be argued by either side is this: Darlene Roberts, admired and respected by her coworkers and loved dearly by her friends and family, lost her life in a truly horrible manner, and she did absolutely nothing to deserve such a cruel, tragic end.

77

When Barbara Ann Roberts began her term in Tutwiler Prison for Women, she found herself in an institution named for the woman who was responsible for early prison reform and improvement in a state known for its harsh early correctional methods.

Julia Strudwick Tutwiler, born in 1841 in Tuscaloosa, Alabama, was a student in the first year of Vassar College when the school opened in 1861. After completing her education there, she then studied with professors of classical languages at Washington and Lee University. She studied abroad in France at the Sorbonne and at the Institute of Protestant Deaconesses in Kaiserworth, Germany. When she returned to Alabama, she was on the faculty of the Tuscaloosa Female College, became the coprincipal of the Livingston Female Academy, and principal of the Alabama Normal College.

Tutwiler first gained nationwide attention when she exerted considerable pressure on the officials of the University of Alabama and got ten of her Livingston graduates admitted to the university, the first women to attend there. From that time on, she was often referred to as the "mother of coeducation in Alabama."

Tutwiler's influence also came to bear when she was instrumental in the establishment of the first Alabama Girls' Industrial School (AGIS). Begun in October 1896, it eventually became the highly respected institution known now as the University of Montevallo.

One of Tutwiler's top priorities, however, was her constant crusade for prison reform within the state. She lobbied incessantly to separate male and female prisoners and young juveniles from older "career" criminals. She also pressured state authorities for improvement of prison sanitation and for providing of religious and educational resources for prisoners. To the great benefit of young convicts in the state, she managed to bring a Boys' Industrial School into being, and she succeeded in her efforts to get laws passed requiring prison inspections.

Julia Tutwiler died in 1916, and in tribute to her constant efforts to improve the lot of women in prison, the state named its first women's facility—Julia Tutwiler Prison for Women— after her. Prior to that, an older version of the prison had existed with primarily female inmates, but the 1942 construction was the first institution built expressly for women prisoners.

The prison cost $350,000 to build using inmate labor, and it was intended to hold four hundred women prisoners in two cell blocks for white inmates and five for black inmates, with separate dining rooms. There was one notable fact to be reported: the prison's first warden, a woman named Nell Farrar, headed an all-woman staff, which was the first time for such a staff in the nation.

These accomplishments were all well and good, but if Julia Strudwick Tutwiler could have seen the prison named after her when it neared meltdown at the start of the twenty-first century due to extreme overcrowding—with over a thousand prisoners in the facility built to house four hundred or less—she would have no doubt been bitterly disappointed.

78

In December 2002, U.S. District judge Myron Thompson, after a visit to the facility and a thorough review of the situation, declared that conditions in the prison violated the Constitution. Four months later, there were still 992 women housed in Tutwiler's dorms, and little else had changed. There were unoccupied inmates standing around, lining the hallways. Others tried to sleep on their bunks, with the noise around them at times rising to levels that would make sleep impossible under most conditions.

Ill inmates were packed the hallway to the medical unit, lying on cots waiting and hoping for their turn at treatment. They were jammed into crowded classrooms and rehab sessions like sardines into a tin. A judge-ordered twelve-month drug-treatment program, similar to those in other state prisons, might or might not make it into existence; in the meantime, some inmates had to start breakfast at 3:40 A.M. in order for everyone to be fed on time.

There was no air-conditioning at the prison,

and the inmates had to rely on fans when temperatures inside the buildings soared to the high eighties in the hot, humid central Alabama summers. There were holes worn through the floor tiles, and most of the exercise yard was a bare dirt surface. There were problems with the prison's equally overcrowded population of roaches and spiders, whose only extermination threat came from the inmates, who stepped on them or swatted them at every opportunity.

It is a decrepit, dismal place, a representative of the Southern Center for Human Rights reported.

The warden at that time even admitted that she could not see how the prison could continue to operate under such harsh conditions.

"We're going to need some relief," she said.

The following year, in 2004, a settlement was filed in the case that had been brought about by the federal lawsuit brought by inmates and ruled on by Judge Thompson, who had called the prison a "ticking time bonb" following his visit in December 2002.

Some media sources cheered the settlement, claiming that the state's female inmates would soon have fewer insect infestations in the dorms, more fans and showers, and additional ice machines. But investigators from the Southern Center for Human Rights remained skeptical.

"The place is a dump and the changes being made by the lawsuit are minimal," said one investigator, and an attorney for the Southern Center said the changes might improve conditions, but would certainly not make the prison a comfortable place to serve out a sentence.

The agreement called for the prison to be monitored for four years by a doctor, a mental-health expert, and attorneys and advocates from the Southern Center to be sure the prison was in compliance with the rules.

One of the primary points of the agreement was an effort to reduce the population at the prison, which would necessarily take place over a period of time. The medical issues addressed included the statement that *sick call shall not be conducted between midnight and 6 A.M.*, and when women entered the prison, they would have to be allowed to continue taking their prescription medications. It would be required that a licensed dentist be on staff, and he or she would provide dentures when necessary. Improved hepatitis treatment, infection control, and specialized care for the mentally ill population, the elderly, and the terminally ill patients would be required.

There were entire sections of the settlement that dealt with pest control, heat issues, and doubling the number of ice machines operated at the prison.

The investigator who called Tutwiler "a dump" remained very dubious about the amount of change that would eventually take place at the facility.

"Until Alabama passes genuine sentencing reform, the prison is going to continue being a warehouse," the woman said. She believed that sentencing reform was a better answer and a more reliable means of correcting the problems caused by the overcrowding.

One of the inmates in Tutwiler might have agreed

with the investigator, but the settlement had unfortunately come too late to give her any hope for improved conditions. The prisoner suffered from severe mental illness and had been often left alone and untreated. She committed suicide earlier in the year.

79

Before signing off on the settlement offered by the state, Judge Thompson toured the prison once again in 2004 and spoke directly to the warden and several of the inmates to determine what changes had been made since he had declared it unconstitutionally unsafe two years earlier. He first asked to speak with the warden, whose statements to him at his first visit had been very frank and forthright about conditions at the prison and the serious problems with assaults, crowding, and inmate idleness. For the most part, she agreed that with what the prison had at hand, as far as resources, the settlement would prove to be a workable solution. One of the most helpful aspects would be the requirement for the state to keep the prison's population at seven hundred or less; it had reached its high of 1,017 in 2002, and was designed at that time to hold 617.

One prisoner testified to the judge that a night hadn't passed in segregation (where she was being housed for disciplinary purposes) when she hadn't had to kill at least ten bugs. She also told the judge that guards had harassed some of the inmates about taking part in the lawsuit, telling them it wouldn't improve their lives.

Another woman told the judge that she had been at Tutwiler for eighteen months, and she had been denied and delayed medical care for her serious problems with high blood pressure, heart disease, and diabetes. Her free-world doctor, she said, had faxed a special request to the prison regarding her treatment. Because of the requirement in the settlement that prisoners be allowed to continue taking their prescription medication once they were incarcerated, she hoped that the settlement would be approved.

Following the tour, Thompson told the press that he was particularly concerned with the issue of mental-health treatment for those inmates who were in need of it. He wanted to be sure the staff understood that the inmates had a problem, and that their needs were recognized. He also spoke about the excessive heat, insect and spider infestations, crowding and understaffing, and shortages of programs that would give the inmates the opportunity for self-improvement and continuing education.

Having toured the prison and heard the testimony of staff and inmates, with a wide majority in favor of the settlement, Judge Thompson gave it his signature of approval, and it became final.

80

Despite the court-ordered changes and the settlement reached between the court and Tutwiler Prison for Women, conditions had not seemed to improve a great deal by the summer of 2007. The state's largest newspaper reported that women had been locked down in dormitories where the heat index reached temperatures greater than 130 degrees, and in the previous winter, the inmates had stuffed toilet paper into cracks in the windows to keep out the frigid drafts.

There had been much recent debate within the state government in Alabama as to whether the prison should be replaced with a larger, new facility that could hold more inmates, or whether it should be replaced with a smaller prison and use the money saved for programs to keep women out of prison. When corrections authorities asked Governor Bob Riley to support their requests for $120 million for a new prison, he declined. Instead, he created a prison overcrowding task force and began to work with reform experts to find answers to the state's correctional and criminal justice dilemma.

The state legislature also enacted voluntary sentencing guidelines, plumped up funding of community corrections programs, and created a Commission on Girls and Women in the Criminal Justice System. The chief justice of the Alabama Supreme Court also came up with a statewide drug court plan, similar to those already in place in some counties. If enacted, it would *treat* criminals with drug addictions—an alternative to a prison sentence.

The media announced that Alabama's criminal justice system would, no doubt, become a model for progressive internal reform. But that claim would remain to be proven true; it would take a long time to improve resources within communities like mental-health treatment programs, drug treatment work programs, and other such programs designed to keep women out of prison.

Tutwiler can then be replaced by something smaller and better, the media claimed. The question that remains is this: the newspaper writers and editors and the other journalists who believe conditions were far better in 2008 than they were in 2002, have they actually toured the prison to see for themselves?

The Southern Center for Human Rights, which brought the original 2002 suit against the state, apparently did not think the conditions had improved nearly enough, and began taking applications for a person to lead a campaign to *close the brutal Tutwiler Prison and transform Alabama's women's criminal justice system into one that is small, family-oriented, community-based and rehabilitative.*

The Southern Center's director said that Alabama needed a real solution, something that could not be litigated into. Two other groups, Aid to Inmate Mothers, Inc., and the Alabama Coalition Against Domestic Violence, joined in support of the campaign to close the prison.

At that time, the prison was holding 982 inmates instead of the 700 required by the settlement agreement, and inmates' attorneys filed to have the state found in contempt of court. This caused the Alabama Department of Corrections to agree to six years of court-ordered monitoring by the Southern Center for Human Rights, instead of the four years originally called for in the settlement.

The corrections commissioner told the press that he wanted to replace Tutwiler within the next year, but that did not happen. There had been a struggle by prison officials to comply with the requirements of the settlement, and the struggle would continue while other solutions to the problems at Tutwiler were sought.

With its long-acknowledged reputation as one of the most harsh women's prisons in the nation, Tutwiler came to be the subject of a documentary episode of ABC's *Nightline,* with one of its reporters going so far as to live in the prison as an inmate for eleven days. The report, when aired, came as a real eye-opener for everyone who viewed it, but there was no surprising information there for the families and friends of the inmates, who already knew what life inside Tutwiler was like. The *Nightline* reporter described it best.

"I was only there for eleven days," she said, "but I will never forget what it's like to be a prisoner—disconnected from the outside world, without control over my surroundings, or contact with the people I care about."

If that eleven-day stretch was hard to take, it should have been easy for the *Nightline* viewers to imagine how it would feel to spend eleven months in lockup, or eleven years . . . or a lifetime.

81

There are several women, along with Barbara
Ann Roberts, who are currently serving life without the possibility of parole at Tutwiler. Some of
them are unknown to the general public, spending day after day in anonymity, serving their time
for crimes that attracted little attention from the
outside world.

Others, however, are from the other end of the
spectrum, still attracting intense media attention,
years after the crimes that put them in prison.
One such inmate, Betty Wilson, was convicted of
capital murder in the 1992 death of her husband,
Dr. Jack Wilson, a wealthy Huntsville, Alabama,
doctor. The murder and the subsequent arrests
of Betty, her twin sister, Peggy Lowe, and the man
prosecutors said the twins had hired to kill
Wilson, a handyman named James White, made
nationwide headlines. Betty was tried, found
guilty, and sentenced to life in prison without
parole. Then, after Betty's trial and conviction,

Peggy was tried for the same crime and acquitted. The verdicts caused a sensation: one twin—rich, promiscuous, and widely disliked—was sent to prison for life, and the other twin—a beloved schoolteacher who was very active in her church—tried for the same crime and acquitted.

James White testified against both sisters but was not tried himself until after their trials. White made a deal with the prosecution; his testimony against the twins in exchange for a life sentence for himself in lieu of the death penalty. Then, after their trials and his own sentencing, he admitted he had lied about Betty Wilson.

After several true-crime books, television news magazine episodes, and an extensive Internet campaign, which netted worldwide attention for the case, support for Betty Wilson's innocence built to a high level. Betty's process of appeals began and eventually worked its way to the Alabama State Supreme Court, where, in 1997, an appeal for a new trial was turned down by a five-to-two vote.

The next step was an appeal to the U.S. District Court, and after several postponements, it was finally presented to Chief Justice Sam Pointer Jr. He denied Betty a new trial.

In 2000, Betty's appeal to the Eleventh Circuit Court was denied, and the following year, in 2001, Betty's appeal to the U. S. Supreme Court was also denied.

Betty's legion of supporters continued to work on her behalf, preparing a petition for Alabama governor Bob Riley that asked him to change

Betty's sentence to life *with* the possibility of parole. Their hope is to present it to him toward the end of his term of office. In the meantime, Betty was married in prison on May 1, 2006, to Bill Campbell.

82

One reason Betty Wilson's supporters pinned their hopes on a commutation of her sentence by Alabama's governor is the shocking and controversial commutation of the sentence of Judith Ann Neelley by Governor Fob James on his last day in office in 1999. Neelley was convicted of the 1982 murder of Lisa Ann Millican, a thirteen-year-old runaway whom Neelley and her husband, Alvin, kidnapped in Rome, Georgia, and later brutally tortured, raped, and murdered at Little River Canyon in DeKalb County, Alabama.

Neelley was tried and convicted, and a DeKalb County jury recommended life in prison without parole, but Circuit Judge Randall L. Cole sentenced her to the death penalty because of the extreme brutality of the crime.

James, on his final day as governor, commuted Neelley's sentence to life in prison without the possibility of parole. When word reached DeKalb County of his action, there was immediate outrage on the part of the public and the law enforcement officers and prosecutors who had handled the case.

At the time of Lisa Ann Millican's death, DA Mike O'Dell was an assistant district attorney, and her murder case was one of the first he helped to prosecute in the county. He was astounded to learn what had happened without his office being consulted or contacted in any way prior to the announcement of James's decision.

"I was shocked and disturbed when I found out Governor James commuted Neelley's sentence," he said. "He did this without speaking to the DA's office or asking our opinion. It is clear he did not want us to be involved in his decision."

As soon as James issued the commutation, he left his office, left Montgomery, and headed out to a duck-hunting vacation in another state. He gave no explanation for what he had done, or why, but rumors abounded that his wife had begged him to issue the order on religious grounds.

James did not explain himself until 2002, when he made a statement to a Cherokee County, Alabama, newspaper, the *Post,* and said he had spent a long time deliberating the issue, examining documents and records, and giving the matter a lot of long, hard thought. He said the primary reason for the commutation was the fact that the jury had recommended life without parole, and then the judge overruled and sentenced Neelley to death.

"That DeKalb County jury, which heard all of the facts surrounding that heinous crime in the months right after the events took place, convicted her to life in prison," he said.

James evidently decided that since a jury reviewed all the evidence in the case, including Neelley's claims that she was following orders from her allegedly abusive husband, Alvin, a life sentence was appropriate punishment.

James's opinion notwithstanding, DeKalb County and most of northeast Alabama and northwest Georgia remain outraged to this day that Judith Ann Neelley's death sentence was commuted . . . on the very day that the district attorney's office asked the state to set an execution date. By the good graces of a former governor, or perhaps by the religious fervor of his wife, Judith Ann Neelley will be staying at Tutwiler Prison for the remainder of her natural life.

83

There are, no doubt, other equally dramatic stories among the inmates at Tutwiler who are serving life without parole. Appeals are a continuing concern, court-appointed attorneys fail to stay in touch with updates, and frustration reigns on a daily basis. The inmates grow impatient because they are unable to take action for themselves and do for themselves the things they must rely on others, on the outside, to take care of for them.

When Barbara Ann Roberts was first sent to Tutwiler, she had an especially hard time adjusting to the conditions there, primarily the constant, incessant noise. It was all but impossible to sleep, she wrote, with the commotion in the dorm. Prison food apparently did not agree with her at all, either. When she returned to Cherokee County for her first appeal hearing after several months at Tutwiler, she had lost a shocking amount of weight and appeared tired and haggard. She had no money in her prison account for soda, coffee, snacks, or anything else, and she had to borrow pens and paper in order to write letters. By the time she was convicted and sent to the prison, she was destitute and had no resources whatsoever, and her appeal attorney had been appointed by the court.

Attorney Angela Cochran Morgan appeared to be very prepared at the appeal hearing, and had familiarized herself with the case quite well by that time. Barbara's impatience for quick action would have to be reined in by the facts of the matter: things just don't move quickly in the legal system, no matter what the circumstances.

As time passed, Barbara began to write about the remorse she felt over Darlene's death. On one occasion just before the trial, she said, Rodney Stallings had brought the crime scene photos taken of Darlene for Barbara to see.

"You really do not know how much I wish that would have been pictures of me, instead of Darlene," she said. "Then no one would be hurting now, no family would be missing anyone, nobody would care at all. Everything would have long since been forgotten, never to be remembered.

"It's not that way, though," she said. She pointed out there were two people without a mother, Vernon without a wife, a family lost a sister, and so much more. If it had been her instead of Darlene, she said, there would be no one in pain.

"Why could that have not been God's choice, why?" she asked. "Why? If you could only imagine how it would have been."

A woman had died a terrible death, Barbara said, and her mother, Irene Comeaux, had died, and so many people were hurt and suffering, and their lives would never be the same again.

Barbara said on one occasion that she had trusted in the system and believed she would not have been found guilty of Darlene's murder.

"I had only seen [how the system works] on TV," she said, "you know, where it was the innocent are always shown as such. I have come to find out that in the real world, things do not always work that way."

People would rather hear lies and twisted truths, she said, not the whole truth and nothing but the truth.

"Truths do not seem to make headlines at any court."

Barbara wrote very often about how much she loved and missed her family, and at one time two of her sisters had planned to come to visit her at the prison. She had been out of contact with them for such a long time, and she looked forward to the visit so much that she shared the news of their expected visit with the other inmates in the chapel services.

"I told everyone how God did answer prayers, just to continue praying and never let go," she said. "I had so much hope."

Barbara's hopes were dashed when arrangements for the trip from Texas fell through due to scheduling and other concerns. It had meant so much to her. But she held out hope that

someday, someway, they might plan another trip
to visit her.

"I really need them," she said. "I miss them all
so very much. Please let them know how much I
love them."

If Barbara's family had, indeed, been able to
come to visit her, they would have undoubtedly
seen a very different person than they had dealt
with the last time they were together, back in
Texas for their mother's funeral, days before Barbara and Schiess were arrested when their plane
touched down at the Atlanta airport.

In addition to the startling weight loss, Barbara's mental clarity seemed to have become a
great deal more focused. Now that she was in
prison, where a court order had ruled that inmates' prescription medication would be administered correctly and properly, her mind was
much sharper, her thoughts were far better or-
ganized, and she seemed to be functioning at a
much better level than prior to the trial, while she
was in the care of the DeKalb and Cherokee
County Jails.

The county jails no doubt were much quieter
than Tutwiler, and the food was probably better,
but being medically regulated for the period of
time at Tutwiler had made a great difference in
Barbara. Thin, haggard, and as tired as she
might be due to lack of proper rest, Barbara
seemed to have gained strength while in the
prison. If she could be patient and work through
the appeals with her attorney, perhaps things
might move faster for her than for Betty Wilson
and other inmates. And Judith Ann Neelley

could tell her that sometimes an unexpected stroke of fate might accidentally come her way.

Hopefully, Barbara will heed her own advice to the other inmates:

"Just . . . continue praying and never let go."

MORE MUST-READ TRUE CRIME
FROM PINNACLE